Destabilizing the Margins

Destabilizing the Margins
An Intersectional Approach to Early Christian Memory

MARIANNE BJELLAND KARTZOW

☙PICKWICK *Publications* • Eugene, Oregon

DESTABILIZING THE MARGINS
An Intersectional Approach to Early Christian Memory

Copyright © 2012 Marianne Bjelland Kartzow. All rights reserved. Except for brief quotations in critical publications or reviews, no part of this book may be reproduced in any manner without prior written permission from the publisher. Write: Permissions, Wipf and Stock Publishers, 199 W. 8th Ave., Suite 3, Eugene, OR 97401.

Pickwick Publications
An Imprint of Wipf and Stock Publishers
199 W. 8th Ave., Suite 3
Eugene, OR 97401

www.wipfandstock.com

ISBN 13: 978-1-61097-675-6

Cataloguing-in-Publication data:

Kartzow, Marianne Bjelland.

Destabilizing the margins : an intersectional approach to early Christian memory / Marianne Bjelland Kartzow.

xii + 204 pp. ; 23 cm. Includes bibliographical references and indexes.

ISBN 13: 978-1-61097-675-6

1. Women in the Bible. 2. Women's studies. 3. Interdisciplinary research. 4. Bible and feminism. I. Title.

BS195 K25 2012

Manufactured in the U.S.A.

Contents

Acknowledgments · vii

Notes on Abbreviations, Texts, and Translations · xi

Introduction: Re-Forgetting the Margins? · 1

PART ONE: Embodying Cultural Complexity

1. Gendered Slave Bodies and "Metaphorical Violence": Thinking with Luke 12:45–46 · 31
2. Borderline Identity: The Contested Body of the Ethiopian Eunuch (Acts 8:26–40) · 46
3. Mapping Sameness and Difference: Virginity in *Joseph and Aseneth* · 59
4. Rediscovering Slaves: Motherhood and Circumcision in the Pastoral Epistles · 70

PART TWO: Sound of Silence? Dynamics of Speech and Talk

5. Challenging Female Communities: Orality and Resurrection in the Gospels · 81
6. Limited Access: Stereotyping the Voice in the Pastoral Epistles · 102
7. Negotiating Power Relations: Talkative Widows out of Place (Luke 18:2–5 and 1 Tim 5:13–14) · 110
8. Talking Pair: Paul and the Fortune-telling Slave Girl (Acts 16:16–18) · 122

PART THREE: **Overlapping Relationships**
9   Conceptualizing Power Structures: Gal 3:28 and the Colossian Household Codes · 135

PART FOUR: **Beyond Intersectionality: Trice Vulnerable but Named**
10   Negotiating Hierarchy: The Slave/Woman Blandina · 157
11   The Memory of Hagar: A Model for Overcoming Marginality · 165
     Conclusion · 174

Bibliography · 181
Subject Index · 197
Scripture Index · 203

Acknowledgments

In October 2008, when still few Biblical scholars worked with intersectionality, the research project I was part of, Jesus in Cultural Complexity, arranged an international conference at the University of Oslo entitled *Methods for the study of the Jesus movement: Intersectionality*. I remember leaving this event encouraged and inspired not only to explore what intersectionality can do to early Christian studies, but also to combine it with recent developments within memory theory. It took almost a year of working with these theories before I realized that I was in fact in the process of writing a new a book, a book about how to destabilize the margins. I wanted to develop how intersectionality and memory theory in combination may represent a possible way to study early Christian texts and their impact on our fast-changing world, in line with what participants at the conference had suggested.

Several people have been lively conversation partners or constructive critics along the way. I am first and foremost very grateful to those who have been part of the research project Jesus in Cultural Complexity for these years (2008–2011). Halvor Moxnes has been the chair as well as my closest scholarly inspiration and co-worker on a daily basis. I would like to thank the Research Council of Norway for funding the project and the Faculty of Theology at the University of Oslo for hosting it. Anne Hege Grung and Rebecca Solevåg have been my conference mates, true friends, and foremost discussion partners from the beginning to the end. Secretaries and PhD students connected to the project have contributed with new perspectives, thought-provoking questions, and fresh comments that have helped me contextualize my perspectives. Ward Blanton, James G. Crossley, Annhild Tofte Haga, and Oddbjørn Leirvik have strengthened the interdisciplinary profile of the project and broadened my scholarly horizon.

Many of the chapters in this book have been presented and discussed at various conferences, in particular at Society of Biblical Literature (SBL) meetings and at the Nordic New Testament Conference. The program units "The Pastoral and Catholic Epistles," which I chaired at the SBL International Meeting 2005–2010, and "The Disputed Paulines" at the Annual Meeting, as well as the new consultation that I chair together with Jeremy Hultin, "Speech and Talk: Discourses and Social Practices in the Ancient Mediterranean World," have been important venues for developing several of the points I make in this book. I would like to thank colleagues who one way or the other have helped me think more clearly or be more critical and creative: Ulrike Auga, Bernadette Brooten, Denise Buell, Jennifer Glancy, Holly Hearon, Jeremy Hultin, Sabrina Inowlocki, Melanie Johnson-Debaufre, Margaret MacDonald, Carolyn Osiek, Todd Penner, and Gail Streete. My fellow Nordic scholars have also been encouraging and interesting to discuss with, in particular Lone Fatum, Fredrik Ivarsson, Kasper Bro Larsen, Hans Leander, Outi Lehtipuu, Antti Marjanen, Jesper Tang Nielsen, and Hanna Stenström.

Another equally important place for finding inspiration and scholarly impulses has been UNISA (the University of South Africa, Pretoria). Through transcontinental conferences and correspondence I have found a stimulating home away from home for intellectual thought, self-critical investigation, and belief in a better future. In particular I would like to thank Pieter Botha for his kind and inclusive attitude, and for sharing so generously of his insights, ideas, and frustrations. Also Loreen Iminza Maseno, Kenya, has come to be a good friend and important discussion partner during this book project.

The spring term 2010 I was a guest researcher at the Centre for Gender Research at the University of Oslo. Although I did not have to travel far, I nevertheless met an international, interdisciplinary, and very creative group of people who gave me much to think about and a lot to laugh about. That semester was indeed very decisive for how this book developed. I would in particular like to thank Jorunn Økland for inviting me into her research group and Oddrun Rangsæter for facilitating the best possible working environment. In 2010 I also had a mentor from the Faculty of Educational Sciences, Kirsten Hofgaard Lycke, who became an important and inspiriting guide in the writing process.

In March 2011 I was invited to the University of Riga, Latvia, to teach at a doctoral course in religion and theology. Thanks to Valdis Teraudkalns for this opportunity, and thanks also to the PhD students who gave me precisely the fresh challenges and inspiration I needed in order to finish this book.

I would also like to express my gratitude to those people I have worked side by side with at the Faculty of Theology, in particular the participants in the research groups I am part of: Vemund Blomkvist, Gitte Buch-Hansen, Åste Dokka, Zoro Dube, Anne Hege Grung, Kirsten Marie Hartvigsen, David Hellholm, Birgitte Lerheim, Hugo Lundhaug, Ole Jacob Løland, Anders Martinsen, Halvor Moxnes, Christina Petterson, Tarald Rasmussen, Turid Karlsen Seim, Jone Salomonsen, Rebecca Solevåg, Terje Stordalen, and Aud Valborg Tønnessen. I am also grateful to the students at the Master course "Jesus in Cultural Complexity" (fall term 2009) for eye-opening discussions and challenging questions regarding how intersectionality can (and cannot!) be useful when interpreting Biblical texts. I have supervised three Master students who have written their theses on issues that I address in this book, and I would like to thank each of them for their devoted interest, creative questions, and stimulating discussions: Stine Kiil Saga, Gaute Granlund, and Katrine Intelhus Lind-Solstad.

I am grateful to Wipf and Stock Publishers and the editors for accepting this book for publication under the Pickwick Publications imprint. Thanks also go to Stig Oppedal for proofreading and to Christer Hellholm for preparing the final manuscript.

A different version of chapter 1 was published in *Acta Patristica et Byzantina* (4/2010), and chapter 9 was published as a separate article in *Biblical Interpretation* (4–5/2010). I am grateful to both journals for allowing me to include these texts in the current book.

Finally, I would like to thank Anders, Nikolai, and Ella, and the rest of my family and my close friends, for giving me reasons for continuing to fight for what I believe in and inspiration to keep on working. Without you this book would never have been accomplished.

Oslo, May 2011

Notes on Abbreviations, Texts, and Translations

ABBREVIATIONS

Bauer	*A Greek-English Lexicon of the New Testament and Other Early Christian Literature*
HTR	*Harvard Theological Review*
JBL	*Journal of Biblical Literature*
JECS	*Journal of Early Christian Studies*
JFSR	*Journal of Feminist Studies in Religion*
JSNT	*Journal for the Study of the New Testament*
JSNTSup	Journal for the Study of the New Testament Supplement Series
JSP	*Journal for the Study of the Pseudepigrapha*
JSOT	*Journal for the Study of the Old Testament*
LCL/Loeb	The Loeb Classical Library
LSJ	Liddell, H. G., R. Scott, H. S. Jones, *A Greek-English Lexicon*. 9th ed. with revised supplement. Oxford, 1996
LXX	Septuaginta
NRSV	*The Harper Collins Study Bible*. New Revised Standard Version (1993)
NTS	*New Testament Studies*
NTT	*Norsk teologisk tidsskrift (Norwegian Journal of Theology)*
SBL	Society of Biblical Literature
SNTS	Society for New Testament Studies
TDNT	*Theological Dictionary of the New Testament*. Edited by G. Kittel and G. Friedrich. Translated by G. W. Bromiley. 10 vols. Grand Rapids, 1964–1976
TLG	*Thesaurus linguae graecae: Canon of Greek Authors and Works*. Edited by L. Berkowitz and K. A. Squitier. 3d ed. Oxford, 1990

TEXTS, TRANSLATIONS, AND TOOLS

Greek texts are downloaded from TLG (font: Unicode). The Perseus Digital Library's Greek and Roman Material (Department of Classics, Tufts University) has provided advanced lexicographical searching facilities, linked up to LSJ online. Translations from Greek to English are taken from NRSV and LCL when nothing else is mentioned.

Introduction

Re-Forgetting the Margins?

The Syrophoenician woman's story invites us to consider the interconnectedness of oppressions—racism is sexism is classism is homophobia.
—Sarojini Nadar, "The Bible in and for Mission," 226

Memory concerns the past, but happens in the present.
—Mieke Bal, *Traveling Concepts in the Humanities*, 183

[We] deconstruct and reconstruct the past as we allegedly know it by questioning the power structures that are embedded and preserved in the archives we have inherited.
—Rowley and Wolthers, *Queering the Archive*, .9

BELONGING TO THE PAST as well as to the present, early Christian texts have a potential for being "texts of terror" or texts of hope and liberation.[1] And it is my belief that overlooked and marginal Biblical characters can contribute with crucial impulses related to identity processes and power struggles in a fast-changing world. This book suggests that ideas taken from recent discussions of multiple identities and intersectionality, combined with insights from memory theory, can renew our engagement with ancient texts.

By use of these perspectives I will re-read selected early Christian texts in what the scholarly community has re-constructed as their historical contexts, and look for alternative ways these texts can produce meaning. Such perspectives may be relevant for those who see the New Testament as religious canon or as cultural canon, or as both. Perhaps a

---

1. See Trible, *Texts of Terror*.

fresh look at marginal Biblical figures—such as male and female slaves who are beaten by a fellow slave, the queer figure of the Ethiopian eunuch, foreign Egyptian women, rebellious widows, or a possessed fortune-telling slave girl—can help us talk in more critical and creative ways about responsibility, identity, injustice, violence, inclusion/exclusion, and the intersections of gender, race, and class?

At times I wonder why the stories of marginal Biblical characters were remembered by their contemporaries and recorded for posterity. However, these characters were not necessarily mentioned because they themselves were so important. They often serve minor purposes, are given stereotypical character traits, or are needed to make an important point. Nonetheless, they were not deleted from the record although they played marginal roles in early Christian memory. The combination of theoretical perspectives employed in this book aims at creating tools that emphasize the destabilizing potential of marginal characters.

I am interested in opposition, transformation, and counter-discourse, and want to contribute to the ongoing and vital task of relating Biblical texts to present-day contexts.

WHOSE BIBLE? READERS WITH DIFFERENT FILTERS

In the public discourse it is occasionally mentioned that the Bible is not only a religious text for believers but is also part of the cultural canon.[2] "Cultural Christians" have their specific ideas about the Bible, at times without having read it. For example, one of the national theaters in Oslo, Norway, plans to present a six-hour marathon performance based on the Bible. The preparations have started and it will be on stage in 2013. When the director actually sat down and read the entire book—the first Bible he had bought in his life—he was surprised at how brutal God was and characterized him as "a terrible mass murderer."[3]

One question has been haunting me while working with this book: Do we really *want* people to read the Bible? What happens if this book is disconnected from an interpretative community, a church or a confession, which normally equips the readers with some sort of interpretative

---

2. The Bible is seen as "a master narrative of Western cultures" in Schüssler Fiorenza, *Jesus and the Politics of Interpretation*, 4.

3. See Christiansen, "Får all makt i himmel og på jord." Online: *http://www.aftenposten.no*.

guide? Religious practitioners sometimes possess a rather fragmented knowledge of the actual texts, and build their ideas about God, Jesus, and the early Christians on a narrow selection of texts, a canon within the canon, created to emphasize the central texts and characters and downplay the textual periphery. Such filters are not in play if the Bible is read as literature on its own terms, for example when it operates as a manuscript for a theatrical performance.

But also other readers lack such filters: for example, new churches or communities aiming at "taking the whole Bible literally," and organizing their life according to texts that promote violence or discrimination, represent a current challenge in many countries. Students have told me that they have read the Qur'an because they want to know what Islam is all about—similarly, if people who are interested in Christianity or Western culture sat down and read the Bible, and in particular the New Testament, I wonder whether their ideas about Christianity would correspond to how "cultural Christians" perceive the role of religion in Western societies. With modern technology the access to online text versions and worldwide discussion groups, with a huge variety in quality and seriousness, are almost without limits.

My point is not to argue in favor of doctrinal or academic control of the Biblical texts, as if religious leaders or scholars are in the position of warning or protecting ordinary people from reading the Bible. Such expert readers should indeed listen to other voices. Rather, this book is an attempt to highlight texts, characters, and perspectives that have been marginal but may have the potential to help various religious and cultural readers to reflect on new challenges that we are facing in the age of globalization. Biblical experts must be prepared to accept that readers without filters, or with other filters, see God as a mass murderer and most likely pick up other texts passages than those with theological importance and gravitas. Perhaps those stories that best correspond to our time—stories that reflect complex social relations, hybrid bodies, or multiple identities—will have most appeal?

But these readers are not the only ones who approach the Bible in "new" ways. Some "readers at the margins," employ the Bible as a text they need in order to survive. I find it crucial to integrate such perspectives when dealing with Biblical discourses. As Musa Dube argues, Biblical studies cannot limit the interest to the history of textual traditions or to the doctrinal aspects of the texts, but needs to extend its scope to issues of domination, Western expansion, and its ideological manifestations as central forces in defining Biblical knowledge.[4] Some of those who consider the Bible a "talking book" need subversive readings and imaginative use of the Bible to deal with subordination and colonialization.[5]

I think that highlighting the growing variety of readers, such as cultural Christians or those suffering from domination and Western expansion, represents a revitalization of Biblical studies. We thereby pay attention to those who have an unknown reception history ("new" readers) and highlight the forgotten reception history of the marginalized.[6]

In this book I want to engage with the Bible by connecting issues of identity construction and global power relations as a challenging but hopefully fruitful approach. Therefore I at times talk about Bible readers, interpreters, or users to emphasize that the impact and effect history of the Bible often involves other practices than the concrete reading act, such as identity construction or legitimating the social order.

New readers and new users mean new perspectives and new questions. These texts are important to religious people, and also to those who suffer from global injustice and who call on us to be sensitive and respectful, but the same texts also have the potential to create meaning outside of faith communities. Instead of considering these perspectives as competing interests, I see the benefits of trying to combine them with the same curiosity, critique, and responsibility.

Further, I see no point in blaming the past for producing texts in which people were valued according to their gender, class, or ethnicity. However, religious texts that have an impact on societies and communities today need to be met with some kind of ethical critique.[7] Instead of looking to early Christian texts to find answers, the best way to approach

---

4. See the introduction in Dube, *Postcolonial Feminist Interpretation of the Bible*.

5. Kwok, *Discovering the Bible in the Non-Biblical World*, 42.

6. I thank Åste Dokka for suggesting this creative conceptualization.

7. I follow David Wright, who argues: "Imposing an outside measure on a text from an entirely different time and culture is questionable . . . In any case, ethical criticism becomes appropriate for a reader when a text like the Bible is brought to bear on public policy and the life of modern religious communities" (Wright, "'She Shall Not Go Free as Male Slaves Do,'" 129). Schüssler Fiorenza writes that "a critical ethical-political rhetoric sees religion and the Bible as sites of struggle over meaning, ethics and theology" (Schüssler Fiorenza, *Rhetoric and Ethic*, 76).

these texts is perhaps to let them present problems and questions for debate.[8]

THE COMPLEXITY OF MARGINALITY

This introductory chapter is entitled "Re-Forgetting the Margins." I will write more about forgetting later, but also "margins" is a complex word. Nevertheless, I am inspired by scholarship aiming at giving "marginalized subjects" an epistemic advantage.[9] In Biblical scholarship, "margin" has become a strong and powerful term for those who consider themselves as outside of the leading discourse in the field.[10] Whether someone or something is "marginal," however, may be contested and challenged. In this book I use the term in order to account for several interrelated discourses, as presented in the following.

First, marginality is both fixed and fluid. Patterns of marginality seem to have certain stable elements related to issues of gender, race, and class. The difference between rich and poor is increasing. The title of the book *Still at the Margins: Biblical Scholarship Fifteen Years after Voices from the Margin* demonstrates that although someone brings to light ethnic, geographical, or economic power structures and speaks up against the dominant force, it does not necessarily change the structures. Some would still argue that the power dynamics between "the West and the rest" have been rather stable for the last decades. Several feminists or LGBT people will confirm similar long-lasting power structures.

On the other hand, ideas about the marginal are also negotiated in a fast-changing world. Discourses about marginality need to take seriously the new urban dominance of the media and internet technology: not only economy, family ties, or politics define who are the powerless and marginal. What about cultural capital, social capital, relational capital, and capital related to sexuality, reproduction, age, body, or health? When all these parameters also interconnect, it is obvious that the power structures will not remain stable.

In recent years the global community has indeed realized that economy is unstable; suffice to mention the huge impact of the financial crises and the states that have gone bankrupt. Former colonial powers or

---

8. Wright, "'She Shall Not Go Free as Male Slaves Do,'" 139.

9. See Nash, "Re-Thinking Intersectionality," 3. See also Schüssler Fiorenza, "Transforming the Margin—Claiming Common Ground," 22–23.

10. Sugirtharajah, *Voices from the Margin*.

empires are in high debt, and former colonies or developing countries are about to take the lead in the global economy. In addition, extreme weather and natural catastrophes disturb the power balance, and those with little resources often suffer the most. New patterns of margins are arising, indicating that we face situations with new peripheries and new centers related to several aspects of life. Accordingly, marginality is contextual and negotiable, although some power structures seem to survive. I will suggest some specific analytical tools in order to deal with these fixed and fluid dimensions of marginality, because these tendencies most certainly will make a huge impact on the future of the Bible.

Second, there is the marginality of Biblical knowledge. Biblical scholarship is for the most part marginal in academia and in the public discourse of secular societies. In contrast, when the University of Oslo was established in 1811, theology, including Biblical studies, was among the few select fields of study, together with medicine, philosophy, and law. This context is completely changed. Recently I introduced myself as a Biblical scholar at an international gender conference, and a Nordic colleague replied, "Wow, that is so exotic!" I replied that it wasn't for me, but I immediately realized that my answer lacked a strong and convincing argument. Although recent critique has argued that the humanities are necessary for democracy, Biblical departments (like other humanistic studies) are suffering from budget cuts.[11] If Biblical scholars work in a theological environment, as I do, we are suspected by other disciplines of being ideological or of "having an agenda," reminiscent of the response feminists are often met with. Still, there are some highly privileged scholars and institutions within Biblical studies that also enjoy high status outside the field.[12] In addition, the rise of a new Christian conservative movement, with access to economic capital, may increase interest for the Bible in the future, but not necessarily for *critical* Biblical scholarship. These aspects of marginality deal with power, control, and hegemony. All practices related to Biblical texts, such as scholarship, translation, and usage, are related to these overall factors, in many ways.[13]

---

11. Nussbaum, *Not for Profit*.

12. See the discussion in Chapter 4 in Vander Stichele and Penner, *Contextualizing Gender in Early Christian Discourse*.

13. The translation industry seems to play an important role related to modern Bible users; see the discussion in Martin, "Womanist Interpretations of the New Testament."

Third—and a very important point in this book, since it is the criterion for the text selection—are the various margins of the Bible. Not only have certain Biblical interpreters or perspectives been marginal, but also certain texts passages and characters in the Bible itself are marginal and have been largely ignored by interpreters. Some Biblical characters have almost been forgotten since they have been of little value for those whose primary interest was the great men of early Christianity, such as Jesus, Paul, Peter, and John. Elisabeth Schüssler Fiorenza has criticized the view of Jesus as a unique personality and religious genius, emphasizing the roles of the participants in the early Christian movement, especially the wo/men.[14] Recent attempts to "de-center Jesus" emphasize the importance of the community for the construction of Christian origins.[15]

In the margins of these de-centered spaces I have found some intriguing texts and characters that might enhance current discussions of identity and power relations. Recent interpretations show that the margins are indeed about to be destabilized: the Ethiopian eunuch, for example, is not marginal at all for the LGBT community or African scholars. For sex workers texts about prostitutes or sexualized slaves may be the most relevant to study.[16] Many "new" readers highlight characters and texts that earlier have been overlooked.

Fourth, those I characterized as cultural users of the Bible may be considered as being at the margins, since Biblical scholarship traditionally has served religious users. As I have argued, however, marginality is fluid; perhaps the growing attention towards the Bible as part of the cultural canon will give those who consider it to be Holy Scripture an experience of being marginalized? Recent trends at conferences and in publishing houses show that themes such as the Bible and film, the Bible and fiction, and the Bible in recent philosophy enjoy prestige within the field. Or should the distinction between those two categories of readers—religious and cultural Bible readers—be downplayed, since both "old" and "new" readers will include people who vary in background, gender, race, class, age, and health? And perhaps it at times would be difficult to decide which group that readers belong to? My guess is that other or marginal

---

14. See, e.g., Schüssler Fiorenza, *Jesus and the Politics of Interpretation*, 36. See also Moxnes, "From Unique Personality to Charismatic Movement."

15. See in particular Part 1 in Johnson-Debaufre, *Jesus among Her Children*.

16. See Ipsen, *Sex Working and the Bible*.

texts may come to the fore when a variety of readers with a mixture of backgrounds and identities approach the Bible.

A pertinent question here is what happens when the margins meet. Do power struggles take place at the margins as well? I will return to this question when reading ancient texts, since both Biblical characters and modern interpreters deal with overlapping marginality in interesting ways. A follow-up question may be whether there are any limits to the marginality, that is, am I interested in any type of cultural or religious user of the Bible as long as they are (or I perceive them as) marginal? In principle, yes, but in this book I will pay particular attention to those who read the Bible as part of the cultural canon and those who consider it to be a useful text in fighting domination and colonialism.

A final reflection concerns myself. Am I by any means a reader at the margins? Since marginality seems to be an open and fluid category, this question needs to be contextualized.[17] I am a white, Norwegian, middle-class, educated woman with a foreign family name; for some I am exotic in being both a feminist and a Christian. But more important than stating who I am is to reflect upon who I am not, as Anne Hege Grung, my colleague in Oslo, does. Like her, I am not a person who faces pressure for my religious identity. I am not poor, politically oppressed, threatened due to my gender, or living amidst violent conflict.[18] I think her arguments can help me to engage in contexts of marginality: as long as we are open for what we cannot represent, are willing to be corrected by other voices, and invite other perspectives that can compensate for what we lack ourselves, we may contribute to an epistemology that aims to construct a better world.[19] This is a shared project; to destabilize the margins is a challenging task that invites all responsible and self-critical people of good will and that is not dependent on any given or stable positioning in the world.

---

17. Note that Scandinavian hermeneutical practices are listed among "other" together with African, Asian, and Latino in Vander Stichele and Penner, *Contextualizing Gender in Early Christian Discourse*, 172.

18. Grung, "Makt og kontekst i Susanna-fortellingen."

19. Ibid.

MEMORY THEORY AND INTERSECTIONALITY AT THE MARGINS

But how can the margins be destabilized? For me, this question deals with the process of challenging "the past as we allegedly know it by questioning the power structures that are embedded and preserved in the archives we have inherited."[20] Related to the Bible, we need tools that can help us see that what we remember from the past is a result of power struggles. Negotiation over memory took place before the texts were written down, but also subsequently, as some of these texts have hardly been noticed by readers and interpreters ever since. Issues of intersecting power relations obviously play a huge role in these processes.

The two theoretical traditions I employ in this book, memory theory and intersectionality, originated outside the field of Biblical studies. Of the two, memory theory has garnered increasing interest during the last ten years within this field.[21] My main reason for employing memory theory regards both concepts and vocabulary; by use of memory theory it is possible to talk in nuanced ways about the relation between past, present and future, but also to explore the complex power dynamics embedded in the memory process. The basic assumption is that remembering the past serves the process of present identity formation. Memory reflects the past, but also shapes the present and the future by providing people with understandings and symbolic frameworks that enable them to make sense of the world.[22]

The other set of analytical tools I will employ both challenges and modifies the concept of memory and develops and expands feminist perspectives. Intersectionality as a theoretical concept has only recently been applied to Biblical scholarship,[23] although the basic ideas and concerns have for some years now been articulated by African American scholarship and womanist Biblical interpreters, in particular. Intersectionality has become essential within recent race and gender theory.[24] Some scholars even talk about "the intersectional turn."[25] Instead of examining gender,

---

20. Rowley and Wolthers, "Lost and Found," 9.

21. For a good overview see Rodríguez, *Structuring Early Christian Memory*.

22. Misztal, *Theories of Social Remembering*, 13.

23. See for example Schüssler Fiorenza, "Introduction" and Kartzow, "Asking the Other Question."

24. See Davis, "Intersectionality as Buzzword," Knapp, "Race, Class, Gender."

25. Mattsson, "Genua och vithet i den intersektionella vändingen."

race, class, age, and sexuality as separate categories of oppression, intersectionality explores how these categories overlap and mutually modify and reinforce each other.[26]

Intersectionality is useful for conceptualizing power aspects of the memory process, but can also help interpret ancient texts in their social, political, and historical contexts. Many of the marginal characters in early Christian memory have complex identities in which these categories intersect. A complex web of identity markers constructs a culturally complex social environment in which concrete persons with concrete bodies were located. Cross-cutting ties and diverse combination of identities describe the Roman Empire at the time when Christianity entered the scene.[27] Several identity categories were subject to constant renegotiation, and identity construction often seems to be a work in progress.[28] A person could change status and position during his or her lifespan due to a variety of reasons, and especially "the blurring distinction between slave and free" was an object for fear or hope.[29] Multiple loyalties could generate conflict, and ancient sources testify to several challenges for those Roman citizens who in addition were Jews or Christians. Categories did not operate in isolation but were interconnected and influenced each other. A brief look at the Ethiopian eunuch (Acts 8:26–40) will immediately illustrate these points. Some of the identity markers were challenging to combine, and sometimes also dangerous, illegal, or downright impossible. In this book I suggest that theories from what has been know as intersectionality can account for some of the complexity of early Christian memory.

Early Christian Memory: Marginality and the Archive

When we remember the past, we are creative and selective in what we choose to mention and how we shape the narratives. The process of remembering serves the challenges of the present. As Mieke Bal says, memory concerns the past, but happens in the present.[30] Early Christian

---

26. P. H. Collins, "It's All in the Family," 63. See also Nadar, "The Bible in and for Mission," 226.

27. See the discussion in Eriksen, "What Is Cultural Complexity?"

28. See Knust, *Abandoned to Lust*, 85. See also Conway, *Behold the Man*, 68–69.

29. See chapter 3 in Glancy, *Slavery in Early Christianity*, 71–101. She focuses especially on Augustine and pays attention to "the open windows in the slave system: enslavement, sale, escape and manumission," 72.

30. Bal, *Travelling Concepts in the Humanities*, 183.

writers constructed their stories to serve the purposes of their own time. Ancient texts can therefore be read as participating in a communication process in which disagreement, conflict, and the struggle for power most certainly were vital ingredients. As readers, interpreters, and users of Biblical texts, we also participate in the memory process.

The theoretical concept "memory" has become a complex, pluralistic, and labyrinthine analytical tool that has been increasingly influential in cultural history and social sciences in recent years, as well as in Biblical studies.[31] I have a rather ambiguous relationship to memory theory: On the one hand, I am intuitively suspicious of a theory that all kinds of researchers embrace and employ. Is it merely because it is convenient, adaptable, and simple that we all use it? We can almost talk about a memory industry; so much is published around it and so many interests (also financial) are tied to it, and yet so little seriously critical scholarship deals with it. On the other hand, I find memory to be a useful concept to theorize certain features of my research. I am among those who need the vocabulary offered, the core ideas, and the various perspectives in order to engage with and challenge the questions I aim at highlighting in this book. I solve this ambiguity by drawing on gender and feminist critique of the concept of memory, and in particular by combining memory theory and intersectionality. Accordingly, my aim is not to give a comprehensive overview of memory theory, but only present a few aspects of the available theories in order to use them in my analysis.

Negotiating Canon and Archive

Memory is never innocent. The past as such is not remembered; rather, small, limited pieces of the past are selected in order to construct new meaning, challenge the present, or rewrite the past in order to better serve present purposes. What is remembered represents the exception, since most of the past is forgotten.

Memory theory offers a language to talk about the complex relation between "past" and "present."[32] According to Aleida Assmann, cultural memory consists of two interrelated categories, remembering and forget-

---

31. Castelli, *Martyrdom and Memory*, 5.

32. See for example the various studies in J. Assmann, *Religion and Cultural Memory*. See also Mendels, *Memory in Jewish, Pagan and Christian Societies of the Graeco-Roman World*.

ting.³³ I am in particular interested in the two subgroups of remembering, that is "canon" and "archive," representing the active and passive side of memory. Assmann imagines these two modes of memory as two separate rooms at a museum, where the prestigious objects are shown to the visitors in carefully staged shows while other paintings and objects are stored in inaccessible cellars or attics. She considers "the show rooms of cultural memory as the *canon* and the attics and cellars as the *archive*."³⁴ Canon can be called "the presence of the past," while the archive represents "the pastness of the past."

These concepts are not stable, however. The archive is part of memory, giving us the opportunity to retrieve lost memory from the archive, to transform the pastness of the past to be relevant for the present; in addition, what is part of the active canon today can be relocated to the archive tomorrow. These are very useful distinctions when focusing on marginality. We may say that the Bible represents memory divided into both canon and archive. By aiming to use intersectionality to destabilize the margins, this book demonstrates that canon and archive are neither stable nor constant throughout time and place.

Other elements, however, are neither inscribed in canon nor archive; they are not part of memory and are lost forever. Most of the past is in fact forgotten.³⁵ The past however, can be re-imagined or reconstructed as recovered memory.

Elizabeth Castelli argues in her book *Martyrdom and Memory* that memory deals with struggles over power, reason, law, and order. She sees memory work done by the early Christians as a form of culture making, where identity was indelibly marked by collective memory of the past.³⁶ A remarkable capacity of collective memory is that it explores the work that the past does in the present.³⁷ When reading two central New Testament texts that deal with hierarchy (Gal 3:28 and the Colossian household codes), I wonder who needed this memory to construct their present identity or for the benefit of culture making.

---

33. See Figure 4 in A. Assmann, "The Religious Roots of Cultural Memory," 274.

34. Ibid. The term canon in this sense obviously has a different meaning than in Christian theology.

35. Ibid.

36. Castelli, *Martyrdom and Memory*, 4.

37. Ibid., 9.

The NT texts constitute parts of the written version of early Christian memory, and I am interested in how the process continued when later texts used the same social motifs or re-interpret the same characters. How is for example the early Christian story of the martyr Blandina, who is called both slave and ideal woman and who performs masculine duties, an example of how Gal 3:28 is negotiated? This perspective generates some new questions: How are the hierarchies remembered—how are they used to construct meaning?

Memory, Storytelling, and Identity Questions

Community and identity formation is shaped by remembering and storytelling.[38] Collective memory works to construct a shared identity, a shared past, a shared reason to live.[39] According to Jeffrey Olick, "Identity...is always a relation between past and present established through the media of memory."[40] The past for early Christian groups was what they remembered and retold about Jesus and his early followers, and the New Testament represents what some of them found most relevant to remember. These written remains, these peoples' selective stories of the past, served various purposes in their present situation, generations after eyewitnesses had passed away. Quoting Stuart Hall, Olick goes on to write:

> "Identities are the names we give to different ways we are positioned by, and position ourselves in, the narrative of the past." This is just another way of saying that identities are projects and practices that individuals and groups undertake rather than essential and unchanging properties they possess.[41]

Accordingly, what the various early Christian groups remembered was kept alive and helped construct their identity. Furthermore, memory also shapes the future, and we are part of the New Testament's future. These texts become our stories of the past, our memory that contribute to shape our present reality. And the Bible represents memory that is important for both the religious and cultural readers, and for readers at the margins.

Since memory is so important for identity and deals with power issues, feminist theory contributes by asking about women in the process

---

38. Boomershine, *Story Journey*, 19. Wire, *Holy Lives, Holy Deaths*, 4.

39. On collective memory, see the new preface in Casey, *Remembering*. See also Connerton, *How Societies Remember*.

40. Olick, "Products, Processes, and Practices," 8.

41. Ibid., 6.

of remembering the past. Feminists often work with recovered memory,[42] and the concept of "memory" is used to define the field of women's studies as a form of "countermemory," focusing on the official "forgetting" of women's history.[43] It has been pointed out, however, that feminist perspectives have not yet reached the majority of publications on memory.[44]

Intersectionality and Early Christian Marginality

Whereas some interpreters have been concerned with criticizing memory theory and memory theorists for ignoring the importance of gender, I try to develop the perspectives by use of intersectionality. It is not only women who have suffered from not being represented in the memory process; mechanisms related to class, race, ethnicity, age, sexuality, or health also play important roles.

The characters described in texts from the ancient world experienced complex social relations, as the text material presented in this book shows. A slave, who himself was considered an owned body, could be given the role as overseer for his fellow slaves, but in one of Jesus' parables, one such slave used his privileges to beat and mistreat his fellow slaves (Luke 12:45). The Ethiopian eunuch was associated with the stigmatized category of eunuchs, but he was nonetheless a treasurer of an important queen and was granted the privilege of reading from a scroll, sitting in a chariot, and returning from a pilgrimage. How can we understand such complex and intersecting social roles?

As argued by the social anthropologist Thomas Hylland Eriksen, leader of the research project at the University of Oslo entitled *Cultural complexity in the new Norway*, we need a new language to talk about cultural complexity.[45] In this book I present several attempts to let intersectionality offer such a new language to talk about the complexity of early Christian memory. The concept of intersectionality has gained increas-

---

42. Hirsch and Smith, "Feminism and Cultural Memory," 3.

43. Ibid., 4.

44. See Schüssler Fiorenza, "Discipleship of Equals". See for example Rodríguez, *Structuring Early Christian Memory*.

45. "Cross-cutting ties and multiple loyalties are typical characteristics of any complex society. An ethnic or religious label does not provide a satisfactory description of the relevant characteristics of a person or group. Although there are implicit rules and norms regulating group membership, diverse combinations of identities are empirically possible." See http://www.culcom.uio.no/forskning/programbeskrivelse.

ing currency within recent interdisciplinary research.[46] It has become the primary analytic tool that feminist and anti-racist scholars deploy for theorizing identity and oppression.[47] When white Western feminists in the 1960s and 1970s started to criticize male-centrism, their insights about oppression "as a woman" tended to conflate the experiences of one particular group of women with those of all women.[48] In the early 1980s African American scholar-activists in particular started to question the hegemony of white women within the feminist movement. They argued that the experiences of African American women are not shaped only by race but also by gender, social class, and sexuality.[49] Awareness of how different social divisions cannot be understood in isolation, but that they mutually modify and reinforce each other, is central to intersectional studies.[50]

Instead of examining gender, race, class, age, and sexuality as separate categories of oppression, intersectionality explores how these categories overlap.[51] Every person belongs to more than one category, and faced with discrimination it might be difficult to articulate which correlative system of oppression is at work.[52] Various oppressive mechanisms can work together and create new hierarchies and systems of discrimination. Intersectionality offers a language to talk about cultural complexity and our role in the production of knowledge.[53]

---

46. See Knapp, "Race, Class, Gender."

47. Nash, "Re-Thinking Intersectionality," 1. See also Davis, "Intersectionality as Buzzword," 68. McCall, "The Complexity of Intersectionality," 1777. Note, however, that "intersectionality" is not mentioned as a keyword in 2001 in Gamble, ed. *The Routledge Companion to Feminism and Postfeminism*.

48. The critique of white feminism's hegemony and exclusive practice was strongly articulated in Crenshaw, *Demarginalizing the Intersection of Race and Sex*.

49. For a critical presentation of how intersectionality relates to feminist theory, see De los Reyes and Mulinari, *Intersektionalitet*, esp. 78–88.

50. See, e.g., Phoenix and Pattynama, eds., *European Journal of Women's Studies*. See in particular their introduction. See also Maseno and Kartzow, "Widows, Intersectionality and the Parable in Luke 18."

51. P. H. Collins, "It's All in the Family," 63.

52. In the UN, as well as in the EU system, intersectionality has become a useful tool to address multiple inequalities and discrimination; see Verloo, "Multiple Inequalities, Intersectionality and the European Union".

53. See also the research project chaired by Moxnes: "Jesus in Cultural Complexity," ([Univeristy of Oslo] www.tf.uio.no/jc).

One important issue to discuss is whether intersectionality inadvertently functions to uphold the given categories. Are categories such as gender, class, and race stable and already given? While some argue that so-called third wave feminism responded to the collapse of the category of "women," intersectionality needs the categories as a premise when highlighting overlapping categories.[54] I think my way out of this dilemma is to use intersectionality to nuance identities and challenge the stability of any group identity. Rather then using impulses from post-structural thinking to argue that categories do not exist anymore, I use intersectionality to destabilize ancient and new power structures and ways of organizing identity that employ gender, class, race, and so forth. This combination of reading strategies seems to follow recent trends in which interpreters embrace multilayered approaches and prefer to draw on a diversity of theoretical thoughts within the humanities as well as the social sciences.[55]

Intersectionality, Biblical Studies and Finding Relevant Social Categories

In a recent publication Elisabeth Schüssler Fiorenza finds it "more than surprising" that scholarship of early Christianity has not embraced the "rich body of critical feminist work on intersectionality."[56] I welcome her challenge and argue that we need to re-think both the category of women and that of memory by use of intersectionality.[57] Although intersectionality obviously has its weak points and pitfalls, it helps interpreters solve essential challenges of complexity when dealing with ancient texts.[58]

---

54. Snyder, "What Is Third-Wave Feminism?" 175.

55. See the introduction in Vander Stichele and Penner, *Contextualizing Gender in Early Christian Discourse*.

56. Schüssler Fiorenza, "Introduction," 4–5.

57. See also various contributions in the recent book Bailey, Liew, and Segovia, eds., *They Were All Together in One Place?*

58. Note that, although embraced, the concept has also generated critique, for example when the use of intersectionality is "motivated by an ethical-political 'will to empower' underprivileged groups," discussed in Gressgård, "Mind the Gap." Some point at the "analytical confusion" that has followed from the use of intersectionality, although some of these issues have already "been tackled by feminist scholars;" see Yuval-Davis, "Intersectionality and Feminist Politics," 206. "[T]o assume an unquestioned similarity of inequalities," where all differences (in class, race/ethnicity, sexual orientation and gender) are incorrectly considered equal, has been one way of facing multiple discrimination. To employ a "one size fits all" approach when confronted with inequality represents

When theories of intersectionality are relocated from studies of current oppression and power to studies of ancient texts, one important task is to find relevant categories. The standard categories of gender, sexuality, class, race, age, and health are not necessarily the most important ones for conceptualizing ancient societies. What categories to include is an ongoing discussion for scholars, often marked by adding "etc." to the suggested list of categories.[59] For example, if we want to understand the role of Hagar, Sarah's slave girl from Egypt who was brought to Abraham because Sarah was apparently barren, the category of motherhood—with all its various intersections with slavery, race, and sexuality—would be essential.

Furthermore, the social categories "gender," "race," and "class" are contested, and in post-war and post-communist contexts the latter two terms in particular may seem problematic.[60] In this book these terms are used to relate to a specific theoretical discourse, although they must be qualified: for example, "class" as understood in Marxist ideology would hardly fit to describe the ancient discourse on slavery or the present power structures in the US.[61] Still, I often use "class" and not merely "social status" when I discuss the power dynamics between slave and free. By emphasizing class, I want to look at the difference discursive practices related to these main characters within a slavery system.[62] These supposedly fixed groups, where free persons owned enslaved persons, may represent different "classes" that do not corresponding to the ideas of class in the political discourse of the last century.

Intersectionality originates from discourses in which it functioned as a tool to understand discrimination and the subordinated, but it may be employed in order to understand difference in general and how identities are negotiated.[63] To move beyond uniformity and simplification is

---

a misuse of intersectionality. See Verloo, "Multiple Inequalities, Intersectionality and the European Union," 211.

59. See the discussions in McCall, "The Complexity of Intersectionality."

60. Knapp, "Race, Class, Gender."

61. See also the editors' introduction in Økland and Boer, *Marxist Feminist Criticism of the Bible*.

62. See the discussion of status in Meeks, *The First Urban Christians*, 51–53.

63. See Sengupta, "I/Me/Mine—Intersectional Identities as Negotiated Minefields".

useful in order to understand identities, regardless of where a person is located in the hierarchies.[64]

Asking the Other Question

Mari Matsuda argues that intersectionality enables interpreters to "ask the other question":[65]

> The way I try to understand the interconnection of all forms of subordination is through a method I call "ask the other question." When I see something that looks racist, I ask, "Where is the patriarchy in this?" When I see something that looks sexist, I ask, "Where is the heterosexism in this?" When I see something that looks homophobic, I ask, "Where are the class interests in this?"[66]

Her insights are compelling, although I will emphasize that it is not only when a form of subordination is made explicit that "the other question," or perhaps rather *questions* in plural, may be relevant.[67] Her insights may help us look for what is not necessarily visible at the surface. When feminist interpreters are enthusiastic about the women at Jesus' empty tomb and their role in the oral transmission, for example, Matsuda may challenge us to ask about female slaves or about those who did not know the language. Intersectionality offers tools to decode complex identities, regardless of where in the hierarchy the given character can be located. In fact, one of the benefits of intersectionality is that it emphasizes the relational nature of identity and highlights interaction between the categories as a separate object for analysis.[68]

Since I started my scholarly work as a feminist concerned with how gender hierarchies work to exclude women in both the past and the present, intersectionality has helped me realize that although I am sensitive to issues of marginality, I am also on top of certain hierarchies. It is not only gender systems that construct dominant discourses, silencing the voices from the margins: sexism, today and in history, overlaps with other

---

64. Burman, "From Difference to Intersectionality," 294.

65. Matsuda, "Beside My Sister, Facing the Enemy," 1183–92. See also Nash, "Re-Thinking Intersectionality," 12.

66. Matsuda, "Beside My Sister, Facing the Enemy," 1189.

67. Various scholars have discussed whether intersectionality can be used to understand oppression only or more broadly to understand all aspects of identity and hierarchy; see for example Davis, "Intersectionality as Buzzword."

68. As argued by Saga, "Teologi for hundene?"

systems of discrimination, and if scholars pay attention to elite women only we risk reproducing and legitimating the oppression of marginalized women and men.[69] Although ancient sources are most interested in the elite, intersectionality can help us fill in the gaps by providing tools to unpack the rhetoric of the given text and suggest different ways of reading.

COMBINING MEMORY THEORY AND INTERSECTIONALITY: TOWARDS A METHODOLOGY

Developing Matsuda's technique of asking the other question, I will take some specific aspects of intersectionality into consideration. First, I will examine intersectional reasoning in ancient texts. Second, I will ask the other question when several categories are not made explicit: when a text deals with women, for example, I will ask about class; when a text talks about slavery, I will ask about gender or ethnicity; and so forth. Third, I will investigate the intersectional aspects of the memory process. I will see the ancient texts as memory, and I will also consider readers, interpreters, and users as contributors to the memory process.

I take the early Christian texts to be "frozen" memory, selective and creative representations of the past for those who wrote, composed, read, or heard these texts. All of them did not necessarily agree on these representations, as the several variations of the story of women and resurrection in the Gospels bear witness to. Perhaps other alternative variations of early Christian memory also existed, and we must assume that some of these stories are lost to us. What is forgotten is lost, but to focus on the archive may be one way to challenge the active canon in order to open up for more variety and complexity.

The memory process indeed deals with intersecting power structures. What is remembered helps construct identity in a given time and place—but whose memory? By employing an intersectional approach to memory, this book will focus on marginalized characters and the dynamics of the archive. Memory theory helps scholars identify and articulate issues related to power, status, and struggle over canon.[70]

---

69. Spelman, *Inessential Woman*, 52–53.

70. See the introduction to Danbolt, Rowley, and Wolthers, eds., *Lost and Found*. See also Olick, "Products, Processes, and Practices."

An important insight intersectionality may generate is related to what has been called a text's destabilizing potential.[71] I have at times found it useful to look for what represents destabilizing discourses of marginality in ancient texts. For example, when Paul is so annoyed by a possessed, fortune-telling slave girl that he heals her, it is a destabilizing element that what she actually says (i.e., that Paul and his men are slaves of God) is the truth according to the logic and ideology of the narrative (Acts 16:16–18). Her function as someone who speaks the truth is actually remembered. To ask critical questions of why Paul is so annoyed will allow the passage's destabilizing potential play a role. Then this strange slave girl is allowed a more ambiguous role, challenging our ideas about marginality within early Christian groups.

When I use the expression "Re-Forgetting" in the title of this introduction, I play with the dynamics of memory. To forget means that we do not remember, and re-forget will accordingly indicate that we forget once more or continue to forget. To re-forget the margins indicates that what is forgotten remains forgotten; we simply reproduce patterns of memory that construct the same ideas about marginality. The nuanced vocabulary within memory theory helps us conceptualize and challenge the power aspects of the archive, and hopefully *not* re-forget the margins. Instead of re-forgetting, this book aims at destabilizing: what is in the archive does not have to remain in the margins forever. By highlighting some of these characters, I hope to increase their visibility as Biblical figures with whom we can fruitfully engage.

I am interested in possible social scenarios that the various New Testament texts may build on or generate when marginal characters are presented. It takes a great deal of social imagination to conceptualize the rhetorical universe. By combining memory theory with what Matsuda calls the "method of asking the other question," I engage with questions of what *could* have happened and how possible listeners or readers of selected early Christian texts *could* have understood them and responded to them. In using the theories presented above, I am interested in the following interpretative practices:

---

71. The terminology of "destabilizing potential" is borrowed from Hornsby, "The Annoying Woman," 83.

1. To theorize the gaps in the archive in order to continue the process of social imagination;
2. To look for destabilizing potential within discourses of marginality;
3. To ask about whose memory these texts may reflect.

I see my attempt at employing intersectionality and memory theory on early Christian discourses of marginality mostly as an experiment. The texts I engage with in this book represent merely a selection of case studies in which some tendencies and patterns occur. Nevertheless, I hope to bring new perspectives into the discussion and to contribute with critical and creative suggestions to enlighten the role of early Christian memory for identity construction and power struggles in our fast-changing world.

METHODOLOGY AND MARGINALITY

I am interested in these theoretical discussions not only to demonstrate that theories "fit" the Biblical material or interpretative practices, but also because I need them to deal with some of the questions I am struggling with related to marginality. My attitude towards theory, inspired by scholars of ethnography who develop theories based on their fieldwork, is to invite the texts to interact with theory, or rather, to acknowledge that interpreters do this work for texts. In this analytical process I try to create a conversation where theory and text meet, cross, or overlap—or perhaps intersect? The reiterative process of reasoning from theory to text and back again is the basic procedure of this book.[72]

However, I see also a danger in this methodology, as all interpretative activities have ethical implications.[73] If we construct useful theories based on other peoples' struggles, because we want to understand ancient texts, we risk reproducing colonizing power relations. Suffering people will easily be reduced to objects; their life situations are merely useful to think with for us. We are in danger of forgetting them as fellow human beings. In this book I will try to account for such tendencies by highlighting that the marginality and suffering of men and women in early Christian memory challenges us to identify and be responsible for structures of

---

72. Craffert, *The Life of a Galilean Shaman*, 79–80.
73. See Schüssler Fiorenza, *Rhetoric and Ethic*.

hierarchy and oppression today.[74] I will look for destabilizing potential within discourses of marginality and thereby also challenge the power relations embedded in all memory processes.

Memory theory and intersectionality used to emphasize marginality have in particular helped me become aware of the female slaves in early Christian texts. Many of the characters I discuss in this book are female slaves. They are marginalized according to parameters of gender, sexuality, and class. Since her groundbreaking book *In Memory of Her*, Elisabeth Schüssler Fiorenza has contributed significantly to the discussion by highlighting and remembering non-elite women.[75] She talks about kyriarchal/kyriocentric (from the Greek term for lord) in order to "underscore that domination is not simply a matter of patriarchal, gender-based dualism but of more comprehensive, interlocking, hierarchically ordered structures of domination, evident in a variety of oppressions, such as racism, poverty, heterosexism, and colonialism."[76] Also Jennifer Glancy's work on slavery takes up the intersections of gender and class, and deals extensively with the body, sexuality, and masculinity.[77] *Beyond Slavery*, a recent anthology edited by Bernadette Brooten, also deals with intersectional dynamics and marginality.[78] Female slaves in early Christianity do not represent a coherent group, and detailed studies of some textual representations of them may give new dimensions to discussions of identity, power relations, social status, and gender.

I am interested in opposition, transformation, and counter-discourse. A fascinating example is the memory of Hagar, the Egyptian slave girl of Sarah and Abraham in Genesis. She is marginalized in early Christian memory, but praised by some rabbinic texts, and she ended up

---

74. I find the epilogue of the book *Beyond Slavery* as exemplifying such a methodology: Mende Nazer, an internationally known anti-slavery activist and former slave in Sudan and London, has read the book and comments on the various articles dealing with Jewish, Christian, and Islamic slavery. She talks about her experiences from enslavement in relation to the religious discourses, urging scholars, jurists, ethicists, and theologians to "continue to do research and to think deeply about slavery" and readers to "find ways to stop slavery and to overcome its legacy." Nazer, with Brooten, "Epilogue," 316.

75. Schüssler Fiorenza, *In Memory of Her*. See also Schüssler Fiorenza, *The Power of the Word*, 159–60.

76. Schüssler Fiorenza, *Rhetoric and Ethic*, ix.

77. Glancy, *Slavery in Early Christianity*. See also Glancy, "Early Christianity, Slavery, and Women's Bodies."

78. Brooten (with assistance of Jacqueline L. Hazelton), ed. *Beyond Slavery*.

being the mother of a new civilization in Islam. Another example is the verse about the male and female slaves who are beaten in the parable in Luke 12:45. This verse is not even mentioned in one of the most influential NT commentaries, and the female slaves are not important characters in various source books of early Christian women (see chapter 1). Can such characters who suffered from violence and oppression be identity figures, because they are survivors? They were at the bottom of the status and gender hierarchies in antiquity and have been ignored in modern scholarship, but they survived in the margins of the archive. I suggest that the best way to challenge marginality is to employ memory theory and intersectionality.

THE STRUCTURE OF THIS BOOK

Jennifer Glancy has pointed out that "[i]ntersectional identities are expressed and negotiated through corporal encounters. Through bodies and embodied exchange, cultural complexity *takes place*."[79] In Part One of this book I focus in particular on some selected bodies employing an intersectional approach to discuss how bodies were remembered. In chapter 1 I use the parable in Luke 12, called the "Watchful Slaves" (NRSV), to think with. The master leaves the house and appoints one of his slaves to run the household. This wicked slave calculates that it may take a while before the master returns, and he begins to beat the other male and female slaves and eat and get drunk (Luke 12:45). The social scenario and household hierarchy represented in the parable generates a whole set of intersectional questions, dealing with social class, gender, generation/age, and violence. This parable is remembered by Luke and Matthew, but only Luke divides the beaten slaves into male and female. Who needed this story to construct their identity? Both evangelists put this parable in the mouth of Jesus, and none of them challenge or condemn the institution of slavery or the gender-divided violence on slave bodies. If early Christian groups included male and female slaves, how would they react to this parable? And how do present-day readers react?

In chapter 2 the Ethiopian eunuch (Acts 8:26–40) is examined in all his complexity. By use of intersectionality, this chapter pays particular attention to issues of social class and masculinity. By comparing the passage

---

79. Glancy, "Jesus, the Syrophoenician Woman, and Other First Century Bodies," 362.

with other ancient texts, I argue that it makes a huge difference whether a eunuch was recruited among slaves or whether he had a background as a free man. A slave eunuch was already before castration a male body outside of the ideal gender discourse—what did castration then do to male slaves' gender? I also focus on how the Ethiopian eunuch's complex identity was remembered by his early interpreters, the Church Fathers, to get an idea about negotiations and struggle over memory. Finally, I discuss the potential role of this text in contemporary discussions of marginal identities.

I include a chapter on a text that is perhaps more contested as representing early Christian memory, the ancient novel known as *Joseph and Aseneth*. Regardless of whether one considers this story "Christian" or "Jewish," I find the text as well as modern interpretations of it an excellent case study for intersectionality and memory theory. It is in particular the tendency to parallel Joseph and Aseneth's virginity—the common observation in scholarship that "they were both virgins"—that generates the discussion in chapter 3. By use of intersectionality I examine how ethnicity/religion, body, sexuality, and gender make a significant difference in constructing the meaning of virginity for the two main characters of this story.

The last chapter in Part One considers the Pastoral Epistles and two specific issues dealing with female and male bodies: motherhood and circumcision. Chapter 4 asks about the role of slaves in discourses of motherhood. When it is argued that women shall be saved through childbirth, can we imagine that also female slave mothers were supposed to be included? In contrast to motherhood, which is a central element of femininity in these letters, a marginal and polemical verse mentions a specific inscription on the male body: the phrase "those of the circumcised" functions as a nametag for Jews, and I ask about the physicality of this expression. Could only free male bodies be represented by such an expression or were also women or male slaves with Jewish origin included in the term?

Part Two emphasizes discourses in which identity construction seem crucial, and asks, Whose voices or words are remembered? I find issues of speech and talk essential in order to understand early Christian power relations and ideology. A whole set of characters are silenced in the sources, some are asked to shut up, and some are given prominent space to speak and talk and are remembered as talking agents. Gender seems to be a key category in these discourses, but by use of intersectionality the patterns have to be nuanced. Not all kinds of women were told to be silent, and not all men were allowed to speak. What about slaves of both genders and how do ethnicity and race construct ideal or disqualified speech and talk?

Chapter 5 engages with the growing field of studies that deal with orality. While examining the various representations of the women at Jesus' empty tomb, I ask critical questions about what categories of women actually had access to the "oral female communities." Building on recent feminist research related to "oral genres," I develop the perspective from gender to intersectionality in a comparative reading of canonical and non-canonical texts about the women at the empty tomb. To question ideas about gender related to resurrection stories may complicate the picture and challenge some present-day preconceptions.

In chapter 6 I follow up scholars who emphasize how speech in the Pastoral Epistles constructs ideal, masculine discourse. It has been argued that gender functions to divide speech and talk into vice and virtue in these epistles, and I add that also issues of social class and ethnicity/religion play a crucial role. By looking at the intersections of several social categories, the picture becomes far more complicated. Who benefitted on remembering Paul in this way, as a person who had limited tolerance of alternative or uncontrolled speech? And how shall we as readers and users handle such stereotypes?

A specific category of women that is mentioned in the New Testament, in two texts in particular (Luke/Acts and 1 Tim), is that of widows. How does the status of a widow as "a woman without a man" destabilize her gender identity? What kind of ideas dealing with for example sexuality or speech were connected to widows? In chapter 7 I compare the parable in Luke 18:2–5, in which a certain widow breaks with conventional gender patterns and approaches a judge, with "the widow's tale" in the Pastorals (1 Tim 5:3–16) and use theories of gossip as feminine speech as my point of departure.

The last chapter in Part Two highlights a marginal female character whose remembrance is far from prominent in early Christian discourse. In Acts 16:16–18, Paul heals a possessed fortune-telling slave girl because she annoys him. My take on this story in chapter 8 is to use intersectionality to compare Paul and this slave girl, since they both are presented as "talking slaves." He is a slave in his relation to God, and she has angry owners who attack Paul since he takes away her profitable talent as a fortune teller. This little story in Acts deals with speech, talk, voice, and silence on several levels. By highlighting the multiple meanings of "slave" in this passage, I conduct an experiment to see what happens if the female slave and the male protagonist Paul, the slave of God, are considered as a "talking pair."

Part Three emphasizes another central element of identity construction and marginality: social relations, which uphold or confirm who we are and where we are located in the hierarchies. In chapter 9 I read two passages connected to Pauline memory that both have played major roles in discussions of power structures and patterns of dominance or liberation in history and even today: the "baptism formula" in Gal 3:28 and the household codes in Colossians. On the surface these passages, which in structure both employ three opposing relationship pairs, seem to contrast each other, as Gal 3:28 proclaims a vision of equality while Colossians requires strict patriarchal order in the household. But when comparing these two passages by use of intersectionality and reading them with other ancient texts, far more complex patterns of social control and possible resistance emerge.

The last section of this book, Part Four, represents an attempt to look beyond intersectionality. Although early Christian texts are based on hierarchical structures, stereotypes, and power regulations, some few and marginal texts and characters destabilize this negative picture. I am in particular fascinated by female slaves, since they seem to represent a threefold oppression related to gender, sexuality, and class. In early Christian texts some of these marginalized characters are nonetheless mentioned by name. With that as a starting point I try to develop the process of social imagination, inspired by theories of recovered memory. Someone within early Christian groups found reasons to remember a few female slaves by name: If they were at the bottom of all hierarchies, why were they named? Slaves were supposed to be cut off from all ties of ethnicity, religion, and origin and were at times re-named. Slaves were also considered genderless, and were not seen as men or women. So why remember some female slaves by name, one of the most important identity markers? The purpose might be to blame them, but the effect is that they are remembered. They are not necessarily prominent characters in the active canon; they are stored away in the archive but are not forgotten.

This naming of female slaves is the point of departure for moving beyond intersectional oppression.

I will contribute to the process of not re-forgetting the margins in Part Four, where the last chapters focus on two named slave women. Chapter 10 reads the story of the slave/woman Blandina in the *Martyrs of Lyon* through the lens of intersectionality. She is among the most fascinating characters in early Christian texts by being both slave and ideal woman, feminine and masculine, and indeed an ideal Christian believer.

Another female slave who is mentioned by Paul is Hagar, and chapter 11 focuses on her as the female slave from Egypt who in the account in Genesis was forced to be a surrogate mother for Sarah and Abraham. In Gal 4, the only place she is mentioned by name in the New Testament, she is not assigned any prominent role at all, but I suggest that the memory of her may nevertheless challenge the massive focus given on Abraham and his children in early Christian discourse. Hagar has become a female hero in several other contexts in spite of how she is remembered by early Christian thinkers.

I divide the discussion of the text material into these four parts, because I think they are relevant for understanding identity and marginality, and because they correspond to issues and topics central to current interdisciplinary discourses. Bodies deal with spatial presence in the world; our bodies represent our appearance in time and place, how we are seen. The aspect of speech and talk relates to how we are able to express ourselves and be heard. Following up, it is indeed in the various social relations that we negotiate, sustain, overcome, or rearticulate identity or marginality. By naming those who are marginalized, we may overcome power structures that reduce human beings to property or objects.

Finally, social relations and identities often seem to be fixed, following given patterns, but I think it is an urgent task for readers, interpreters, and users to search for the unexpected. Although the body, social relations, naming processes, and speaking and talking are essential places where power structures are upheld, interpreters are responsible for creating a room for flexibility, de-stability, and the imaginary.

PART ONE

Embodying Cultural Complexity

As Jennifer Glancy has argued, it is through bodies and embodied exchange that cultural complexity *takes place*. How are such bodies remembered, and how do they construct meaning, identity, and community? Several ancient texts present identities that are hard or challenging to classify according to our categories. Detailed studies of some selected texts may function as case studies that help us reflect further on our own ways of thinking about or being bodies. By paying attention to discourses of bodily processes in antiquity, we do not get access to the actual bodies—we are unable to touch them or see them. Rather, the theories used to reflect on bodies enable scholars to pay close attention to the physicality and materiality of human life and identity and to the various relations and conditions that shape these identities. Physical violence, castration, virginity, motherhood, and circumcision, as inscribed in early Christian memory, also help construct meaning, identity, and bodily practices among readers, interpreters, and users of these texts today, in complex ways.

1

Gendered Slave Bodies and "Metaphorical Violence"

Thinking with Luke 12:45–46

INTRODUCTION

THE PARABLE IN LUKE 12:35–48 may be a good place to start reflecting on how intersectionality and memory theory can contribute with new perspectives by highlighting marginal characters. In contrast to interpreters who use this parable to say something about God and humans, represented by the relationship between master and slave, I am interested in the gendered slavery structures that construct meaning and memory in the narrative universe.

In this parable a master leaves his house, but his entrusted slave misuses his privileged position and starts to beat his fellow slaves, only to be cut into pieces when the owner returns. In Luke's words, Jesus tells the disciples this parable in order to teach them to be prepared. These verses may function as a thought provoking but brutal point of departure.

Slaves represented the margins of the ancient household, with an ambiguous role in the family, and they could be beaten or mistreated. But Lukan terminology opens up for a variety of scenarios: either the trusted slave strikes his fellow slaves, as the synoptic parallel in Matthew says (without mentioning any gender distinction), or the trusted slave strikes boys and girls. Such physical punishment was probably common in ancient households, where slave bodies were part of their owner's property, and children had to obey they parents. Luke constructs ideology and meaning by use of violence and abuse according to power structures in which class, gender, and age intersect.

What about beaten slave bodies? In a slave-holding culture, family values are only for free persons;[1] slaves are only footnotes in great men's biographies.[2] The New Testament and other sources mention male and female slaves among the early Christian groups, and although their "family life" is never discussed in the New Testament, we will draw an unsatisfactory picture of the family if we fail to take into consideration that the Roman Empire was a slave-holding culture. However, in spite of the paucity of the sources, we may nevertheless theorize the gaps.[3]

In her book *Slaves and Other Objects,* Page DuBois treats "the occultation of slavery in the presentation of objects in various institutions of classical studies," arguing that "everyday life" of antiquity is presented without attention being paid to slaves.[4] DuBois examines some museum exhibitions with objects from antiquity, showing that slaves are made invisible. Although slaves were ubiquitous, and production, reproduction, and the ideal family life would be impossible without them, their contribution is not part of what is remembered from the past. They are left in the archive.

The parable in Luke 12:35–48 encourages the disciples to be patient, by comparing God with a master of a household and using the contrast between a good and a wicked slave as an illustration. By using this parable "to think with," I will relate the parable's social reality and ideology to ancient discourses of slavery, gender, and family.[5] I am interested in the historical scenarios and discursive strategies that might be reflected in the parable, as well as in how we as interpreters handle such challenging texts.

I start by reflecting on the complex relation between a parable and "reality." Then I discuss the role of slaves in household and family life and reflect on gender and sexuality in relation to ancient slavery. Finally, I suggest some theoretical tools that may help us to reflect upon how we

---

1. Spelman, *Inessential Woman,* 43.
2. Butler, "Notes on a *Membrum Disiectum,*" 230.
3. I am inspired by Steven Johnstone's reflections on how to write the histories of slaves and women from an earlier period. He suggests that we take the gaps in the ancient sources as facts to be understood and incorporated into historical accounts, in order to link ideology to lived experience. Johnstone, "Cracking the Code of Silence," 223.
4. DuBois, *Slaves and Other Objects.* See section 1, in particular chapter 2.
5. See Vander Stichele and Penner, *Contextualizing Gender in Early Christian Discourse,* 6.

think, talk, and write—or remain silent—about slavery and structures of slavery, in antiquity, and today.

CONTEXTUALIZING THE PARABLE: SLAVERY AND FAMILY

What is this parable about? Parables talk about the relation between God and humans, and in this parable the relation between the master and the slaves has received the most attention. How would "new" readers understand this story? How would they react to the violence of this household?

Some theological interpretations overlook those persons who actually populate the narrative universe of the story. It is striking that commentaries on Luke have nothing to say about the beaten male and female slaves mentioned in verse 45, as if these slaves, or servants as they often are called in modern translations, had no relevance.[6] Translation practices that prefer servant and not slave, interpretative bias, and lack of intersectional sensitivity reduce these male and female slaves to being things or property, making their humanness and victimhood invisible and unimportant.[7] Bringing them out of the archive forces us to acknowledge that these male and female slaves actually are part of the history of early Christian families.

Before I discuss what kind of household this parable may be referring to, I want to briefly comment on the challenge of using a parable as a text that reflects real-life social arrangements. Characteristic of the parable genre is that it uses one reality to talk about another reality, integrating both into a rhetorical unit in which the two worlds simultaneously merge and are kept apart. William Herzog challenges the conception that the parables of Jesus are either theological or moral stories, and argues that they rather are political and economic ones. According to him, parables are not stories about how God works, but how exploitation worked in ancient Palestine.[8] When the parable tells how slaves are beaten according to the magnitude of their perceived transgressions, some real-life slaves probably had such experiences in everyday life, if the parable is to produce meaning for its original audience. The characters and events of

---

6. See for example Fitzmyer, *The Gospel According to Luke: Introduction, Translations and Notes*, 990. Note also that this parable is not commented upon in the chapter on Luke in Blount et al., *True to Our Native Land*.

7. See the strong arguments in favor of translating with "slave" in Martin, "Womanist Interpretations of the New Testament."

8. Herzog, *Parables as Subversive Speech*, 7.

this parable most certainly corresponded to the experiences of both slave owners and slaves within early Christian groups. The bodies of beaten slaves function as metaphors, but for real-life slaves with real bodies violence did affect the integrity of their personhood. I would therefore like to suggest that the family and household parables can be used as relevant material in order for us to think about early Christian families and their rhetorical and strategic functions.

Luise Schottroff has criticized other scholars for reading and interpreting such slave parables in Luke as merely allegories or parables with allegorical elements (see also Luke 17:3–10 and 19:11–27), adding that "[t]his tradition of interpretation has justified slavery and identified the slave owners with God."[9] Interpreters who do not problematize violence against slaves participate in a process that justifies and legitimates that some people were able to own other people. Allegorical or metaphorical slavery language depends on real slavery to make sense, as several scholars have pointed out.[10] Accordingly, slave parables may function to uphold and re-inscribe relations of slavery, in both the past and the present, when one-dimensional theological approaches are applied.

What kind of household is mirrored in Luke 12:35–48? In this parable, the master of the house departs, leaving it up to slave morality to run the house. The master is probably thought to have brought along his wife and their children and other free members of the household, and perhaps some of the other slaves. A framework of an ideal household with husband, wife, children, and slaves constitutes the social environment,[11] a similar structure to what we have in the Pauline and post-Pauline household codes.[12] It is sometimes argued that slaves, as considered part of property, could be part of the household but not the family.[13] In this parable, however, it seems as though the good slave is part of the family, representing family values such as care and responsibility, while the

---

9. Schottroff, *The Parables of Jesus*, 171.

10. On the metaphorical use of slavery in Christian discourse, see Glancy, *Slavery in Early Christianity*, 92–101. In relation to the use of slavery in Pauline letters, Elizabeth Castelli argues that "the use of social relations to make a theological point is successful to the degree that the metaphor reinscribes the social relation, rather than calling it into question," in Castelli, "Romans," 294.

11. Spelman, *Inessential Woman*, 38.

12. M. Y. MacDonald, "Slavery, Sexuality and House Churches," 94–113.

13. Challenged by Johnstone, "Cracking the Code of Silence," 230.

wicked slave, with his cruel intentions and violent and drunken behavior, cuts himself off from family life and is "cut into pieces."[14]

SLAVE AND CHILDREN—AND SLAVE CHILDREN

The Gospel of Matthew (Matt 24:42–51) recounts much of the same parable, but refers unambiguously to "fellow slaves" [τοὺς συνδούλους] (Matt 24:49) while Luke's terminology opens up for a more flexible interpretation, since the Greek term *pais* is used [τοὺς παῖδας καὶ τὰς παιδίσκας].[15] The phrase in Luke 12:45 can be translated as either "male slaves and female slaves" or as "boys and girls" whom the slave manager starts beating.[16]

The common terminology for slaves and children reflects common nature and function, but the various social relations between slaves and children in antiquity were rather complex. Slaves were like children in many ways: they were not considered grown up, but were rather thought to be immature, impulsive, irresponsible, and so forth. Since both slaves and children moved rather freely between households, both groups were expected to spread news and gossip.[17] Regardless of their age, slaves were thought of as children and treated accordingly, although there was a huge difference related to future roles: free children would themselves be part of the slave-holding class. The male slave endured the permanent status as a boy, never entering manhood. According to Roman mentality, the slave remained forever under the *potestas* (power) of the owner, although some slaves could have education and positions.[18]

In addition to the parents, most people who nourished and instructed upper-class children were slaves.[19] Slaves were their pedagogues, care-takers, and protectors.[20] For freeborn children, some of the most

---

14. Literally, διχοτομέω in verse 46 means "cut in two," see LSJ and Johnstone, "Cracking the Code of Silence," esp. 205.

15. Note the similar open interpretation of either slave or boy in Matt 8:5–13, by use of same Greek term *pais* (translated with "servant" in NRSV).

16. The Greek term used is τύπτειν, translated in LSJ as "to beat, strike, smite."

17. See Kartzow, *Gossip and Gender*, 191.

18. Glancy, *Slavery in Early Christianity*, 24. But see Harrill, *Manumission of Slaves*, 51–53.

19. Joshel and Murnaghan, *Women and Slaves in Greco-Roman Culture*, 13. See also M. Y. MacDonald, "A Place of Belonging: Perspectives on Children from Colossians and Ephesians," 303.

20. Lohse, *The New Testament Environment*, 214.

important people in their childhood must have been slaves. To strike children was most probably an integrated part of this relation, although some ancient thinkers found it "against nature" that slaves sometimes struck the freeborn children they had in their protection.[21] In Luke's parable it might well be boys and girls who are mistreated by the wicked slave, since slaves often took care of children. How does it influence us as readers, interpreters, or users of this text today if *pais* is translated as "children," indicating that this parable talks about the physical abuse of children, of boys and girls, and not slaves?[22] Would that make the parable even more problematic? After all, slaves belongs to the past (at least formally), while children remain ever present. To beat children is unacceptable in many cultures today, a positive development in the last generations. Interpreters most likely prefer to imagine that slaves and not children are beaten in this parable, but we need to reflect on other possible translations too.

But what about slave children in antiquity?[23] Did free and slave children have anything in common? As Carolyn Osiek and Margaret MacDonald have so realistically described in their book *A Woman's Place*, free and slave children shared social space: both slave babies and free babies could be nursed by the same woman, slaves grew up playing with their owners' children and the friends of these children (and sometimes even went to school together), and slave and free children may even have had been half-brothers or sisters, if the husband of the house had made one of his female slaves pregnant.[24]

Why Luke uses *pais* in this context will remain an open question, but it nevertheless helps us see how slaves and children, two important groups in the ancient household, at times shared functions and roles, but also had very different opportunities. In the following I take these characters from Luke to be slaves, as Matthew does in the synoptic parallel. This parable uses a wicked slave and his mistreatment of other slaves as a bad

21. For example Quintilian, discussed in Gilhus, Seim, and Vidén, *Farsmakt og moderskap i antikken*, 161.

22. See also the discussion in for example Corley, *Women and the Historical Jesus*, 66, Lind-Solstad, "La de små barna komme til meg? En analyse av Markusevangeliets fortellinger om barn," 60. From the growing field on childhood studies and the Bible, see for example Bunge et al., *The Child in the Bible*.

23. See the discussion under the subtitle "Children of varying statuses," in Dixon, *The Roman Family*, 123–30.

24. Osiek and MacDonald, *A Woman's Place*, esp. ch 4. See also M. Y. MacDonald, "A Place of Belonging," 299.

example, but the slave-holding system as such is neither condemned nor criticized in Luke and Matthew.

FAMILY MATTERS

The institutions of both slavery and family varied greatly in terms of ideals and practices, and the variety of sources, both written and material, leaves us with a challenging work of interpretation. Throughout the Empire and over time, Roman law and social practice interacted in various ways with local rules and customs, and there were most certainly significant variations from region to region. Besides, as argued by Catherine Hezser, Jewish discourses on slavery had great similarities with the Roman attitudes, and did not represent a completely different ideology, as some have argued.[25] Early Christian slavery and gender have recently been the subject of much scholarly attention,[26] and many books on family in early Christianity also discuss the role of slaves.[27] In the following I will discuss the insights gained from such research, some of it obviously contested.

In the parable, the overseer slave is told by his master to take care of the other slaves. Apparently, although enslaved himself, a man could reach a position of power. When he abuses his position, Luke writes that he strikes male and female slaves. Some translations write "men and women" (see NRSV), leading us to think that these slaves are almost like regular hetero couples, as if they were husbands and wives. But the picture is far more complex when it comes to slaves' possibility to form their own families. According to Roman law, they had access to neither marriage nor legally recognized parenthood.[28] Their owners could split families and move or sell however many slaves they wanted.[29] Although they were biological fathers, male slaves did not have access to legal fatherhood,[30] and

---

25. Hezser, *Jewish Slavery in Antiquity*. See in particular her introduction.

26. Just to mention a few: Briggs, "Slavery and Gender," in *On the Cutting Edge: The Study of Women in Biblical Worlds*; Schüssler Fiorenza, "Slave Wo/Men and Freedom"; Brooten, *Beyond Slavery: Overcoming Its Religious and Sexual Legacies*.

27. See, e.g., Osiek and Balch, *Families in the New Testament World*.

28. According to Harrill, "Slaves could not start their own families. To be sure, slaves had what they (and their masters) considered spouses and families, but such unions had no recognition in the law, and so were subject to separation by sale to different owners" (Harrill, *Manumission of Slaves*, 55). See also Osiek, "Female Slaves, *Porneia*, and the Limits of Obedience," 258.

29. See Joshel and Murnaghan, *Women and Slaves in Greco-Roman Culture*, 3.

30. Glancy, *Slavery in Early Christianity*, 26.

slaves born by slave mothers had no legal father, regardless of whether the biological father (when known) was slave or free.[31] Slave babies increased the property of their mother's owners,[32] and to separate mother and child could be one possible means for owners who wanted to maximize the production and reproduction activity of female slaves.[33] We may say that instead of forming their own families, slaves helped to run their owners' families.

However, although slaves legally had access to neither marriage nor parenthood, some epigraphic sources point at how slaves at times formed couples and could live in long-term relationships.[34] If we conclude that slaves were not involved in family life because the public discourse said so, we confuse ideology and lived experience.[35] We must assume that there were huge variations, and that our sources are incapable of giving any complete picture of the situation.

Another important issue, discussed in particular by Jennifer Glancy, is slaves' roles as surrogate bodies.[36] Slaves were considered as both things and persons. They could be imprisoned or beaten on behalf of their owners, and both male and female slaves were sexually available for both their owners and others.[37] The most important sign of free male status was bodily integrity, that is, that they were not subject to sexual penetration or corporal punishment, a privilege also held even by the poorest among free men, in contrast to slaves.[38] Concerning this parable, it is noteworthy that the slave who strikes the other slaves is blamed for doing so, whereas when the master at the end cuts this slave into pieces, it seems to be "according to procedure." Physical violence was a means of discipline within

---

31. Ibid., 4.

32. According to Glancy, "[s]ome slave children grew up in the same household with their mothers, but many others were not so lucky," and furthermore that "slaveholders were certainly aware of the potential of female slaves to increase household wealth by bearing future generations of slaves" (ibid., 5, 18, cf. 26, 73–74).

33. Dixon, *The Roman Family*, 128.

34. See D. B. Martin, "Slave Families and Slaves in Families."

35. See Johnstone, "Cracking the Code of Silence," 223.

36. She writes: "Slaveholders in the first century characterized their slaves as bodies, and their treatment of their slaves was commensurate with that characterization," Glancy, *Slavery in Early Christianity*, 3.

37. Ibid., 10–16. See also Joshel and Murnaghan, *Women and Slaves in Greco-Roman Culture*, 7.

38. Joshel and Murnaghan, *Women and Slaves in Greco-Roman Culture*, 18.

the ruling male discourse but a sign of uncontrolled behavior when performed by a slave. As Saller has noted, "the application of the whip generally marked slave from free."[39] We may ask what the wicked slave is actually blamed for: for taking on the master's role of beating, or because he transgresses his subordinate role?

Some slaves were born by slave mothers, while others became slaves later in life. Even the elite seem to be haunted by the constant fear and threat of becoming enslaved: they could be taken as prisoners of war, kidnapped, or enslaved due to high debt.[40] If prisoners of war were sold to a slave owner far away, they would have to mix with a group of slaves who had a different language, culture, skin color, and custom. They became part of the same serving class of a household, some with a past as free persons while others born into slavery. Were they all treated as owned and available bodies? What if some new slaves were already married and had children? How did the variety in background influence the slave hierarchy?

For ancient thinkers it seems to be important to keep a clear-cut distinction between slave and free. Free status was a fixed category, neither negotiated nor contested. The discourse of family concerned freeborn persons, while other rules regulated the serving class. Still, as we have seen, a person could move between the two statuses: free persons could be enslaved and slaves could either be manumitted or flee and become "runaway slaves."[41] Apparently, the hierarchies were not stable and secure.

GENDER AND SLAVERY

In this Lukan parable, slaves are gendered. When we add gender to the discussion of family and slavery, we are confronted with certain complex challenges of interpretation. It seems crucial to reflect again upon what we mean by family. Although slaves could not form legal families, according to political and religious codes in antiquity, we can nevertheless ask questions about slave families. Denied official family status, we can still

39. Quoting Saller, in ibid., 6.

40. Note also that some freeborn babies who were not acknowledged by their fathers could be exposed, and if they were found by slaves they grew up among slaves, Glancy, *Slavery in Early Christianity*, 74–77. See also the discussion on voluntary enslavement, J. Byron, *Recent Research on Paul and Slavery*, 77–80.

41. See in particular Harrill, "The Dramatic Function of the Running Slave Rhoda (Acts 12:13–16)."

assume slaves had some "family life." What kind of dilemmas occurred for a slave, whose body belonged to a master, to be part of a couple with another slave, in a hetero or a same-sex relationship? How could slaves, whose production and reproduction were owned by someone else, form their own families? How did gender influence a slave's role in the family and the household?

The parable that I use to think with here is rare in that it, together with a few other NT texts, mentions female slaves.[42] Luke, in contrast to Matthew, felt for some reason the need to gender the slaves he mentions. By use of a heterogender dichotomy, he gives a glimpse into a gender-divided slave culture. Luke Timothy Johnson explains this by stating that "[i]t is typical of Luke to notice both genders," a solution that does not take into account that gender has a different meaning for slave and free.[43] In the overall discourse of slavery in antiquity, several scholars have pointed out that "[s]laves of both genders were supposed to be only the passive objects of their master's will and desire."[44] The distinction between male and female was important only for free persons, for slaves it was irrelevant.[45] To some extent, slaves were without gender and their sex did not matter.[46] Accordingly, female slaves were seen as slaves, not women.[47] But if this is correct, why does Luke mention both male and female slaves in verse 45?

Slaves were owned by others, indicating that also their bodies and sexuality were owned. Nevertheless, the gender difference between slaves actually played a role in relation to sexuality and reproduction. For female slaves the hope of manumission was closely connected to sexual relations.[48] By marrying her owner or another free man, or by surviv-

---

42. See for example the stories in Acts of the possessed slave girl whom Paul heals from her possession/talent in fortune-telling (Acts 16:16–18) (see Part Two, chapter 8), and of Rhoda, the slave girl who encounters Peter and is accused by the others of being mad (Acts 12:13–15).

43. Johnson, *The Gospel of Luke*, 204.

44. Butler writes: "Slaves of both genders were supposed to be only the passive objects of their master's will and desire, though in practice (and even in theory) things seldom were really that simple." Butler, "Notes on a *Membrum Disiectum*," 248.

45. Spelman, *Inessential Woman*, 42.

46. Ibid., 55.

47. See also Osiek and MacDonald, *A Woman's Place*, 96.

48. M. Y. MacDonald, "Slavery, Sexuality and House Churches," 96.

ing many childbirths, a female slave could be freed.[49] Male slaves did not have similar hopes.[50] If they formed couples with other female slaves, they could never be sure of their fatherhood, since the pregnant mother probably would have several possible fathers, at times including the male owner. In fact, not only did male slaves lack access to legal fatherhood, but also access to biological fatherhood was most uncertain. I wonder whether male slaves were more excluded from family life than female slaves, since female slaves at least could take part in the bodily process of child production and nursing. This tentative observation seems crucial when dealing with the ancient household, slavery, and gender, and I will return to these issues later on, in particular when discussing the household codes in chapter 9.

In the parable, both male and female slaves are beaten, not by their owner but by another slave who stands in for their owner. Since Luke mentions it, what role did gender play when slaves were beaten? Were they beaten differently? When a male person beats female slaves, was it in any ways sexualized?[51] Could beating also lead to sexual violence, as if the way was short to other forms of penetration, such as sexual penetration, when the body's integrity was attacked through striking?[52]

New Testament interpreters have recently discussed in what way the Christian community followed the conventional moral values by which masters could sexually use their slaves, or whether "sexual violation of slaves and the break-up of slave families . . . was something to be avoided by masters in the *ekklesia* who sought to treat their slaves 'justly and fairly.'"[53] Margaret MacDonald argues, on the basis of recent research

---

49. Osiek, "Female Slaves, *Porneia*, and the Limits of Obedience," 259–61.

50. Osiek discusses in what way it was shameful for a female slave owner to have a sexual relation with her male slave, and argues that such marriages were discouraged; see for example ibid., 261.

51. Note that Johnson translates *tuptein* with "abuse"; see Johnson, *The Gospel of Luke*, 204.

52. See how female slaves are described as extremely powerless and vulnerable (also sexually), functioning as a vehicle for addressing others' concerns, in Joshel and Murnaghan, eds., *Women and Slaves in Greco-Roman Culture*, 7.

53. M. Y. MacDonald, "Slavery, Sexuality and House Churches," 112. See also MacDonald's discussion with Glancy, where she writes that "Paul's failure to clarify whether sexual contact with one's own slaves constitutes *porneia* raises the question of whether Paul's silence was due to an unspoken expectation that the sexual use of slaves is abhorrent or, conversely, to an expectation of cultural norms regarding the sexual use of slaves."

into the Roman family, that sexual treatment of slaves "must have varied widely" given "the complexity of familial arrangement in general."[54] Nevertheless, in Luke's parable male and female slaves are objects of violence that is legitimated by gender and class, with sexual overtones. The parable describes a household hierarchy that practices physical violence. Whatever theological meaning this parable may have, it uses corrupted relationships, violence, and sexual differences in the everyday lives of real slaves as rhetorical devices.

THEORIZING FAMILY, SLAVERY, AND GENDER

Early Christian families can be studied from many different angles. What we find in our sources is always also part of our strategy or context as interpreters. We decide what questions to ask, we choose what perspective to read from, we decide what to look for and where to look. How we search in the texts will also reveal much about ourselves, and challenge our ethics of interpretation.[55] Scholarship is not an isolated world in which some neutral persons can present what happened in the past without also contributing to how it is re-imagined or remembered.[56]

I am interested in slaves because I think we will only fully understand early Christianity and family life in antiquity by paying attention to them. Slavery structures must be made visible, in the past as well as in our time. I am particularly interested in female slaves as emblems of marginal characters since they suffer a threefold oppression. Elizabeth Spelman points out that a woman is never treated according to her gender only, but also according to her class and race.[57] But we cannot simply combine information about slaves with information about women in order to find information about female slaves in antiquity.[58] We need a more complex, analytical approach, as offered by intersectionality.

---

54. Ibid., 94.

55. See the various discussions in Schüssler Fiorenza, *Rhetoric and Ethic*.

56. See the recent discussion in Vander Stichele and Penner, *Contextualizing Gender in Early Christian Discourse*, esp. ch 4.

57. Spelman, *Inessential Woman*, 53. I use Spelman's words (38), only replacing Aristotle with Luke: "An account of *Luke's* views about women that doesn't inquire seriously into what he says about slave women not only announces that the position of slave women is theoretically insignificant, it also gives a radically incomplete picture of what he says about women who are not slaves."

58. Ibid., 49.

Although the New Testament does mention a few female slaves, feminist commentaries have been little concerned with them.[59] The female slaves mentioned in Luke 12:45 are not central characters when women's history is written—due to political or theological challenges, feminist exegesis has been most interested in women with leadership roles. Some of these women were probably slave owners themselves or belonged to slave-holding families.[60] Also feminist classical scholars have shown greater interest in elite women.[61] Of course, the sources are few and often brief, but if researchers concerned with women or family in the past are primarily interested in privileged women, we ignore that women are also part of hierarchies in which other women are oppressed. If our interest in gender leads our attention towards women who are only oppressed "as women," we may overlook that such women are subject to "pure sexism" because they are on top of other hierarchical systems.

The crucial point here, as I see it, is to map how various social categories work together and mutually construct each other. The parable in Luke 12:35–48 is here particularly interesting to think with, since it operates within a complex web of social relations. Awareness of how different social classification systems cannot be understood in isolation, but mutually modify and reinforce each other, is central to intersectional studies.[62] Instead of examining gender, race, class, age, and sexuality as separate categories of oppression, intersectionality explores how these categories overlap. Not only slaves are beaten in this parable, but different *kinds* of slaves. It is not a parable about how women are beaten but about a specific, vulnerable group of women, together with vulnerable men.

CONCLUSION

I started by referring to Page DuBois, who did not find slaves in museum exhibitions from antiquity. If we use the language of memory theory, extant stories of slaves and slavery are stored away in the archive while the

---

59. See Osiek's telling comment: "Female slaves as a group have been very little studied" ("Female Slaves, *Porneia*, and the Limits of Obedience," 260). A recent contribution that pays attention to female slaves as one such group of "women" is Osiek and MacDonald, *A Woman's Place*. Note in particular the chapter called "Female Slaves: Twice Vulnerable."

60. See Osiek, "Female Slaves, *Porneia*, and the Limits of Obedience," 258.

61. Spelman, *Inessential Woman*, 52–53.

62. See, e.g., Phoenix and Pattynama, "Intersectionality."

slave-holders' stories have become part of canon, our active memory.[63] Slaves had their place—that is, *no* place—in ancient domestic space, but they were actually all over the place, since the whole social machinery depended on them. Similarly, when New Testament or classical interpreters focus on elite women only, we may say that the feminist memory has stored away slavery in the archive.[64] DuBois wants to write slaves into history and memory—and not just add them, but let them disturb and disrupt our narratives from the past.[65] This is crucial, since our memory not only reflects the past, but also shapes the present reality by providing us with understandings and symbolic frameworks that help us make sense of the world.[66] It is not only women who are left in the archive; what is remembered from the past must not be challenged from a gender perspective only, but from an intersectional perspective as well.

In museums, curators and researchers choose on behalf of our societies what to present as our common memory, what to include in the active canon, and what to store in the archive. As I have pointed out in the introduction, the Bible is both canon and archive. Some stories are considered more central, some particular characters are remembered. Memory is selective; what is not remembered is almost forgotten, because it is never in use, it is never made visible.

When we talk about family in antiquity, certain crucial questions arise: Who did not belong to the family? Who is not remembered as family? How did gender and class determine who was excluded from the family discourse? As Elisabeth Schüssler Fiorenza points out, focusing on the memory of elite families only entails the risk of increasing the gap between the "haves" and "have-nots," in the past as well as the present.[67] In the age of globalization this represents an urgent challenge that Biblical scholars must take seriously. We must theorize the gaps in the ancient sources, and engage with the structures that uphold the hierarchies. How the Bible can be used in current discussions of family values will be affected by which Biblical texts and characters are either stored in the archive or considered

---

63. A. Assmann, "The Religious Roots of Cultural Memory," 274.

64. See Schüssler Fiorenza's usage of "feminist memory" in Schüssler Fiorenza, "Discipleship of Equals," 77.

65. DuBois, *Slaves and Other Objects*, 81.

66. Misztal, *Theories of Social Remembering*, 13.

67. Schüssler Fiorenza, "Transforming the Margin—Claiming Common Ground," 37.

part of the canon when the concept of family is scrutinized. The conservative nuclear family ideology based on Biblical texts faces some major challenges when confronted with early Christian slave bodies.

In addition, class, race, age, and gender intersect also today to construct certain power relations, within or outside of families, which look much like slavery. Victims of trafficking, illegal immigrants, and some domestic servants today live under conditions in which they lack basic human rights and dignity.[68] Their services, bodies, and lives are owned by others, and they suffer from psychological violence and sometimes also physical and sexual violence.

Slaves in antiquity were needed to help free families live proper family lives. Extreme ways of practicing the au pair institution, in which women from poor countries leave their own children and family to take care of children and housework in career families in rich countries, share some basic elements with ancient slavery. Although slavery as an institution is illegal, slave structures survive and re-appear in new contexts and situations.[69]

By employing an intersectional approach to Biblical memory, I suggest that we pay attention to the margins of the family and highlight some forgotten fragments and characters by moving them from the archive into the canon. Another important task is to make slaves visible in Bible translations, not pretending they are servants. The parable in which male and female slaves are beaten may help us see patterns of marginality also in present-day families and communities. Awareness of marginality and slave structures at the roots of Christianity challenge Bible users to speak up against similar structures today.

---

68. Schüssler Fiorenza mentions present day relations and how "millions of people . . . have been forced by traffickers into prostitution or debt bondage," in Schüssler Fiorenza, "Slave Wo/Men and Freedom," 123.

69. A recent Norwegian documentary (in English) argues that around 37 million people live in structures of slavery today, and issues related to family are indeed strongly involved; see Robsahm, "Modern Slavery."

2

Borderline Identity

The Contested Body of the Ethiopian Eunuch (Acts 8:26–40)

INTRODUCTION

THE ETHIOPIAN EUNUCH WHO was baptized by the apostle Philip on his way home from a pilgrimage to Jerusalem (Acts 8:26–40) is one of the most complex and challenging characters in the whole New Testament. This queer character—a "black Jew, castrated man," as Virginia Burrus describes him—seems to be an incarnation of multiple identities.[1] As a minor and marginal character he is too often stored away in the archive, and I think he has great potential for playing an important role in our complex and fast-changing world.

The scholarly discussion about the eunuch most often circles around the issue of whether the Ethiopian eunuch was a Jew, whether by birth or as a proselyte.[2] He has become an example of an early convert into Christianity, and what he went through has been conceptualized primarily as a case study of baptism, something that is of course important when read within a theological paradigm. His ethnic origin as an Ethiopian and the gender/sexuality stigma of being a eunuch make him hard to classify within fixed categories,[3] but with "new" Bible users his complexity and marginality have been given renewed attention.[4]

---

1. Burrus, "The Gospel of Luke and the Acts of the Apostles," 149–50.
2. See the overview in Shauf, "Locating the Eunuch," 763–65.
3. See Moxnes and Kartzow, "Complex Identities."
4. See for example G. L. Byron, "Ancient Ethiopia and the New Testament." For recent gay/lesbian interest in the Ethiopian eunuch, see for example http://www.geocities.com/

To the ongoing discussion of his ethnicity and gender/sexuality I will use intersectionality and add the dimension of class by reading this text in comparison with a poem of Catullus. I highlight "class" here and not merely "social status," since I am interested in the dynamics between slave and free. By emphasizing class I want to look at different bodily practices related to these two main groups within a slave-holding society. In the last part of this chapter I employ memory theory and ask how the eunuch was negotiated by some early interpreters of Acts, namely the church fathers. Although he was not a marginal character for them, they nevertheless tried to negotiate all the various elements of his complex character in fascinating ways that can help readers today to remember not only certain elements of him but his queer and boundary-crossing identity.

INTERPRETATIONS OF THE EUNUCH'S STATUS

Scott Spencer asks about the "social status" of a eunuch in the ancient world, and shows that even those who managed to rise to position and power could not wholly escape the stigma associated with their peculiar position.[5] For the most part, eunuchs were viewed negatively in the sources we know. Spencer points out that eunuchs often "were slaves who had been brutalized by other men as a form of punishment or subjugation."[6] Studies of eunuchs place them in the gendered world of antiquity as castrated men, most of them involuntarily, many as slaves and prisoners at war.[7] As Halvor Moxnes argues, eunuchs "occupied an ambiguous place in various respects: They did not fit into common ways of making boundaries and drawing borders. They could not be placed securely either as male or as female."[8] Eunuchs could also voluntarily be castrated, they could be eunuchs by birth, or they could symbolically be considered to be castrated.

WestHollywood/Heights/2554/kallos/walstudy3.html.

5. Spencer, *The Portrait of Philip in Acts*, 167–68.
6. Ibid., 167. See also Roller, "The Ideology of the Eunuch Priest," 118.
7. Roller, "The Ideology of the Eunuch Priest," 118.
8. Moxnes, *Putting Jesus in His Place*, 80. He suggests (90) that Jesus' use of "eunuch" can be a parallel to those today who identify themselves as "queer" in protest against fixed male or female identities. He is inspired by Lee Edelman's description of the queer movement, as it "does not choose a consistent and strategic form of politics"; rather, "its vigorous and unmethodical dislocations of 'identity' create [. . .] a zone of possibilities in which the embodiment of the subject might be experienced otherwise," ibid., 5.

If the Ethiopian eunuch was supposed to be a eunuch in the physical sense, we do not know in what way his male genitals were impaired. As for his status, the Ethiopian eunuch might have been born as a slave, castrated by a former owner, and then recruited to the queen's court. As was the case with the enslaved overseer I discussed in the last chapter, a man did not necessarily have to be free in order to have an influential position. On the other hand, the Ethiopian eunuch in Acts is portrayed as having an important service in the Queen's court, as δυνάστης, and he travels in a chariot (Acts 8:27–28). He is even called a man. Most interpreters agree that εὐνοῦχος not only refers to his title and official role as treasurer of the Ethiopian Queen, but describes a castrated man. He has an important position, but this indicator of wealth and high status does not describe why he is a eunuch and whether he is freeborn, freed, or a slave. Regarding this eunuch's social status, scholars highlight two aspects in particular: a eunuch represented a troublesome gender position, and many eunuchs were slaves. By looking at the intersection of gender, sexuality, and class, I will in the following show how it is difficult to reconcile these two aspects when confronted with ancient notions of masculinity. They must be discussed together, and intersectionality offers a theoretical framework to do so.

AMBIGUOUS CLASS STATUS

In order to understand the social status of eunuchs, I will argue that their class background makes a huge difference and influences what gender expectations they had experienced before they became eunuchs. If eunuchs were slaves, it indicates that they were already considered outside the ideal gender system that freeborn males were part of. A male slave was physically born with a penis, but, as Jennifer Glancy phrases it, "Symbolically, no slave had a phallus."[9] They did not take part in the masculine discourse; they were not in control of themselves, but were owned property. They had no role in the ongoing struggle to negotiate and defend masculine standards and values.[10]

In antiquity, masculinity was not a birthright given to all persons born as males. It was only possible to achieve for free men and had to constantly be fought for and proved.[11] Slaves were owned bodies that

9. Glancy, *Slavery in Early Christianity*, 25.
10. Gleason, *Making Men*. See also chapter 6 in Kartzow, *Gossip and Gender*.
11. See, e.g., Gleason, *Making Men*, 159.

were available for hard labor, sexual use, and vicarious physical punishment.[12] In many ways male slaves were hard to classify: As slaves they were sometimes grouped together with children and described by similar terminology, as I showed in the previous chapter. Although they were ascribed feminine traits, they were not considered women, though they were not real men either. As Lynn Foxhall argues, male slaves belonged to a "subaltern" category of men.[13] When such male persons who were not real men were castrated, what kind of gender position did they achieve?

This complex picture generates a whole set of new challenges in which the intersection of gender and class becomes crucial. I use Matsuda's technique of asking the other question:

1. In what ways was the gender identity of a eunuch influenced by whether he was freeborn, freed, or a slave?
2. Was the class distinction erased or did it remain through castration?
3. Did a eunuch who earlier had been free and voluntarily castrated himself belong to another social class than eunuchs who were slaves?
4. If competition over masculinity was so central to public discourse, who was most male: a free man who was a eunuch, or a slave?
5. Did castration lead to a decline in prestige for free men and a rise in prestige for slaves?

Accordingly, we cannot talk about the social status of eunuchs without paying attention to the complex relation between class and masculinity. For slave eunuchs, their class already made them unqualified to be called men, while free eunuchs were considered outside the masculine discourse due to their castration. This obviously had a huge impact on the identity of a eunuch. When it comes to the Ethiopian eunuch in Acts he is called a man, but we have no clear indicators of what the eunuch stigma did to his masculinity and whether he was castrated voluntarily or by force.

In order to think more in depth about these questions that are relevant for how the Ethiopian eunuch is remembered, I will now dwell on a text that deals with some of these dilemmas. Many sources talk about men who for various reasons, often religious, voluntarily castrate them-

---

12. Glancy, *Slavery in Early Christianity*, 50–51.
13. Foxhall, "Introduction," 5.

selves.¹⁴ Castration, however, seems to do something not only to gender identity but also to class.

STRUGGLING EUNUCHS

From Free Man to Female Slave: Catullus 63

To read Catullus' poem 63 may provide some useful insights related to the gender and social status of eunuchs in order for us to understand the complex identity of the Ethiopian eunuch in Acts. Marilyn Skinner argues in a recent study that this poem is an important "source of information about ancient gender attitudes" and the complex position of a eunuch.¹⁵ In poem 63, the narrator uses the eunuch to explore his own ambiguity about the social restraints, including gender restraints, that define his world.¹⁶ In his description of the young Attis, who eagerly castrates himself in honor of the Magna Mater, the eunuch's alien status challenges the masculine values. When Attis wakes up after his ecstatic and ritual castration, with wild dance and music, he regrets his action, comparing his new role to that of runaway slaves who leave their masters—he has left his place and his country. The poem starts to use feminine pronouns when referring to him, and the emasculated Attis realizes that she will no longer play a role in what formerly shaped him: the social context and the male space. Attis is out of place related to "my country, my possessions, my friends, my parents" (63.59), and misses "the market, the wrestling place, the racecourse, the playground" (59, 60), male spaces in which a man had to prove and confirm his masculinity. By leaving male relations and male space, Attis reflects on what kind of human being he now is: *Ego mulier*, I . . . a woman (63). Attis is a handmaid of the gods, a mistress of Cybele, a pseudo-woman, and a barren man. Britt-Mari Näsström observes:

> The specific state of Attis is confusing and contradictory: In fact he has become neither male nor female, but at the same time holds a position of both sexless and androgyne state. As a eunuch he is obliged to deny sexuality and as androgyne he had the possibilities of total experience. He is no longer a member of the ordinary

---

14. Also slaves could castrate themselves voluntarily, in particular in cultic contexts, according to Roller, "The Ideology of the Eunuch Priest," 124–25.

15. Skinner, "*Ego Mulier*," 451.

16. Roller, "The Ideology of the Eunuch Priest," 127.

world of men but in a state of betwixt and between which is characterized by the indefinite sex-determination.[17]

Attis has sunk below the status of both man and woman and become a non-person—indeed, a complete outcast.[18] Towards the end of the poem, there is no mercy for Attis, and he is told to spend the rest of his life as a slave girl for Cybele (63.90). Regardless of his prominent social biography—he has a past as a privileged man—there is no way back for him.[19]

The ecstatic eagerness that transformed Attis into a new person has given him a different identity, but dragged him down the status ladder. He has changed from being a man to becoming a person with no masculine value, and from being a free citizen to becoming a female slave of the Magna Mater. His loss can be described by use of the intersection of gender, sexuality, class, and origin: The eager and ecstatic act of castration had power enough to remove all the indicators of male status. His greatest shame in becoming a eunuch is that he voluntarily gave up the privileged status that constructed his identity, and after relinquishing this position there is no point of return at all. Compared with a runaway slave he will be haunted his entire life.

It almost seems as if what is written on his body through the act of castration can never be wiped out, like a slave's tattoo in which the owner's name was inscribed. Castration can be read as an identity marker inscribed by use of the eunuch's impaired genitals: this body is out of its male control. In Catullus' poem 63, slavery language is used to describe an ambiguous gender position. Castration influenced both class and gender. The eunuch stigma controlled all areas of Attis' new identity. His prominent background was erased in the act of castration, and ultimately he was like a female slave.

THE EUNUCH STIGMA

How did the eunuch stigma control the identity of the Ethiopian eunuch in Acts? We cannot understand his ambiguous gender or sexual position without paying attention to class issues. There is no clear indication of whether he was a slave, a former slave, or a freeborn man, and we know

17. Näsström, *The Abhorrence of Love*, 45.
18. Roller, "The Ideology of the Eunuch Priest," 128.
19. I use the expression "social biography" as an indicator of how his personal social history was shaped by, and contributed to construct his present identity.

nothing of his social biography before he became a eunuch for the queen. But we have to emphasize how his social status intersects with other features of his identity such as gender and ethnicity.[20]

What kind of memory performance is taking place when the Ethiopian eunuch rides in the chariot with Philip, as described in Acts 8? Maybe the experiences and emotions in Catullus 63 also "talk this eunuch's mind"? There is something striking about the particular passage from Scripture (Isa 53:7–9) that Luke depicts the eunuch as reading in Acts 8:32–33: What did it mean for a castrated man, perhaps with the experience of having his genitals involuntarily excised, to read about a sheep that in silence and humiliation was slaughtered? Perhaps the eunuch asks Philip who this text is all about because he recognizes his own experience in this Biblical text? A slave or a eunuch had bodily experiences that could correspond to these verses from the prophet Isaiah, although it is obvious that it was the suffering of Christ that Philip reads into it. The turning point in the chariot came when the eunuch's personal biography was integrated into the collective memory of the early Christians. There is something about the interplay between "eunuch," "Ethiopia," and the reading of the Book of Isaiah that constructs multilayered meaning in this text.

We have of course no access to the eunuch's experiences, if he ever existed, but early interpreters of Acts 8 may say something about how his complex identity was remembered and negotiated. The afterlife of this story shows the ambiguity of early Christian memory. These first readers, interpreters, and users had to handle the fact that such an ambiguous and for the most part stigmatized character was included in their Holy Scripture. The Ethiopian eunuch was a marginal character, but the earliest interpreters of the passage seem to downplay certain aspects of his identity and highlight others. The way he was read by church fathers may function as an illustration of his negotiated personality.

THE MEMORY OF THE ETHIOPIAN EUNUCH IN THE CHURCH FATHERS

The act of remembering the past contributes to the self image of the group and produces knowledge that secures their identity. The church fathers emphasized in very different ways the memory of the Ethiopian

---

20. See Moxnes and Kartzow, "Complex Identities."

eunuch and negotiated various aspects of his character in order to serve their specific projects of constructing Christian identity. In general, the attitudes towards eunuchs were ambiguous also among early Christian writers. Many church fathers wrote commentaries to Acts, and the figure of the eunuch is dwelled upon and used to raise a variety of religious and cultural questions. The Ethiopian eunuch was mostly appropriated as a sympathetic figure, often used as an introduction in discussions of baptism.[21] I will look at some of these authors in order to find patterns and tendencies of how they remembered the eunuch.

A comment in one of Jerome's epistles, in which he suggests that he and his friends should travel to the fountain where Philip was supposed to have baptized the eunuch, might mean that this place "was something of a tourist stop in late antiquity."[22] The main character of the story seems to work as a person from the past who contributed to identity construction in the present, remembered in ritual and storytelling.

Some church fathers find reasons to explicitly state that this figure was indeed a man, as if his masculinity was under question. The ambiguous gender identity of eunuchs, in which their castrated bodies disturbed the classification, might have been a challenge to early Christians, in particular to the male community of church fathers. Jerome, for example, refers to "the holy eunuch," but then corrects himself and says: "or rather the man, since that is what Scripture calls him" (*eunuchus, immo vir*).[23] The Benedictine monk Bede the Venerable (c. 672/673–735) claims in his commentary to Acts that the Ethiopian eunuch is called a man because of his virtue and integrity of mind, and since he devoted his study solely to the Scriptures. As part of the eunuch's ideal behavior Bede mentions the fact that he showed such religious devotion that he even left behind the queen's court in Ethiopia.[24] Chrysostom also comments on the Ethiopian's virtue: Not only did he reply Philip with restraint, but he also invited him to be seated in his chariot. The eunuch thereby invited "the barbarian," "a man of lowly mien," to ride with him.[25] Chrysostom considers the eunuch to be of a higher rank than Philip and praises the eunuch for his inclu-

21. Kuefler, *The Manly Eunuch*, 270.
22. Ibid., 270–71.
23. See translation and interpretation in ibid., 271 and notes.
24. Bede, *Commentary on Acts of the Apostles* 8:27a.
25. Chrysostom, *Homilies on Genesis* 35:5.

sive attitude towards a stranger. But this positive evaluation could also be contrasted: Athanasius argues that the eunuch lacked manhood and came from a low rank.[26]

By use of the image from Jer 13:23 ("Can an Ethiopian change his skin, or a leopard his spots?"), Bede says that the Ethiopian eunuch "with the stains of his sins washed away by the water [of baptism], he went up, shining white, to Jesus."[27] His transformation from black to white as a result of the baptism ritual bear witness to how the religious metaphor for the pure and clean (shining white) interacts with discourses of skin colors. Ephraim Syrus describes Christian brotherhood in similar terms, and says about the Ethiopian eunuch that "he made disciples, and out of black men he made men white."[28] Such notions about skin color and peoples from Africa influenced ethnic reasoning among early Christian thinkers.[29]

Some texts dwell upon the association between the eunuch and the queen of Ethiopia, the one who they assume sent him on the mission. Bede praises her for this generosity.[30] The allegorical and mystical exegesis of Arator (490–550), the only Western writing on Acts before Bede, praises the Ethiopian queen for her beauty and her faith, as an image of the church.[31] As Moses united with an Ethiopian woman in marriage and the Song of Songs praises this everlasting bride, the queen's best treasure is "the glory of the font." Such a female character is "black and beautiful," and "she comes from the south." Arator considers it right that her herald is precisely a eunuch, using the association to eunuchs as non-sexual beings: "As [faith] proceeds, lust is driven off, and the chaste capture the heavenly kingdom."[32]

---

26. According to Lawrence, "The History of the Interpretation of Acts 8:26–40 by the Church Fathers Prior to the Fall of Rome", 84–91.

27. See translation of the Bede, *Commentary to the Acts of the Apostles* 8:27a, 97.

28. See Lawrence, "The History of the Interpretation of Acts 8:26–40 by the Church Fathers Prior to the Fall of Rome," 47–48. See also similar motif in Jerome, ibid., 39 and 50.

29. See Buell, *Why This New Race*.

30. 8:27c in Oden, *Ancient Christian Commentary on Scripture: Acts*.

31. Arator, *On the Acts of the Apostles* 1.

32. Arator, *On the Acts of the Apostles* 1, in Oden, *Ancient Christian Commentary on Scripture: Acts*, 97–98.

Chrysostom emphasizes the fact that the Ethiopian eunuch reads the Holy Scripture during his journey, even while sitting in his chariot. He uses this as an ideal for those who always find excuses for not reading: they live with a wife, perform military service, care for children, attend to domestic chores, and look after the concerns of others.[33] The eunuch is here constructed as a person who is freed from such duties, which normally represented the ideal for free men and women in antiquity. He functions as an ideal since he reads from the Bible and finds no hindrance even when sitting in his chariot on a long journey.

Athanasius and Bede use this story to blame the Jews for their ignorance and for causing the death of Jesus, respectively.[34] The eunuch "was not ashamed to confess his ignorance" when he asks Philip to guide him in his reading, in contrast to some Jews who "persisted in their ignorance," according to Athanasius. As a comment to the scene when the eunuch reads from Scripture, Bede repeats that the Jews and Pilate are to be blamed for what happened to Jesus, when he was "slaughtered like a sheep."[35]

NEGOTIATED COMPLEXITY

This brief look at a few Church fathers shows that among early interpreters of the story of the Ethiopian eunuch, several features of the main character could be emphasized. I will in particular highlight five points that deal with the intersection of gender, sexuality, class, and race:

1. First, it seems important for some of the Church fathers to confirm that *the eunuch was a real man*. The focus on the eunuch as being a proper male, due to his virtues and behavior, places him within the ancient discourse of masculinity. Perhaps this was an attempt to meet the critique that eunuchs were in the borderland between male and female, and thus difficult to classify and categorize.

2. Second, *he also represented a wealthy queen's court*, and was praised for his inclusiveness toward Philip, as if the eunuch was an elite male. This positive attitude towards the eunuch also met criticism

---

33. Chrysostom, *Homilies on Genesis* 35:4 in ibid., 98.

34. Athanasius, *Festal Letter* 19:5, and Bede, *Commentary on the Acts of the Apostles* 8:33a, in ibid.

35. Bede, *Catechetical Lecture* 10.3.

from those who granted him a low social rank and emphasized his lack of manhood.

3. Third, the eunuch is interestingly constructed as *freed from sexual lust and family responsibilities*. His gender and sexuality play a further role when he is praised for reading Scripture and not busying himself with the ordinary family life of free men, and since his "lust is driven off." In opposition to these ascetic and non-sexual values, he is also associated with the queen of Ethiopia in a loosely connected *heterogender alliance*. She is almost constructed as a bride, as she is the beautiful sexualized female other. The male fantasy about her exotic character contributes to construct her as an object for erotic dreams, but as the same time she is a powerful and respected woman, as the eunuch seems to be a respected man.

4. Fourth, their *skin color* seems to contribute to this exotification process. He as a eunuch and she as a woman are in different ways idealized, with their skin color used in the argument: she is black and beautiful, and also his skin color is highlighted when his sins are said to be washed away in baptism and he appears shining white.

5. Fifth, he is used as a rhetorical device in *religious anti-Jewish polemic*. The eunuch is better than (other) Jews since he admits his ignorance and is baptized, and his act of reading and the content of what he read open up space for blaming the Jews for the death of Jesus.

What kind of social contexts needed to remember the Ethiopian eunuch as he is reflected in each of these early Christian writers? To answer that question will be too broad a task for this chapter, but they must indeed have been culturally complex contexts. He seems to be a flexible and negotiable character from the past.

CONCLUSION

The Ethiopian eunuch crosses boundaries and is not easily categorized. Was he part of the male elite or was he stigmatized, marginalized and feminized? What about his castrated body? Was he considered a man? The challenge for interpreters is not to answer all these questions but to accept that he is a unique character in the Biblical landscape, difficult to categorize and understand, but still playing a role in early Christian memory. In a fragmented world, stories about characters who cannot easily be classified by use of one-dimensional categories may have great potential for identification. In particular, the issue of class seems to be crucial in order to understand who this figure is supposed to be in the narrative of Acts, since it deals with the body, gender, and ethnicity.

Issues of class and how the Ethiopian eunuch is remembered by some church fathers add new fragments to the growing interest for this queer character. One of the most productive and fruitful discussions related to the Ethiopian eunuch the last years has highlighted issues of race and ethnicity. The Ethiopian eunuch has had a central role in discussions of ethnicity, since he is among the few characters that are explicitly connected to the continent of Africa. Clarice Martin examines how the Ethiopian's ethnographic identity and geographic provenance has been neglected in various interpretations of this story.[36] Through what she calls a "politics of omission," ethnographic data in particular have been considered irrelevant for Luke's theological purpose with Acts. She finds that Biblical atlases often neglect this part of Africa, and she lobbies for Ethiopia's inclusion, arguing that the "evangelistic outreach of the Church...should, in fact, depict those regions to which New Testament narrative texts allude."[37] It seems as if the contribution of particular groups or peoples have been historically marginalized or ignored, but Martin argues that such ethnographic and geographic data are theologically significant and that Black Africa should not be overlooked as part of the Biblical heritage. The continent of Africa should not be left in the archive.

Martin's observations are indeed important; they deal with the power structures of the production of knowledge and the ethics of interpretation.[38] But I see a tendency among scholars, in that those who employ this story to challenge Christianity as a "white man's religion"[39] pay remarkably little attention to what it meant to be a eunuch. I will argue that it is exactly the intersection between several identity markers such as

36. C. J. Martin, "A Chamberlain's Journey and the Challenge of Interpretation for Liberation".

37. Ibid., 121.

38. See Harding, *Is Science Multicultural?*, in particular the introduction.

39. See Lawrence, "The History of the Interpretation of Acts 8:26–40 by the Church Fathers Prior to the Fall of Rome," 77. See also A. Smith, "A Second Step in African Biblical Interpretation."

race, class, sexuality, and gender that points at new ways to understand this text and its memory with great potential for identification for "old" and "new" users of the Bible.

Another tendency to reduce the ambiguity of the Ethiopian eunuch has to do with the praxis of translation. In Biblical translations in Norwegian (both variants), Sami, and Swedish, the Ethiopian eunuch is said to be an *embetsmann* or *hoffmann* (civil servant, lit. "man of office" and "court man"), emphasizing his role in the Queen's court, without showing that the Greek term includes some ambiguous information about his sex, gender, class background, and body. The argument that "no one today knows what a eunuch is anyway" is also falling apart: for LGBT people he is seen as an important identification figure in the New Testament. Complex sexualities are indeed part of the new internet and media world. By using the term "eunuch," similar to how I preferred "slave" to "servant" in the previous chapter, some of the strangeness and ambiguity of early Christian memory is highlighted.

If we consider the ongoing process of remembering ancient texts still working today, perhaps some of the most rich and flexible Biblical figures should be taken out of the archive and recognized, for example the Ethiopian eunuch. As I have argued here, not only does he destabilize the picture by representing a marginal racial/ethnic background and a stigmatized gender position, his uncertain class background and bodily experiences also make him an even more relevant character with whom to engage.

3

Mapping Sameness and Difference
Virginity in Joseph and Aseneth

INTRODUCTION

IN THIS CHAPTER I engage *Joseph and Aseneth*, a text with a more contested relation to early Christian memory since most scholars consider it to be of Jewish origin. Although I will not go deeply into the classification of this novel as either "Christian" or "Jewish," since such terms have recently been challenged as problematic and imprecise when talking about the first and second centuries, I will employ memory theory to argue that *Joseph and Aseneth* represents a possible version of the past that aims to construct the identity for some people influenced by the Jewish narratives in antiquity. I focus on questions that seem to have a broader meaning for discussions of religion, gender, group identity, and mechanisms of inclusion and exclusion. It is particularly striking how the body in *Joseph and Aseneth* is constructed as the place where negotiations and adjustment take place, and the overall challenge is: How can a foreign body be transformed and integrated? I will look at the intersections of a variety of social categories in order to suggest an answer.

In the novel about Aseneth a whole set of strategies are used in order to negotiate how an important forefather could marry a non-Jewish wife. Aseneth is mentioned in the Hebrew Bible three times (Gen 41:45; 41:50; and 46:20). According to Genesis, she is the daughter of Potiphera, the priest from On, giving birth to two sons after Pharaoh gives her as a wife to Joseph. The novel is a re-working of this information, and re-interprets Biblical figures in a way that tells an elaborate new story about

Joseph and Aseneth.[1] The relation between the Aseneth of Genesis and the Aseneth of *Joseph and Aseneth* may be articulated as the following: from being a marginal character mentioned only in passing, *Joseph and Aseneth* retrieves her from the archive and constructs her as part of the canon, worthy of a whole novel.

I will focus on one particular aspect of this novel, and discuss how virginity relates to issues of gender, class, sexuality, ethnicity, race, and religion. These categories work together to construct Aseneth as a proper wife for Joseph, and Matsuda's other question is particularly helpful to challenge a one-dimensional focus on gender. I am fascinated by this ancient text because it is so rich of small strange details and deals with challenging issues of sameness and difference, but also because scholars have spent so much energy in recent decades in interpreting, categorizing, and situating it.

JOSEPH AND ASENETH—TEXT AND SCHOLARSHIP

In the following I will use Burchard's text version, which is the longer version, since it gives more information relevant for an intersectional analysis.[2] Many studies have focused on this novel, including a whole issue of *Journal for the Study of the Pseudepigrapha* in 2005[3] and recent works that deal with gender.[4] However, I believe that insufficient attention has been given to how male and female virginity work differently in the novel, and I suggest that complex intersections of virginity, gender, and religion are used in order to construct the narrative logic of this novel.

In *Joseph and Aseneth*, Aseneth is presented as an exceedingly beautiful 18-year-old woman. She lives in her parents' house, surrounded by her seven female virgin slaves. Many men want to marry Aseneth, including Pharaoh's son, but she remains a virgin. She lives in a world of women, worshipping the gods of the gentiles, but is disturbed by her father's suggestion that she shall marry Joseph. She refuses her father because she has heard malicious rumors about Joseph, but when she casts her eyes on him

---

1. Wire, *Holy Lives, Holy Deaths*, 3–4.
2. Burchard, "Joseph and Aseneth."
3. *JSP* 14:2 (2005).
4. See for example Kraemer, *When Aseneth Met Joseph*. Standhartinger, *Das Frauenbild im Judentum der hellenistischen Zeit*. Stenström, "Masculine or Feminine? Male Virgins in *Joseph and Aseneth* and the Book of Revelation."

she falls in love. Joseph is also a virgin and is sought after by all women in Egypt, who are desperate to get hold of him. When he sees Aseneth for the first time, he refuses to kiss her as a pagan woman, but prays for her conversion instead. She undergoes a weeklong process of fasting and crying, and the foremost of God's angels comes to see her and declares her reborn. Following this transformation she meets Joseph again and he accepts marriage. She plays an important role in the second part of the novel as "the city of refuge." Joseph and Aseneth are threatened by various attempts to kidnap and kill them, but they survive through the aid of divine intervention and some of Joseph's brothers. Pharaoh and his firstborn son ultimately die, and Joseph subsequently reigns over Egypt for forty-eight years.

There are many unsolved scholarly problems of this text concerning issues related to date, place, genre, and whether the long or short version is older. The text is most often dated between the first century BCE and the second century CE and is located in Egypt.[5] *Joseph and Aseneth* shares common characteristics with other ancient novels or romances, but has some features that are atypical for the genre.[6] Most scholars agree that it was composed in Greek, we have sixteen Greek manuscripts, falling into at least four groups.[7] The question of religious milieu for this story is still debated: when it first was published for an academic audience it was classified as Christian (Batiffol, 1888), but most scholars have rejected this hypothesis and consider it Jewish.[8] Although many challenges still remain, the novel's core element is Aseneth's conversion and her relation to Joseph, and both these issues pertain to her virginity.

---

5. Ibid., 177. See also Chesnutt, who proposes "around the turn of the eras," Chesnutt, "Joseph and Aseneth," 969. But see Kraemer, who argues that it could have been written anywhere where Greek was spoken, since it draws heavily on the "common cultural currency of the Greco-Roman world." Kraemer, "The Book of Aseneth," 860.

6. See Humphrey, *Joseph and Aseneth*. For a more thorough treatment, see Standhartinger, *Das Frauenbild im Judentum der hellenistischen Zeit*.

7. Burchard, "Joseph and Aseneth," 178–81. See also the textual history, 180ff.

8. Kraemer finds the arguments for its Jewishness, held by several scholars, to be largely unfounded, and makes a strong case for its Christian composition and redaction; see Kraemer, *When Aseneth Met Joseph*, ix., and Kraemer, "The Book of Aseneth," 858. See others who argue for its Jewish origin, e.g., Lieu, *Neither Jew nor Greek?*, Inowlocki, *Le Roman D'aséneth*. For a recent update and discussion, see J. J. Collins, "Joseph and Aseneth." See also Kee, "The Socio-Religious Setting and Aims of 'Joseph and Aseneth,'" 183. Humphrey, *Joseph and Aseneth*, 18. Burchard, "Joseph and Aseneth," 187.

AN INTERSECTIONAL APPROACH TO *JOSEPH AND ASENETH*

I find intersectionality useful in order to map the complexity of how categories intersect in the narrative about Joseph and Aseneth, and to show how negotiations between different positions construct logic and meaning.

Ideal Hetero-Gender Discourse

On the surface this novel seems to focus on a woman and her life perspectives. Aseneth is the most important (human) character. Although the novel has a female heroine, her significance emerges through her relations with others: primarily Joseph in the first part and his extended male family in the second.[9] This novel indeed deals with a hetero-gender discourse in which the male is the dominant.[10]

In Aseneth's prayer of forgiveness to the Lord God, one of the central issues is that she regrets that she has despised every man on earth and hated all men who wanted to marry her. She praises God because Joseph freed her from this arrogance and demoted her from her "dominant position" (21.10–21). In contrast to other female protagonists, she rejects the marriage her father arranges, but at a certain point she experiences the common fate of most heroines in ancient romances: love at first sight.[11]

It is primarily men who are active and initiate progress, namely Joseph, Pharaoh, and Aseneth's father. They follow proper standards for masculinity in antiquity, while Pharaoh's firstborn son and some of Joseph's brothers born by slave mothers base their plans and activities on sexual passion, envy, or evil vengefulness. Their masculinity is questionable, and to some extent they seem to be aware of the problem, as they are repeatedly described as giving in to wicked plans because they do not want to die like women (e.g., 24.7–8 and 25.8).

The story of *Joseph and Aseneth* is concerned with the elite of society.[12] Aseneth herself is attractive for Pharaoh's son and other wealthy men of high rank, although Pharaoh initially advises his son to marry the

---

9. Humphrey, *Joseph and Aseneth*, 65.

10. This tendency has also been classified as "compulsory heterosexuality" by feminist theorists Gamble, *The Routledge Companion to Feminism and Postfeminism*, 249.

11. Pervo, "Aseneth and Her Sisters," 150.

12. Burchard notes "upper brackets of Jewish society, or perhaps not top level" in order to localize this story; see Burchard, "Joseph and Aseneth," 188.

daughter of another king, and "not seek a wife (that is) beneath you" (1.8). Aseneth as a married woman is portrayed as someone who follows female ideals in antiquity, as being a wife and a mother. But her wifely duties and motherhood do not constitute any central part of this novel, and it is only mentioned in passing that she gave birth to two sons (21.9). Aseneth's motherhood is never dwelled upon, and neither is Joseph's fatherhood. It seems that Aseneth's role as "the city of refuge" for all is more important than her role as a mother. A woman of her rank and social position probably charged her slaves and servants with raising and educating her children. In that respect she is an ideal mother according to particular standards for upper class women in antiquity.

The patriarch Joseph is presented in a positive light as the man of God, with an important task entrusted him by Pharaoh. The only exception comes when Aseneth rejects her father's suggestion to marry Joseph and reports malicious rumors that Joseph is a foreigner, a slave, an adulterer, and that he interprets dreams like old Egyptian women (4.10–11).[13] He is a stranger to her, beneath her rank, and his sexuality, class background, and masculinity are questioned. When she sees him for the first time, however, she forgets all these accusations.

Issues of Sexuality and Virginity

One of the most fascinating aspects of this novel is "its blend of chastity and eroticism," as Howard Kee phrases it.[14] By employing several characteristics from a Greek romance it deals with love, sexual attraction, and passion between a beautiful man and a beautiful woman. This heterosexual erotic pattern, however, is creatively combined with the ideal of virginity.

Ross Shepard Kraemer notes that virginity is "a universal trait of heroines in ancient romances," and finds in this novel an "extraordinary stress on Aseneth's virginity."[15] Her virginity is established with the greatest security: her seven virgins had never even talked to a small male child, and prior to Joseph no man had ever seen Aseneth. Her sexual purity is also described in terms that may challenge the overall heterosexual structure of the novel: Aseneth slept in her bed alone, and to emphasize

---

13. On Aseneth's gossip, see Kartzow, *Gossip and Gender*, 101–03.
14. Kee, "The Socio-Religious Setting and Aims of 'Joseph and Aseneth,'" 190.
15. Kraemer, "The Book of Aseneth," 863–64.

this point it is added that "a man or another woman never sat on it, only Aseneth alone" (2.16).¹⁶ By not even talking to a male child, being seen by any men, or having other women sitting on her bed, the novel establishes beyond doubt that Aseneth is a pure woman. It might generate scholarly curiosity to consider whether a male child or a woman were expected to represent sexual pollution, since the novel explicitly mentions that such contact did not appear.

Uniquely for this novel, virginity is not considered an ideal only for women, but is also applied to Joseph (4.9, 8.1). Before they meet both he and Aseneth scorn the other sex. Joseph is constantly harassed by utterly brazen Egyptian women who fall in love with him, but Aseneth, although being an Egyptian woman, is by no means like them.¹⁷ Joseph can neither touch pagans, nor eat with them. He is a virgin when he meets Aseneth, as the novel mentions twice. Although they kiss and hold hands, Joseph insists on not sleeping with Aseneth the night after they have made plans for the marriage, saying that "it does not befit a man who worships God to sleep with his wife before the wedding" (21.1). Joseph's virginity has puzzled scholars. It was in fact the use of the Greek term "virgin" used for Joseph, παρθένος, that first introduced this novel to New Testament scholarship, since this term is used also of the 144,000 elected in Rev 14:4 who have "not defiled themselves with women."¹⁸ Christoph Burchard claims that these two occurrences are the earliest references to this term used on men.¹⁹ In a recent article, Hanna Stenström discusses whether there is something particularly Jewish or Christian about the "male virgins," relating the phenomenon to ancient ideals of masculinity where active male sexuality was expected of a proper man, including before and outside of marriage. Stenström suggests that Joseph's "virginity is something positive: it is a way of speaking about the positive aspects of integrity, pride and faithfulness."²⁰ She further asks whether Joseph, who guards his

---

16. Greek text: ἐν ταύτῃ τῇ κλίνῃ ἐκάθευδεν Ἀσενὲθ μόνη, καὶ οὔτε ἀνὴρ οὔτε γυνὴ οὐδέποτε ἐκάθισεν ἐπ' αὐτῆς πλὴν τῆς Ἀσενὲθ μόνης.

17. Pervo, "Aseneth and Her Sisters," 150.

18. For more on the use of this term in Rev, see Økland, "Sex, Gender and Ancient Greek," 130–39.

19. Burchard, "The Importance of Joseph and Aseneth for the Study of the New Testament," 102.

20. Stenström, "Masculine or Feminine?," 213.

individual body against all Egyptian women, is an image of how the social body of the community guards itself against the dominant culture.[21]

FEMALE CONVERSION AND TRADITIONAL CRITERIA FOR JEWISH IDENTITY

John Collins has some intriguing comments related to Aseneth's conversion. He notes that the "traditional criteria for Jewish identity, descent or circumcision," are not decisive in this novel, and that circumcision is "conveniently avoided because of Aseneth's sex." The basic requirement for group membership, as he sees it, "is acknowledgement of the living God, not ethnic descent." He also finds it "noteworthy that even before her conversion Aseneth is devoted to chastity and shuns aliens."[22] How do these observations relate to how gender, sexuality, and religion intersect in this novel?

Gender plays an important role in ancient rhetoric of religious difference and conversion, as scholars such as Judith Lieu and Daniel Boyarin have shown.[23] In the beginning, Aseneth is the incarnation of the religious other: she belongs to the pagan other, as a priest's daughter and as being involved in idolatry.[24] She cannot function as Joseph's wife if she does not change her religious practice. Nickelsburg suggests that contact between Jews and gentiles meant pollution, and argues that the novel constructs pollution from idols in a very specific and unusual way.[25] Aseneth was polluted by her engagement with pagan idols, but her sexuality was not influenced by this pollution, as is the case when other pagan women are described.[26]

Female idolatry and sexual immorality often go hand in hand in ancient texts. In this novel, however, Aseneth's virginal seclusion has a specific function in the story, serving to prove that there is no such con-

---

21. Ibid., 215.

22. J. J. Collins, *Between Athens and Jerusalem*, 234.

23. Lieu, *Neither Jew nor Greek? Constructing Early Christianity* Part III, and Boyarin, "Thinking with Virgins".

24. Kraemer, *When Aseneth Met Joseph*, 193–96.

25. Nickelsburg, "Joseph and Aseneth," 69.

26. To this point on pagan women, see Joseph's father commandments to his sons in 7.5: "guard strongly against associating with a strange woman, for association (with) her is destruction and corruption."

nection in her case.²⁷ This story negotiates Aseneth's past of religious misconduct, but clearly expresses that there was no sexual misconduct. She could take off the bracelets and buskins where "the names of the gods of the Egyptians were engraved everywhere," (3.10) but her body was pure from the start. Apparently, paganism could be left behind when a woman became a new creation, while sexual purity was non-negotiable.²⁸

If we follow Collins, one of "the traditional criteria for Jewish identity" was circumcision—"traditional," that is, for men. Circumcision could transform male bodies to be full members of the community. Since a woman could not be circumcised, Aseneth's body had to be marked in other ways, namely with extraordinary chastity even before the conversion. It seems as if fasting and repentance were insufficient to repair a broken female body, and that she therefore had to be pure and intact also as a pagan.

As an elite woman her body was proper, but as an Egyptian worshipper of idols her bodily practices and rituals made her a second-class citizen who needed a transformative fix in order to be accepted. Gender and sexuality did not intersect with ethnicity and religion, since that obviously would have disturbed her future role as a Jewish wife. To be blamed for religious practice or ethnicity could pass, while questionable connection to sexual practice would add to the image of her as a foreigner. In the Jewish tradition, another Egyptian mother—Hagar—was only a concubine, and did not have to undergo a similar transformation. She was remembered merely as Sarah and Abraham's foreign and troublesome female slave and the mother of Ishmael. I will discuss her case in a later chapter.

Gendered beauty and race/religion

It was not only Aseneth's chaste sexuality that was proper even before her conversion. Also her appearance was extraordinary already from the start, and by emphasizing this aspect the novel uses ethnic reasoning that might qualify the idea that group membership depends on "acknowledgement of the living God, not ethnic descent."²⁹

27. Nickelsburg, "Joseph and Aseneth," 71. See also Boyarin, "Thinking with Virgins," 217.

28. Also in rabbinic material that deals with Aseneth, her character seems challenging, and various strategies are used in order to explain why Joseph married her. See Kraemer, *When Aseneth Met Joseph*, 307–21. Kraemer, "Recycling Aseneth," 239–40.

29. See above, J. J. Collins, *Between Athens and Jerusalem*, 234.

As is stated in the beginning of the novel (1.5), Aseneth's beauty is not typically Egyptian, but resembles that of the daughters of the Hebrews, such as Sarah, Rebecca, and Rachel.[30] Although Aseneth is a pagan woman born to Egyptian parents, her beauty is so promising that it qualifies her to be compared with the Jewish foremothers, even before her conversion. She is Egyptian, but her beauty is atypical for her race. Bloodline and religious practice are important features, but female beauty seems to be emphasized when it comes to evaluating who can be listed among the Hebrew women. Following the conversion, Aseneth is transformed into a heavenly beauty when she meets Joseph for the second time.

But also other characters are depicted in ethnic terms as extraordinarily beautiful: When Aseneth meets Joseph's father, it is pointed out that she was amazed by his beauty: "Jacob was exceedingly beautiful to look at, and his old age (was) like the youth of a handsome (young) man, and... the hairs of his head were all exceedingly close and thick like (those) of an Ethiopian" (22.7–8). Here age and ethnicity function as essential beauty ideals: a young man is handsome, and Ethiopians have close and thick hair. Male beauty in this novel is not only found among the Hebrews, as is the case for female beauty. "Ethiopian" represents beauty for a male religious insider, while "Egyptian" represents lack of beauty for a female religious outsider. The relation between Ethiopia and Egypt as symbols for black Africa are here valued rather differently.[31] The connection to Ethiopia, as in the case of the eunuch treated in the last chapter, is highly interesting. Ethnicity, religion, and gender intersect in this novel in a rather complex way: male beauty is constructed by use of a more inclusive attitude to African nationalities as ethnic metaphors than the case is with female beauty.

CONCLUSION

Given that *Joseph and Aseneth* is a unique combination of a romance and a conversion story with a female protagonist, gender is necessary as an analytical tool, but it also requires a more complex approach that integrates several perspectives. The novel uses gender, virginity, race, and reli-

---

30. Pervo, "Aseneth and Her Sisters," 149.

31. See the overall discussion in G. L. Byron, *Symbolic Blackness and Ethnic Difference in Early Christian Literature*.

gion in complex and intersecting ways in order to legitimate the marriage between Joseph and Aseneth.

The novel belongs to the Greco-Roman gender system in which the male was the norm and represented the controlling power. The gendered class system is not challenged, but taken for granted. Gender is also interwoven with religion and race. Aseneth undergoes a transformation in order to move from the sphere of one man to another, when she leaves the Egyptian paganism of her father to join the Judaism of her new husband. Though circumcision is not an option in Judaism for a woman, Aseneth can nonetheless be a proper member of the community through conversion and marriage, since she is sexually pure and is beautiful like Hebrew women.

Joseph is portrayed as a man according to ideal standards for masculinity and religious customs, and uniquely also by use of his virginity. Joseph's foreignness and slave background, and the accusations against him of adultery and soothsaying, do not really challenge his genuine masculine standards.

Although virginity was a conventional requirement for women, extraordinary emphasis is placed on Aseneth's virginity. In contrast to other romances in which female virgins appear, however, *Joseph and Aseneth* offers a male virgin to compare with. Both times Joseph's virginity is mentioned, it is in fact connected to Aseneth's virginity, as if they were two equal "virgins who refuse to mix with foreigners."[32] The function of their virginity, however, is different: Joseph does not touch pagan women due to his religious obligations, while Aseneth's virginity continues although her religion changes.

Based on an intersectional approach I am tempted to suggest that virginity is *a premise* for female conversion in this novel. Aseneth is not a virgin due to religious obligations, as Joseph is; rather, religious practice is disconnected from her sexuality since it is stressed that paganism did not pollute her virginal body. For Joseph virginity is a consequence of his religion, while for her, access to his religion requires virginity. Her gender forces her to be a virgin, while virginity gives him religious credit. For Aseneth as an elite pagan woman, conversion would be impossible if her body was not intact, pure, and untouched at the moment she met Joseph. She is devoted to chastity even before her conversion and mar-

---

32. Sentence borrowed from Stenström, "Masculine or Feminine?," 210.

riage, because that is the only option for a woman who wants to convert to Joseph's religion.

The memory of Aseneth has made her a possible identity figure for proselytes. What is striking in contrast to other proselytes is the centrality of her virginity. Female conversion deals not only with faith or religious beliefs and practices, it also deals with the body and sexuality. Women who are not married need to be pure and untouched. The question then is, who needed to remember one of the foremothers this way? The focus on virginity has similarities with early Christian texts on asceticism and celibacy. But after the conversion, Aseneth becomes a wife and a mother and does not remain a virgin. This mixture of female ideals is fascinating; it is as though Aseneth could fit into both monastery and household, church and synagogue.

Although this novel has no central status in the cultural and religious canon today, I think it has potential to be an important text. In fact, *Joseph and Aseneth* finds a character in the margins of Genesis, this wife of Joseph; perhaps we can use memory theory and consider the story as recovered memory that was created by people living a long time ago because they needed it for their own identity work and culture making. This novel is to some extent the result of how memory works. It is based on storytelling, fantasy, a need for ideal figures from the past, and it aims at bringing an almost forgotten woman out of the archive. And the character they remember is called "the city of refuge," a highly relevant metaphor in a world where many people are looking for protection and freedom. Perhaps it is time to re-introduce Aseneth to the active memory, to canon, and let her marginal role in the Bible be destabilized as it is in this novel.

4

Rediscovering Slaves

Motherhood and Circumcision in the Pastoral Epistles

INTRODUCTION

IN THIS CHAPTER I will ask new questions related to gender, sexuality, social status, race, and ethnicity in the Pastoral Epistles. I am interested in possible social scenarios that these epistles may build on or generate, and I will pay particular attention to the two bodily processes and practices of motherhood and circumcision. One of these embodiments, namely motherhood, is constructed as central and ideal in these letters, while circumcision is mentioned briefly as a negative connotation of opponents. It takes a great deal of social imagination to decode the Pastorals' rhetorical universe, and my aim is to read these epistles and ask about the role of slaves.

In many ways the Pastoral Epistles are marginal texts in the New Testament: they are "late" and supposedly not authentic Paulines. Recent interpreters of the Pastoral Epistles often see themselves as marginal to the scholarly discussion, such as feminists and conservative Christians.[1] These epistles are surrounded by several overlapping discourses of marginality.

EMBODIED MEMORY

In contrast to most feminist readings of the Pastoral Epistles, I will not only investigate how gender constructs structures of control and patterns of problematic difference, but also emphasize other social categories and

---

1. As argued in Solevåg and Kartzow, "Hvem bryr seg om Pastoralbrevene?"

their intersections. I find Matsuda's questions and insights compelling and highly relevant when reading the Pastorals or recent interpretations of these letters. For example, instead of looking at issues of "woman" in the Pastoral Epistles separate from issues of "slaves," as is the tendency among interpreters, I will inquire into the social status of the women in question and into the gender of slaves.[2] By combining intersectionality and memory theory the main research questions to the Pastoral Epistles will be:

1. Who needed this memory of Paul?[3] For whom did these values, ideas, and images of the past construct their present reality? If we accept the theory of pseudoepigraphy, it appears that the epistles intentionally pretend to be written from Paul to Timothy and Titus, while they actually represent *a selective memory* of Paul three generations later.[4] Can intersectionality help us draw up a social profile of the community for whom this memory constructed identity?

2. Are there any "archival" elements within the Pastoral Epistles, some small fragments that few modern readers have noticed and that may clue us into the negotiations and struggles over memory that did take place? Can we find elements that differ from the active canon?

3. What would the recovered memory of the Pastoral Epistles look like? To use an intersectional approach, how would for example a female slave mother of Jewish origin talk about asceticism?

Before I pursue these questions, some text examples from the Pastorals may help us reflect more on the complexity of these letters. I have chosen two topics and text groups, the first dealing with slavery and motherhood, the second with circumcision, race, gender, and class. I do not take these texts from the Pastorals as testifying to any concrete social reality, but I ask questions based on social-historical knowledge of antiquity in order to unpack the rhetorical constructions and re-imagine possible social scenarios.

---

2. In the recent postcolonial commentary, slaves and women are treated in isolation with no attention to intersections of gender and social status; see Broadbent, "The First and Second Letters to Timothy and the Letter to Titus," 325–26.

3. Gillian Beattie considers the Pastoral Epistles to be among Paul's earliest interpreters; see Beattie, *Women and Marriage in Paul and His Early Interpreters*.

4. See Marshall, "'I Left You in Crete.'"

DISCOURSES OF MOTHERHOOD: INCLUDING SLAVE MOTHERS?

In the infamous passage 1 Tim 2:9–15, the Pastoral Paul states that "women shall be saved through childbirth" (v. 15). Much has been discussed related to this complex verse, and a recent PhD dissertation at our faculty in Oslo takes this as the point of departure for an intriguing work on women, childbirth, and salvation in early Christian discourse.[5] Elsewhere in the Pastorals, older women are to be treated as mothers (1 Tim 5:2), they shall teach younger women to love their husbands and children (Tit 2:3–5), and the young widows shall produce children (1 Tim 5:14). But what kind of mothers would be included in these ideals? Would for example female slaves who gave birth be considered mothers in the sense that they were granted salvation or given praise for their reproduction? What about prostitutes or women without legal husbands? Or widows who gave birth more than nine months after their husbands had died?[6]

In antiquity, only free or freed women were considered part of the ideal gender system. They could marry and were expected to follow proper standards for women, keeping their bodies intact until their husbands needed them for producing legitimate children, preferably sons. Aseneth is an example of such a mother. These women were protected by their households, in which they had to follow the orders of the head of the family, either their own husband or another male relative. Procreation was indeed part of the hierarchical fabric of the empire: to produce legitimate offspring was a duty for free men and women, and childlessness could be a scandal for a wife.[7]

Although only free persons had legal access to marriage and family, also slaves, who were left out of the ideal discourse, produced children.[8] Slave fatherhood could be hard to prove, since female slaves could have several possible fathers of their children. The bodily process of pregnancy

---

5. See Solevåg, "Birthing Salvation."

6. Who made the widow pregnant, and how many months after her husband died she gave birth, appear as issues for gossip and rumors; see Kartzow, *Gossip and Gender*, 398–412.

7. Dixon, *The Roman Family*, 120.

8. Harrill, *The Manumission of Slaves in Early Christianity*, 55. See also Hezser, *Jewish Slavery in Antiquity*; in her introduction she argues that "the view of slaves as fatherless aliens without a genealogy and a past was an intercultural commonplace in the ancient world" (28).

was obviously hard to hide for female slaves. Certain theories have been put forth, based on analyses of legal and narrative sources, regarding how slaves' lives were shaped at the time when early Christian texts were written.[9] Slaves of both genders were owned bodies, and sexual penetration could be part of the owners' way of exercising control.[10] Legal parenthood, as legal marriage, depended in general on class: children of enslaved mothers became the owner's property.[11] In this complex situation, one question is particularly important to ask when reading these passages: Was a female slave's motherhood acknowledged as part of the ideal female behavior in the Pastoral Epistles?

Regardless of whether slaves' reproductive capital is praised in these letters, slave motherhood was not necessarily a privilege. Although many women throughout the ages and across cultures have done an admirable and exhausting job as mothers, the picture for female slaves in antiquity is surrounded by much ambiguity. Motherhood represented a risk for all women, due to high mortality rates for both infants and childbearing women. Phenomena we would call rape, incest or sexual violence were probably often part of the picture for slave mothers, with no legal consequences for those who mistreated them. To challenge the stereotype of motherhood by asking about female slaves' reproductivity is important in order to highlight that the category of woman (or mother) is not a homogeneous one. If some women were forced to be silent and subordinated mothers and wives in the Pastorals, as feminists have pointed out, some slave mothers, who might have been owned by these wives or their husbands, suffered a worse oppression.

Did the Pastoral Epistles' way of talking about motherhood contribute to identity formation for female slaves? How was it for a female slave in an early Christian group to hear Paul's teaching be remembered this

---

9. For discussions of female slaves and wives, see Joshel and Murnaghan, *Women and Slaves in Greco-Roman Culture*.

10. These issues are discussed in Brooten, *Beyond Slavery*. The editor writes in the introduction that "slaveholders' control of the sexual and reproductive functions of enslaved girls and women was central to the institution of slavery" (10). An important research question is whether Christian slave owners continued to use their (Christian) slaves sexually or whether the new inclusive fellowship in Christ brought about alternative ways of organizing sexual relations; see M. Y. MacDonald, "A Place of Belonging." Compare Glancy, *Slavery in Early Christianity*, esp. 59. See also Osiek, "Female Slaves, *Porneia*, and the Limits of Obedience."

11. Glancy, *Slavery in Early Christianity*. See in particular 18, 26, 73–74.

way? Were the words of these letters about motherhood a useful memory for the mothers of slaves?

CIRCUMCISION, GENDER, AND SOCIAL STATUS

Lone Fatum argues that "Jewishness and women's participation in charismatic teaching activities are rejected by the author of the Pastorals with the same sort of discriminating contempt and by means of remarkable congruent criteria."[12] A follow-up question based on intersectionality would then be: What about Jewish women, and what about Jews who were slaves?

In the Pastoral Epistles it is both hinted at and explicitly stated that "Jewishness" is a category that names what the believers shall leave behind or avoid. Expressions like "those of the circumcision" (Titus 1:10),[13] "endless genealogies that promote speculations" (1 Tim 1:4), and "Jewish myths" (Titus 1:14) function to characterize certain people and the content of what they believe negatively. In these letters a ranking system constructs various aspects of Jewish custom and tradition as subordinate to what "Paul" describes as his sound teaching. The Christian religious system is far more attractive, and what Jews believe in is described in stereotypical and hostile terms. But using Matsuda's technique of "asking the other question," I wonder who were considered to be Jewish in these letters. These characteristics are merely parts of the margins and used polemically, but still, I think a critical reflection by use of intersectionality challenges our ideas about who could be included in these groups of "opponents."

First of all, the category "Jew" is a problematic one, as scholars such as Steve Mason have pointed out.[14] If the Pastorals deal with a third-generation Christian group after Paul, it is hard to tell whether they still considerer themselves part of the Jewish group, and such statements should accordingly be read as internal Jewish criticism. Or do the letters promote a clear "departing of the ways," and can they be read as anti-Jewish polemic?

---

12. Fatum, "Christ Domesticated," 185.

13. Greek text Titus 1:10: Εἰσὶν γὰρ πολλοὶ [καὶ] ἀνυπότακτοι, ματαιολόγοι καὶ φρεναπάται, μάλιστα οἱ ἐκ τῆς περιτομῆς.

14. Mason, "Jews, Judeans, Judaizing, Judaism."

Second, when circumcision is used as the sign of inclusion and exclusion, what about women?[15] In the case of Aseneth, as I discussed in the previous chapter, a profound transformation was needed in order to afford her the status of a Jewish insider. When the Pastoral Epistles talk about circumcision as a sign of disliked bodily practice, is it to be understood as if women were not included in the group, or is "those of the circumcision" merely a metaphor for all Jews?

Third, circumcision is a sign on the male body, but could also male Jewish slaves be considered part of the group? If enslavement, at least legally, severed ties to an *ethnos* and *genos*, as Denise Buell has pointed out, we may question whether it make sense to talk about the ethnic or religious status of a slave.[16] Catherine Hezser argues that "[e]nslavement constituted a total uprooting from one's family, religion, and society of origin."[17] She suggests that this was characteristic for all variations of ancient slavery, also for Jewish slaves own by Jews, non-Jewish slaves owned by Jews, and Jewish slaves owned by non-Jews.[18]

If freeborn Jewish men who were circumcised as babies were sold into slavery due to economic crises or wars, their bodies were marked with their ethnic/religious origin regardless of who owned them and where they lived. Perhaps circumcision secured them some ethnic status if they were enslaved, and if so, female Jewish slaves lacked this privilege. Or were the attitudes towards Jews hostile, so that women, who had no sign of Jewishness inscribed on their bodies, were better off?[19] And further: were boys born of Jewish slave mothers circumcised? These questions deal with ideas of masculinity, race, the body and gender, which also influenced the complex identity of the Ethiopian eunuch in Acts 8 (discussed in chapter 2).

Hezser also discusses the possible Jewish custom of circumcising slaves of non-Jewish origin, so they could participate in the everyday life of the Jewish household, such as the preparation of food. If foreign male

15. See in particular Lieu, "The 'Attraction of Women' in/to Early Judaism and Christianity."

16. For a discussion of the terms *ethnos* and *genos*, see Buell, *Why This New Race: Ethnic Reasoning in Early Christianity*. On Jewish slaves see also Stein, "A Maidservant and Her Master's Voice," 375–97. Ilan, *Jewish Women in Greco-Roman Palestine*, 205–11.

17. Hezser, *Jewish Slavery in Antiquity*, 21.

18. Ibid., in particular chapter 1.

19. See a discussion on how Jews were frequently persecuted and despised in Briggs, "Slavery and Gender," 182.

slaves were circumcised when bought by a Jewish slave owner, slavery indeed had a "homogenizing effect," as she argues.[20]

Another point related to slavery and religion is that slaves could keep aspects of their integrity by continuing their religious practice although they were not considered to belong to any particular religion. Ritualization, prayer, or fasting can be one way of performing resistance to slavery, although the owners or others in the community would not recognize them as fellow believers.[21] Would slaves who were Jewish, by birth and family and not by force, by able to express their religiosity although enslaved? A similar question has been asked in relation to what kind of "Christianity" slaves who converted to Christianity were able to practice, even when they had Christian owners.[22]

Apparently, the relation between slavery and ethnicity/religion was rather complex. I dwell with it here since I am interested in how different categories may intersect, and when terms like "Jew" or "the circumcised" are used in the Pastoral Epistles, I wonder who could potentially be part of these groups. If the answer is "only free men," I think this should be made explicit when we talk about these passages or use these categories.

CONCLUSION

By use of intersectionality I have asked about how concrete people may have related to the Pastoral Epistles' reasoning about two specific topics: motherhood and circumcision, which deal with female and male bodies, respectively. These two bodily practices are ambiguous: they both include and exclude slaves. Although female slaves did of course produce babies, their motherhood was not an obvious part of the ideal reproductive discourse of the Roman Empire, though they could not in any case escape their reproductive bodies. Similarly, male slaves who were born Jews or circumcised by Jewish owners could not escape the impact of the ritual on their bodies.

The memory of Paul is used in the Pastoral Epistles to construct a true divine group who marked distance and self-justice and promoted a very low level of acceptance for difference. What kind of collective

---

20. Hezser, *Jewish Slavery in Antiquity*, 34.

21. A point made in response to the recent book on slavery; see Nazer, "Epilogue," 311–12.

22. See a recent discussion on sexual use of slaves related to the household codes in M. Y. MacDonald, "Slavery, Sexuality and House Churches."

memory is this when so many groups are excluded from the collective? Although we do not know how new readers, interpreters, and users will conceptualize these epistles, it is perhaps acceptable that the Pastorals for the most part are defined according to what they are not and stored away in the achieve? The theory would be: Pay as little attention as possible to these epistles with their destructive hierarchies and stereotypes, because they are "texts of terror."[23]

On the other hand, I am generally skeptical of theories that are self-evident or that purport to explain the whole picture: there is always more to say, and there are always exceptions to the rule. Theresa Hornsby has inspired me to look for a text's "destabilizing potential,"[24] though after working with the Pastoral Epistles for many years, I find it hard to uncover and be enthusiastic about anything that destabilizes the picture.

However, some elements do not follow the hierarchical structure in detail, and they may give us a hint about the struggle over memory and the dynamics of the canon and archive. In the Pastoral Epistles, the most interesting comment pertaining to slaves is a small fragment almost lost in the archive: "slave traders" appear in the list of vices in 1 Tim 1:10, together with negative figures such as fornicators, sodomites, and liars.[25] How does this point impact on slave motherhood or slave circumcision? To oppose the slave trade would at the time have been a radical social statement, and may be a de-stabilizing element in the overall requirements elsewhere in the Pastorals, telling slaves to obey their masters (1 Tim 6:1–2; Titus 2:10). If slaves could not be sold, they would lose their value as property. If they remained slaves, they would at the outset live in the house where they were born, granting them some household stability and continuity. A prohibition of the slave trade would mean that young female slaves would not be sold as sex workers, that slave mothers' children would not be sold, and that slave families would not be separated. Then also male Jewish slaves born in a Jewish household would retain some of their religious and ethnic markers of identity. Do we see a fragmented glimpse in 1 Tim 1:10 of a Pauline memory that considered slaves not only as property or useful bodies, but as human beings, just as Gal

23. See Trible, *Texts of Terror*.
24. Hornsby, "The Annoying Woman," 83.
25. See the discussion of "slave dealers" in this passage in Harrill, "The Vice of Slave Dealers in Greco-Roman Society," 97–122. See also Glancy, *Slavery in Early Christianity*, 87–88.

3:28 may destabilize the Pauline ideology? If so, this minuscule element should be lifted out of the archive and relocated in the active memory, representing the Pastoral Epistles' destabilizing potential.

For the most part, the Pastoral Epistles use the memory of Paul to construct a community of free women and men who follow standardized notions of behavior. By asking the other questions, we have seen that social categories overlap, probably leaving very limited space for female and male slaves in the community. The negative judgment of slave traders in 1 Tim 1:10 functions as a destabilizing potential in an overall depressing exclusion of slaves from ancient society. Ethnic reasoning combined with negative ideas of "the Jewish" make these letters challenging for modern readers. These epistles, however, will never be excised from the Bible, and they seem to attract certain groups of people today, in particular those who appreciate hierarchy and gender seclusion—and those who actively fight against such restrictions. The main challenges, as I see it, is to read the Pastoral Epistles with intersectional perspectives, in order to be responsible for the discriminative aspects of the history of interpretation, be critical to our cultures' memory, and to engage with our own stereotypes.

Slaves were obviously involved in the bodily processes of motherhood and circumcision, but the Pastoral Epistles are primarily concerned with the ideal discourse of free men and women. Interpreters must examine slaves' roles in these processes in order to find them and uncover similar power dynamics today. For example, why are some mothers more important and valuable than others? Perhaps we can find some possible parallels. In some parts of the world, children of illegal immigrants, Roma women, or asylum seekers are considered to be too numerous and they face an uncertain future, while mothers who are privileged citizens in democracies are praised for helping construct the future. This is racism, sexism, and classism, in attitude and practice, and an urgent problem for global society. When talking about the possible brutality of slave motherhood in antiquity with consternation, we cannot close our eyes to our own social embarrassment. Similarly, slavery and circumcision deal with processes of religion and inclusion and exclusion. The relation between nationality/ethnicity/race and religion is rather complex at several continents where people move and travel and cross boundaries, by force or voluntarily. Issues of classism, racism, and xenophobia represent current challenges for worldwide religions, such as Judaism, Christianity, and Islam.

PART TWO

Sound of Silence?
Dynamics of Speech and Talk

Discourses about speech and talk seem essential in order to understand power relations and ideology. Whose voices or words are remembered in the various early Christian sources? A whole set of characters are silenced—some cry out loud and some are told to shut up—while others for their part speak and talk, and their agency is therefore remembered. But not only texts deal with speech and talk; the recent scholarly perspective of seeing early Christian groups as aural-oral communities suggests that these texts are part of complex communication processes. This part of the book looks into the dynamics of speech and talk by studying a variety of texts and genres, including a whole set of expressions, recommendations, and verbal exchanges. Using memory theory and intersectionality, I try to challenge the uniform category of women related to texts about the women at Jesus' empty tomb, examine speech in the Pastorals, highlight gossipy widows, and compare a possessed, fortune-telling slave girl with the apostle Paul. My aim is to open up the landscape and highlight marginal texts and characters, more than to come up with new solutions and answers complex questions.

5

Challenging Female Communities

Orality and Resurrection in the Gospels

INTRODUCTION

DISCOURSES AND SOCIAL PRACTICES related to speech and talk in the ancient Mediterranean world have recently received interdisciplinary attention.[1] In this chapter I will use intersectionality to investigate the various accounts of the resurrection of Jesus and the empty tomb in the Gospels and other ancient texts. The discrepancies in these accounts form a useful case study for discussing complexity, contested memory, and marginality related to dynamics of speech and talk.

Using theories of storytelling, orality, memory, and gossip—what I will call "oral genres"—I will reconsider the participation of various characters in the resurrection stories. I am intrigued by the fact that these stories vary considerably when it comes to women's roles, but influential theories of gender and exclusion in New Testament texts somehow do not fit into the picture:

> [...] [O]ne major reason for the paucity of women's stories in the canon is that while early Christianity was an oral phenomenon in which women could participate relatively fully, the composition of Christian texts and their selection for inclusion in the canon was the work of the small minority of literates who were mostly men.[2]

---

1. See the new consultation at SBL Annual Meeting, "Speech and Talk: Discourses and Social Practices in the Ancient Mediterranean World," http://www.sbl-site.org. Together with Jeremy Hultin I am the chair for this program unit.
2. Dewey, "From Storytelling to Written Text," 72.

When it comes to the empty tomb, however, the problem is not merely the paucity of women's stories, but rather the strikingly different positions women are given: some texts place them at the center of attention, at times by using feminine stereotypes, while others leave them out of the scene altogether. These women are named and seem to be rather important persons, but what potential roles did male and female slaves play in the event? I will employ theories of orality and gender, but confronted with the various texts about the resurrection, it seems crucial to consider intersectional perspectives.

Accordingly, I do not approach the synoptic problem so much as a literary one, but see the variety in resurrection accounts as a result of a complex communication process related to issues of representation.[3] The differences among these stories are not traced to a complex editorial process, but to different oral situations. In addition, I am also interested in the effect these gospel stories have: since the resurrection scene is one of the "foundation stories" of many societies, how it is remembered still contributes to constructing identity and community.

In the following, after discussing identity and community in relation to oral traditions, I present the New Testament text material and other ancient sources. In order to deal with the variety in these texts, I then engage with some models suggested by feminist scholars and ask who had power and access to the communication process. It will require a great deal of social imagination and attempts at theorizing the gaps in the sources. Towards the end I will use intersectionality to rethink the differences in the stories of the women at the empty tomb.

DEFINING "ORAL GENRES"

In my recent book *Gossip and Gender: Othering of Speech in the Pastoral Epistles*, I engaged with the growing interdisciplinary field of gossip studies, often benefitting from insights from the more established scholarly areas of storytelling, orality, and memory.[4] Although these four concepts have their own distinct meanings, functions, and interpretative discourses, they sometimes appear as synonyms for "oral genres"; they are all seen as means of transmission, elements of identity construction, or ways to keep the tradition alive.

---

3. Kelber, "The Case of the Gospels," 80–81.
4. Kartzow, *Gossip and Gender: Othering of Speech in the Pastoral Epistles*.

But what do we benefit from combining gossip, storytelling, orality, and memory? First, and most importantly, all four concepts insist on the oral nature of the New Testament and force us to think of early Christian groups as oral-aural communities.[5] According to Joanna Dewey, "Early Christianity was a largely oral phenomenon in a mostly oral world."[6] Second, the interdisciplinary discussions of these concepts tend to emphasize the critical importance of gender and power. Third, and highly relevant for this chapter, they all contribute with useful tools when investigating the differing accounts of women and the resurrection and what role (other) marginalized persons may have had.

IDENTITY, COMMUNITY, AND ORAL TRADITIONS

In the last ten years or so, theories of oral genres have been embraced by New Testament scholarship as highly relevant when studying the processes that shaped early Christian communities.[7] Although it is essential to "recognize our complete lack of access to ancient oral performance,"[8] we may benefit from using theories of oral traditions to understand more of the social dynamics, power relations, and identity formation processes among early Christian groups. Holly Hearon argues that

> the application of studies in oral tradition to Biblical texts has begun to foment a shift in thinking among Biblical scholars by encouraging us to look at the Biblical texts in relation to their oral-aural contexts and by considering how these oral-aural texts functioned in the ancient world.[9]

Community and identity formation is shaped by remembering and storytelling.[10] A basic tenet of memory theory is that the stories of the past influence the present and shape the future. Storytelling from the past is

---

5. See also Fowler, "Why Everything We Know About the Bible Is Wrong".

6. Dewey, "From Storytelling to Written Text," 73. See also Horsley, "Oral Traditions in New Testament Studies". But Gerhardsson does not think that "the Israel of NT times can be characterized as an *oral society*." Gerhardsson, "The Secret of the Transmission of the Unwritten Jesus Tradition," 17.

7. Draper, "Orality, Litracy, and Colonialism in Antiquity". See also how this oral perspective has much older roots, in Gerhardsson, "The Secret of the Transmission of the Unwritten Jesus Tradition," 1–3.

8. Rodríguez, *Structuring Early Christian Memory*, 4.

9. Hearon, "The Implications of 'Orality' for Studies of the Biblical Text," 96.

10. Boomershine, *Story Journey*, 19. Wire, *Holy Lives, Holy Deaths*, 4.

not only something communities do but also what they are.[11] For early Christian groups, the past was what they remembered about Jesus and his early followers. The New Testament represents what some of them found most relevant to remember. These written remains, these peoples' selective stories of the past, served various purposes in their present situation. Some of the stories that circulated about Jesus or the first witnesses were fixed into written text, but continued to be kept alive in an oral-aural culture.

Feminist theory contributes by asking about women and other subordinated persons in this process. I want to contribute to this dialogue by connecting orality and intersectionality, arguing that this interdisciplinary exchange may enlighten texts dealing with women and the empty tomb. To "question [. . .] the power structures that are embedded and preserved in the archives we have inherited" is a key task in this chapter.[12]

STORIES OF WOMEN AND THE RESURRECTION

I will start with the text material in which we have "oral-aural written remains" that include women when talking about the resurrection of Jesus.[13] But when Luke in Acts and Paul in 1 Corinthians 15 retell the resurrection event, no women are mentioned.[14] Finally, when Celsus mentions the same scene for the purpose of caricature and blame, a female figure resembling Mary Magdalene is included, dealing with some of the controversy we find in the Gospel of Mary. I find this variety in how the resurrection was remembered highly intriguing.

Women remembered, but with different names

The canonical Gospels, the Gospel of Peter, and the Ethiopian and Coptic versions of the *Epistula Apostolorum* all give women roles in the resurrection scene.[15] However, the way they present this scene and what charac-

---

11. Olick, "Products, Processes, and Practices," 6.

12. Rowley and Wolthers, "Lost and Found," 9.

13. For more on the expression "oral-aural written remains," see Hearon, "The Implications of 'Orality' for Studies of the Biblical Text," 99.

14. See the discussions in D. A. Smith, *Revisiting the Empty Tomb*.

15. For more on the Epistle of the Apostles, see Hornschuh, *Studien Zur Epistula Apostolorum*. On the fragmented Gospel of Peter, see Bernhard, *Other Early Christian Gospels*; Miller, *The Complete Gospels*.

ters they mention differs greatly.[16] The fact that the names of the women varies is striking and unique for the canonical Gospels: in no other story do we find so many versions of names given to the characters involved. The effect of naming a character cannot be underestimated: to give a person a stable and unchangeable name gives him or her a lasting social identity that guarantees existence and gives that person place and time in history, including a memory when the individual life comes to an end.[17] Of course, figures such as Judas and Barabbas are inscribed in memory not due to their positive contributions, but because their actions, persons, or behavior had such an impact. What about the different lists and huge variety of named woman at the resurrection? Few other early Christian sources are populated with so many named women, or so many women at all. Can we take this as a sign of importance, or as a caricature? I am particularly interested in the name lists, and how various women's presence and function differ in these sources.[18]

TABLE 1. Women at the empty tomb.

	Mark 16:1	Matt 28:1	Luke 24:10	John 20:1	Gos. Pet. 12:50	Ep. Ap., Ethiopic 9	Ep. Ap., Coptic 9
Mary Magdalene	X	X	X	X	X	X	X
Mary, mother of James	X		X				
Salome	X						
The other Mary		X					
Joanna			X				
Others with them			X				
Women friends of Mary Magdalene					X		
Sarah						X	
Martha						X	
The daughter of Martha							X
Mary							X

16. See Kartzow, "Resurrection as Gossip".
17. See for example Walton, *Skaff deg eit liv!*, 192.
18. See Bauckham, *Gospel Women*.

Several scholars, including myself, have discussed possible reasons for why the names vary among these sources.[19] Scholars working with oral traditions would be most interested in socio-historical explanations, and not trace these differences to any editorial process. In order to understand the relationship between the Gospels, one has to focus on performance rather than written texts, in order to see how the shared tradition is transmitted as oral texts.[20] The difference in names may be explained by the fact that several groups kept alive their own specific oral tradition in which different female characters had central roles.

Although these women are named, they are not exclusively portrayed in a positive light; Mark recounts that these women were afraid and said nothing to anyone (Mark 16:8), as the Gospel of Peter also does,[21] while Luke reports that the disciples accused them of talking nonsense (Luke 24:11). Neither in the "longer ending of Mark" (Mark 16:11) nor in the Epistle of the Apostles are the women believed when they tell the disciples the news. Though women are not excluded from these masculine discourses, they are represented as typically female, including a whole range of vices and failures.[22]

The Neglected Memory of the Women at the Empty Tomb (Paul and Acts)

Although all the sources presented in the table above seem to agree that some women did witness the empty tomb, it is striking that when Luke in Acts and Paul in 1 Corinthians 15 deal with the memory of the resurrection (so-called *kerygma* summaries), nothing is mentioned about the empty tomb or the women's role related to the resurrection. Paul summarizes that Christ died and was buried, was raised on the third day, then appeared to Cephas, then to the twelve apostles, and then he appeared to

---

19. Kartzow, "Resurrection as Gossip," 4–5. Kelber, for example, argues that it was precisely the great importance attributed to these traditions that accounts for their variability. See Kelber, "The Generative Force of Memory," 20. See also Byrskog, *Story as History—History as Story*, 77.

20. Hearon, "The Implications of 'Orality' for Studies of the Biblical Text," 98.

21. The Gospel of Peter, in which the women only came to the empty tomb long after several other people, has a similar comment about them: "Then the women were frightened and fled" (57). For Greek text and translation, see Bernhard, *Other Early Christian Gospels*, 79.

22. See the discussion of masculine discourses and speech in Chapter 6 of Kartzow, *Gossip and Gender*.

more than five hundred brothers (1 Cor 15:4-7).²³ Nothing particular is mentioned about any women, whether named or anonymous. When it comes to Luke's account in Acts (e.g., 2:31-33 and 13:29-37), it cannot be argued that this tradition was unaware of the role of women in the resurrection scene, since they are included in the account in the Gospel of Luke. Why, then, are the women not mentioned explicitly in Acts?²⁴ It seems as if the central element in the accounts in Paul and Acts is the rising of Christ, and the scene at the empty tomb and thereby the women are not needed to prove his resurrection.²⁵ Still, it is interesting that women's central role in this Gospel story seems completely irrelevant in 1 Cor and Acts.

The Controversial Memory of Women (Celsus and the Gospel of Mary)

One important source for whether women were or were not included in resurrection stories is Celsus, a second-century critic of Christianity. What is known of the lost polemic *True Doctrine*, probably written by Celsus, has been pieced together from Origen's citations when he argues against him. One of Celsus' arguments against Christianity concerns women followers and their role as witnesses to the resurrection. He argues: "But we must examine this question of whether anyone who really died ever rose again with the same body . . . But who saw this? A hysterical woman, as you say, and perhaps some other one [masc.] of those who were deluded by the same sorcery, who (. . .) wanted to impress others by telling this fantastic tale" (Origen, *Contra Celsum* 2:55, 16-20).²⁶ Although this woman is not named, the text most probably refers to the memory of Mary Magdalene. But who is this other one, a man who is deluded by the same sorcery?

23. If *adelfoi* here is interpreted as also including sisters, Paul could have intended to include women among these five hundred, but they are not mentioned as being the first witness at the empty tomb.

24. In Acts 13:31 some women may implicitly be included among those who followed him from Galilee to Jerusalem and who now are witnesses to the people. See also Bauckham, *Gospel Women*, 305.

25. Osiek, "The Women at the Tomb," 102.

26. Greek text: Ὅτι δὴ ζῶν μὲν οὐκ ἐπήρκεσεν ἑαυτῷ, νεκρὸς δ' ἀνέστη καὶ τὰ σημεῖα τῆς κολάσεως ἔδειξε [καὶ τὰς χεῖρας ὡς ἦσαν πεπερονημέναι], τίς τοῦτο εἶδε; Γυνὴ πάροιστρος, ὥς φατε, καὶ εἴ τις ἄλλος τῶν ἐκ τῆς αὐτῆς γοητείας . . . For translation and broad discussion, see M. Y. MacDonald, *Early Christian Women and Pagan Opinion*, 104ff.

In the version of Christianity that Celsus knew, at least one woman was central to the resurrection scene. To describe her, this text has similar characteristics as the canonical Gospels: here the female is hysterical, while in Mark, for example, women flee away in fear and say nothing to anyone, or, as in Luke, they were accused of talking nonsense. For Celsus, a female witness showed how ridiculous and little trustworthy this faith was. His rhetorical weapon is taken from the gospel traditions in which women are included but caricatured, rather than from the summaries in Acts or 1 Corinthians 15, and he plays on conventional female stereotypes familiar from other masculine discourses.

Celsus uses the role of the female witness to blame and caricature the Christians. The Gospel of Mary shows that the role of women was controversial also among Christian groups. The other disciples cannot believe or accept that Jesus revealed his secret message to Mary Magdalene, a woman, and not to them.[27] According to the Gospel of John, Mary was alone in the garden when Jesus appeared, not in the company of any other women and or any male disciples. The unique discussion between Mary and the disciples in the Gospel of Mary is in itself an illustration of how memory was contested and negotiated, and shows how women's roles were controversial.

All the sources mentioned above refer to the same event in the past, but they most certainly use it to serve very different purposes in their present. As argued by Kelber, "each gospel constructs a new representation of the sacred past in order to meet the demands of a changing present."[28] It makes sense to argue that each text refers to different oral traditions, memory circles, or storytelling communities. What these groups included in their stories corresponded to their various needs, and we get access to one step in each of these processes through the written remains.

Related to this memory process, scholars who are alert to gender have asked about representation: Whose storytelling or oral traditions triumphed and became part of the text? Who needed to remember, forget, or criticize that women were the first witnesses? What is not remembered or stowed away in the archive, or forgotten altogether?

---

27. King, *The Gospel of Mary of Magdala and the First Woman Apostle*.
28. Kelber, "The Case of the Gospels," 57.

FEMINIST EXPLANATIONS BY USE OF ORAL GENRES

Several challenges and questions appear upon reading these ancient texts. I will now discuss some suggestions that explain how these sources may have related to the social environment that produced early Christianity.

The gender divide between female orality and male written text has influenced several interpreters. Thanks to Elisabeth Schüssler Fiorenza's groundbreaking work, which introduced feminist theory to the field, early Christianity has been seen as starting out as a "discipleship of equals" and ending with the subordination of women when the canonical texts were written down.[29] It has been suggested that in the early phase, female oral traditions kept alive the memory of Jesus, and that the women involved should be remembered for their contributions although they were denied central roles in the written texts. When paying attention to orality, feminists would not only emphasize, as Birger Gerhardsson does, that the early Christians were "Jews in Hellenistic times in Palestine," but also situate women within these groups.[30]

Carolyn Osiek suggests that Paul in 1 Corinthians 15 simply did not know the empty tomb tradition, because this story was preserved in women's groups and only later made its way into the male "mainstream" canonical tradition. Using ethnographic data, she argues that "women have their own oral traditions and storytelling practices, passed on from generation to generation, that portray life and events from the women's point of view."[31] The gospel stories of the empty tomb originate from the "private" world of women, in contrast to the "public" version that Paul knew and reported in 1 Corinthians 15. She suggests that Paul's silence about women is not because the story is secondary but "because it has not yet made its way from the 'private' female *kerygma* tradition to the 'public' male *kerygma* traditions."[32]

This explanation uses historical arguments and is not so much concerned with power and access: when Paul describes the resurrection without mentioning any women, it was thus without misogynic intent—

---

29. Schüssler Fiorenza, *In Memory of Her*.

30. Gerhardsson, "The Secret of the Transmission of the Unwritten Jesus Tradition," 6.

31. Osiek, "The Women at the Tomb," 103.

32. Ibid. See also Bauckham, who discusses this private-public dichotomy as a relevant explanation, Bauckham, *Gospel Women*, 291–92 and 308.

unlike the later gospel traditions, he simply had no access to the female oral network and was therefore unaware that women were the first witnesses to the empty tomb. I find this suggestion interesting, but it can be pushed further by intersectionality. The various representations of women in the Gospels do not put them in an exclusively positive light, as one would expect of a female network if the intention was to remember the female heroines of the past. Would private, female storytellers emphasize that women fled away in fear and said nothing to anyone, or dwell upon how women's words were dismissed as empty chatter or how the male disciples were sent to confirm the facts? Women are remembered as the first to witness the resurrection, but some sources play on female stereotypes when portraying them and their behavior. It is also difficult to operate with "a point of view" in singular when the term "women" is in plural, since all women did not necessarily have the same point of view. Were for example female slaves or foreign women included among these women? I will return to this question later.

Using studies of European folktales, Joanna Dewey suggests that the active role of women in the resurrection scene was reduced and limited as time passed by.[33] When the oral tradition became a fixed, written canon, "women and other marginalized people" lost their influence. The process was dominated by those few who were literate,

> that is, predominately by educated, relatively high status males, not by a cross-section of all early Christians. In the process of writing and authorizing texts, women's voices and women's stories were omitted, marginalized, trivialized, and at times suppressed altogether.[34]

As seen through the lens of gender, the canonical process is described as a struggle over memory, and women, who originally were equal partners, lost their influence and were controlled by men.[35] In contrast to Osiek, who talks about two separate spheres of private female and public male traditions that did not know about each other, Dewey suggests that the "educated, relatively high status males" knew about a female tradition, but on purpose limited women's role and importance. Paul might have had several reasons for leaving women out when remembering the resurrec-

---

33. Dewey, "From Storytelling to Written Text," 76.
34. Dewey, "From Oral Stories to Written Text," 20.
35. See also Torjesen, *When Women Were Priests*.

tion of Jesus: either as a response to unfavorable reactions from outsiders, or, as Antoinette Clark Wire contends, because he in the Corinthian context did not want to provide support for women prophets who he thought had too much influence.[36]

Dennis MacDonald uses theories of storytelling and gender, and is also concerned with the oral tradition of women that lived as a parallel tradition alongside what became the authoritative and canonical writings of Paul. He is especially interested in the *Acts of Paul and Thecla*, and suggests that an oral ascetic tradition existed among the early Christians where women "storytellers" had a central function.[37] Women had important roles in these communities, something that was not necessarily made apparent in written texts.[38] Some of the same theories inspired me to look for female gossip in the Pastoral Epistles as representing a counter discourse, in contrast to the hierarchical and patriarchal *oikos* codes of these epistles.

As I understand the various research positions there are at least three possible and partly overlapping explanations for why some resurrection stories include women and others do not:

1. The different traditions are a result of the fact that Paul did not know the female oral tradition.
2. Oral traditions were kept alive by women, but when these stories were written down, it was men who decided what to mention and what to leave out.
3. The male elite wanted to control and limit women's influence by downplaying their roles (as known in a variety of oral traditions) and omitting them from what was written down.

Perhaps a combination of the latter two suggestions would be the most relevant when using intersectionality and memory theory: the variety of representations of women bear witness to the fact that they actually played a central role. Different oral communities needed their own particular version of this story in order to construct their present identity, something that shows that the memory process is flexible and negotiable.

---

36. See Wire, *The Corinthian Women Prophets*. See also Bauckham, *Gospel Women*, 307.

37. D. R. MacDonald, *The Legend and the Apostle*.

38. Ibid., 35.

Instead of attributing the Gospels to a gender inclusive community and Paul and Acts to male dominance, I would like to draw attention to the difference among the canonical Gospels as a possible destabilizing potential: while Mark and Luke (and the Gospel of Peter and the Epistle of the Apostles)[39] play on similar female stereotypes as Celsus, and Acts and Paul "forget" these women, Matthew and John do not seem to be so obsessed with masculine rhetoric when they place women/Mary Magdalene near the empty tomb.

CONCEPTUALIZING INTERPRETATIONS THAT APPLY GENDER AND ORAL TRADITIONS

For many feminists, gender is not only a category for explaining or studying difference, but also a tool for generating change,[40] and I see rather different ways of using feminist theory in the various positions related to the role of women at the empty tomb. Osiek, for example, uses gender to explain historical facts such as the difference between private and public traditions. For some interpreters of oral genres, the aim is to listen to silent voices and to find a space for remembrance, re-imagination, and storytelling. Feminists often work with recovered memory.[41] Modern theories are used to argue in favor of an original gender inclusive storytelling Christian group, with relevance for how people today remember the past. As Dewey puts it, "Spaces begin to open up in which forgotten stories may be remembered, re-imagined, and told again, and voices long unheard may once more exercise their authority to speak of Jesus and the life of the new community of faith."[42] Dewey is not merely interested in the past as such, but wants to use ancient texts to speak about Jesus in new ways to the present.[43] Oral traditions and feminist theory work to write a new history in which women are included on equal terms. The memory of women is retrieved and used to explore oppression.[44]

---

39. Kartzow, "Resurrection as Gossip," 5.

40. See different perspectives in the various articles in "Roundtable Discussion on the Future of Feminist Biblical Studies."

41. Hirsch and Smith, "Feminism and Cultural Memory," 3.

42. Dewey, "From Storytelling to Written Text," 76.

43. See also Dewey, "Women on the Way."

44. Schüssler Fiorenza, "'What She Has Done Will Be Told . . . ,'" 5.

But this is not the only way memory can serve a feminist, liberating project. It is not only strong women with their own voice and agency who can function as objects of identification and be worth remembering. To remember the past as a time of oppression and injustice can also serve present-day concerns. A memory of exclusion and silencing, of stereotyping and othering, may have the potential to inspire today, as being the memory of the past that we do not want to repeat or revitalize. Lone Fatum argues along similar lines when she asks one of her many concise questions: Why invoke a different past as an excuse for demanding a different future?[45] Jennifer Glancy articulates her defense when she is blamed for interpreting New Testament texts as describing social realities, with little liberating potential for suffering people: "Do I want theological uplift and liberation? Sure. But you can't always get what you want."[46]

These different arguments, which are relevant for the discussion of female oral traditions and the women at the empty tomb, can greatly enhance the ongoing conversation about what the main purpose of early Christian studies is. Some would say it is to be concerned with the world *behind* and *in* the text, in order to reconstruct the most reasonable scenario.[47] We do not need historically unrealistic portraits of the past in order to legitimate any struggles for change today, the argument goes. Interpreters should not project their own liberating ideas upon the early Christians, confusing historical investigation with wishful thinking or false memory. It is not relevant to the field of New Testament studies to serve women and men today who need stories from the past to support their own liberating agendas.

Another possible approach for New Testament scholars is to highlight the connections between the historical fabric of the text and the world *in front of* the text.[48] My way of combining memory theory with intersectionality deals with these issues. What is the text doing to us or to other readers, interpreters, and users? How can these texts destabilize discourses of marginality? This way of doing exegesis corresponds to the

---

45. Fatum, "1 Thessalonians," 252.

46. Glancy, "Review Essay," 223.

47. For this concept, see Vander Stichele and Penner, *Contextualizing Gender in Early Christian Discourse*, 193–203.

48. See in particular Schüssler Fiorenza, *Jesus and the Politics of Interpretation*.

feminist task of recovering memory. The combination of oral genres and gender looks at the texts' destabilizing potential.[49]

The "historical" core of the oral tradition is that women were the first witnesses to the empty tomb, even though they at times are described as mistaken disciples or omitted from the written sources. Using Elizabeth Clark's work, we may further ask what an isolated interest in the "historical" aspects of the Biblical texts would mean.[50] To challenge a text's own perspective for not representing "historical facts" is indeed an important task within Biblical research after the linguistic turn and of course also after the intersectional turn.[51]

New Testament scholars also help construct the present by studying the past, and an important contribution of New Testament scholarship may be to theorize the gaps or search for early Christian dreams, visions, and possibilities that correspond to present-day hopes. If we want to take the interdisciplinary character of Biblical studies seriously, we cannot embrace merely historical or literary approaches, but also open up for a variety of other impulses from different disciplines, such as philosophy, poetics, political science, and feminist liberation theology. As I argued in the introduction (citing Musa Dube), Biblical studies cannot limit its interest to the history of textual traditions or to the doctrinal aspects of the texts. When studies of oral traditions engage with gender theory, a new, dynamic dialogue with challenging potential may be the result.

INTERSECTIONAL CHALLENGES: RECONSIDERING THE CONNECTION BETWEEN FEMINIST THEORY AND ORAL TRADITIONS

Although I see the variety of feminist perspectives as essential to early Christian studies, the task of recovering the forgotten memories of women builds on some presumptions and ideas that I would like to discuss. There are several intersectional questions to ask regarding the hypotheses that early Christian storytelling was mostly done by women and that women kept the memory alive and were responsible for the oral traditions. As

---

49. Dewey, "From Storytelling to Written Text," 76.

50. E. A. Clark, "Ideology, History, and the Construction of 'Woman' in Late Ancient Christianity."

51. E. A. Clark, *History, Theory, Text*; Mattsson, "Genua och vithet i den intersektionella vändingen."

Olick argues, we need analytical tools that are sensitive to the oral traditions' variations, contradictions, and dynamism.[52]

Is it likely that women participated in storytelling more than men? On one level, yes. Most women were left out of public discourses and had to form their own circles and networks. Private space was female space, and public was male. This is one of the central hypotheses in my book on gossip and gender. The memory of Jesus was kept alive for many years in informal private circles, far away from formal religious structures and political discourses in the Roman colonies.[53] But can gender explain the whole picture? It was not only women who were left out of the public discourse, and not all women had equal access to the informal female networks. I will investigate this by asking some related questions:

1. What kind of women did participate in these oral communities?
2. Who else contributed to the oral traditions?
3. What role did conflict, power struggles, and disagreement play in the processes, products, and practices through which early Christian groups remembered their past?[54]

The Homogenous Category of Women

Intersectional perspectives may challenge the idea that all women in antiquity represent one group with the same point of view. Oral traditions may open up for different ways of constructing power relations and hierarchies, but perhaps we push it too far if we imagine that oral authority is blind to the social order in the broader society.[55] Some women would have access to these oral communities, but I will challenge the idea that full participation and leadership among early Christian groups were open to all regardless of status and gender.[56]

---

52. "Collective memory is something—or rather many things—we *do*, not something—or many things—we have. We therefore need analytical tools sensitive to its varieties, contradictions, and dynamism. . . . How can we begin to untangle the diverse processes, products, and practices, though which societies confront and represent aspects of their past?" Olick, "Products, Processes, and Practices," 13.

53. Also a central point in Torjesen, *When Women Were Priests*.

54. See title of Olick, "Products, Processes, and Practices."

55. "Oral authority is inherently democratic or egalitarian: the opportunity to gain oral authority is open to most people." Dewey, "From Oral Stories to Written Text," 22.

56. Dewey says: "The world of early Christianity was a world of oral communication in which women were full participants as active proclaimers and storytellers as well as re-

We need a theoretical vocabulary that can help us talk about difference among early Christian women and men. Intersectionality may offer useful tools in this context. In order to re-imagine the female oral communities that kept alive the memory of Jesus and the women at the empty tomb, issues of social class, ethnic background, and language seem to be particularly relevant.

Cultural Complexity and Oral Traditions

I will use intersectionality and ask the other question regarding the connection between women and early Christian storytelling. Did only free or freeborn wives keep the oral tradition alive, or were also their slaves or servants included? And what about the subordinates' influence? Were their voices heard, or were they primarily silent listeners who followed their mistresses' will? And were those women who came from wealthy families that supported the Roman occupation included on equal terms only because they were women?

Some sources present wives, nurses, and midwives as storytelling groups, sometimes with children of both genders present, but how was the power dynamic among these various categories of women and children?[57] Some of these wives were probably literate, and this may have influenced their role in this "oral female community."[58] A related intersectional challenge is whether those males responsible for writing down the text were all members of the male elite, or whether also male slaves, who at times were literate, did participate.[59] If so, did slaves merely function

---

ceptive listeners." Dewey, "From Storytelling to Written Text," 74. She also writes: "Early Christianity began as an oral subculture, with full participation and leadership open to all regardless of status and gender." Dewey, "From Oral Stories to Written Text," 23.

57. Hearon, *The Mary Magdalene Tradition*.

58. Literacy was the norm for the upper class, the rulers, owners of large estates, probably the top 2 percent of the population. Dewey argues that "[Among the upper class], literacy would have been normal for the men and probably fairly common for the women." Dewey, "From Storytelling to Written Text," 73.

59. "When we speak of the close relationship between oral and written texts, therefore, we need to recognize that the 'written texts' were relatively few—those responsible for the creation of these written texts made up less than a handful of the population, and of this group the vast majority were male." Hearon, "The Implications of 'Orality' for Studies of the Biblical Text," 102–3. According to Horsley, "[L]iteracy was extremely limited in Mediterranean antiquity," Horsley, "Oral Traditions in New Testament Studies," 4. On literate slaves, see Tsang, "Are We 'Misreading' Paul?" 210.

as secretaries/scribes, or did they contribute to the discussions, negotiations, and selections of what to include and what to omit? Another issue is what characteristics were shared by the handful of literates among the male urban elite who presumably wrote down the texts.[60] Did they have the same needs, agendas, and perspectives?[61]

Early Christian groups had deep roots in what we call "Jewish traditions,"[62] but also other ethnic/national groups contributed in the formation process. Was the Jewish "oral tradition" that has been considered so central for early Christian storytelling, accessible also for others, both men and women?[63] And further: Some slaves came from far away and did not know the language. How could foreign female slaves contribute to the storytelling process? Early Christian groups lived in a Hebrew culture, where some spoke Aramaic, and texts were written in Greek. Sam Tsang has argued that when dealing with orality, "confronting the problem of the multilingual reality is unavoidable." In the empire, several languages were present (Greek, Latin, Getic, Lycaonian, Punic, Libyan, Gaelic, and countless others), and the Romans did not discourage the diversity of language.[64] It is evident that "in some societies languages may mark off one sector from another, intercourse being restricted to a few people who can interpret."[65]

Perhaps some foreign slaves and other ethnic strangers within early Christian groups needed translation, but how did that influence the informal character of oral communication? And did anyone bother to translate if it was only a female slave from far away who did not understand? Female slaves seem to have had rather limited possibilities to speak and talk; in chapter 8 I will highlight all the intersecting challenges that a fortune-telling and prophesying female slave could generate in early Christian discourse.

---

60. Hearon, "The Implications of 'Orality' for Studies of the Biblical Text," 102.

61. See Hearon, "The Storytelling World of the First Century and the Gospels," 27–31.

62. This phrase is problematic, however, as discussed in several chapters of this book. See also Camp, "Oralities, Literacies, and Colonialisms in Antiquity and Contemporary Scholarship," 212–13.

63. Wire, *Holy Lives, Holy Deaths*, Gerhardsson, "The Secret of the Transmission of the Unwritten Jesus Tradition," 6.

64. Tsang, "Are We 'Misreading' Paul?," 213–14.

65. Millard, *Reading and Writing in the Time of Jesus*, 132.

We must examine other categories than only gender if we are interested in access, power, and influence among early Christian storytellers. The various intersections of gender, social status, ethnicity, and language seem especially relevant.[66]

Another related issue is how oral traditions and texts relate to each other, as two interrelated (rather than distinct) media. It is too simplistic to say that text represents hegemony and orality the subjugated peoples.[67] Hearon argues that written texts are instable since different audiences, performers, and contexts shape how the written text appears as oral-aural.[68] Orality and aural reception were built into the New Testament texts.[69] The oral and the written text are bound together in a dynamic relationship, making it irrelevant to talk about a clear distinction between an "oral phase" and a "written phase."[70] As Richard Horsley argues, literacy and orality should not be understood in terms of a great divide.[71] In addition, we cannot talk about one text surviving from the earliest Christians to us; several versions of the same text existed, and our oldest manuscripts are relatively late.[72] Somehow the whole idea of female/oral and male/written collapses, if we start questing both the gender categories and the concepts of textuality and orality.

NEGOTIATED AND CONTESTED MEMORY

In this final section I will use memory theories in order to think more concretely about what kind of oral traditions the New Testament reflects. We can imagine a historical scenario where several socially varied groups had their own oral traditions, as argued above. Those traditions reflected in the Gospels knew of some important women at the empty tomb, heroines or not, while others remembered the resurrection without any women involved. Whose memory won out, and why? Whose voices were

---

66. Also addressed in Camp, "Oralities, Literacies, and Colonialisms in Antiquity and Contemporary Scholarship."

67. But see Draper, "Orality, Litracy, and Colonialism in Antiquity," 3.

68. Hearon, "The Implications of 'Orality' for Studies of the Biblical Text," 100.

69. Tsang, "Are We 'Misreading' Paul?" 211.

70. Hearon, "The Implications of 'Orality' for Studies of the Biblical Text," 98. See also Hearon, "The Interplay between Written and Spoken Word in the Second Testament as Background to the Emergence of Written Gospels."

71. Horsley, "Oral Traditions in New Testament Studies," 4.

72. See Bernhard, *Other Early Christian Gospels*.

heard?[73] What was forgotten and what ended up deep down in the archive, left out of the active canon for later generations? I am interested in patterns of which individuals or groups set their marks on the collective memory. Whose "contemporary interests shape what images of the past" that were remembered?[74]

According to Kelber, "[p]recisely what keeps the tradition a living one, then, is this negotiation of the present with the past so as to make the latter speak to the former."[75] But who was in a position to negotiate? Olick points out that memory has always been a central medium of power:

> Collective memory has thus become more and more a mechanism through which dominant groups seek to control their futures by linking them to pasts within self-consciously eschatological frameworks that legitimate present positions and programs.[76]

Memory involves sharing, discussion, negotiation, and often conflict, and deals with identity, power, authority, cultural norms, and social interaction.[77] Inherent in the memory process, therefore, is the active labor of selecting, structuring, and imposing meaning on the past rather than the mere reproduction of inherent historical truths.[78] Whose dominant interest is the New Testament text reporting? Whose voices are not heard in the extant texts?

In regard to the text material studied in this chapter, I believe it is too unsubtle and indistinct to argue that the Gospels reflect a gender inclusive attitude since they mention women in their resurrection stories, and that Paul's and Acts' accounts, which omit women, represent the dominant male discourse. The role of women was contested, as shown by Celsus and the Gospel of Mary. It was not only the role of women as witnesses to the empty tomb that was controversial, but also the capacity of women to

---

73. Doran Mendels points out that "[t]he past is used in a recycled manner in different forms of memory, that can tell us a great deal about the cultural, political and social structure of a society." Mendels, *Memory in Jewish, Pagan and Christian Societies of the Graeco-Roman World*, xv–xvi.

74. Olick, "Products, Processes, and Practices," 13.

75. Kelber, "The Generative Force of Memory," 21. Olick looks at memory as "a fluid negotiation between the desire of the present and the legacies of the past." Olick, "Products, Processes, and Practices," 13.

76. Olick, "Products, Processes, and Practices," 7.

77. Brundage, "Introduction," 4.

78. Ibid., 5.

receive divine messages or have leadership positions. But who were these women, and how did they operate? Were they slaveholders, and if so, did they involve their slaves in their female storytelling community? I think it is urgent and essential when working with early Christian memory to ask whether the gender inclusive communities in which female oral traditions were kept alive also represented alternative ways of organizing social hierarchy related to class, ethnicity, language, and age.

CONCLUSION

When we use memory theory and intersectionality to examine different accounts of women and the resurrection, it becomes clear that some of the presumptions on which the arguments are built invite to further discussion. The idea that the early Christian oral traditions were kept alive by women as storytellers and were then written down by men has been challenged in various ways:

1. Not all women had equal access to the female oral community, with marginalized women being excluded.
2. It was not only women who were excluded from the small group of literates who took part in the text production process.
3. There were significant social differences among the literate elite as well as among the non-literates: some women were literate, some men were not literate, not all men had access to the written tradition, those who did not know the given language had less access to the communication process, and so forth.
4. The category of women is not a uniform one, and gender is insufficient as the only analytical tool. The various intersections of gender, social background, language, and age seem more relevant.
5. It is hard to draw a distinctive line between an oral and a written phase.

It might be that it is typical for all subordinates to talk in informal ways, but did they talk together? Did male slaves hang out with freeborn wives and storytellers (that is, with people who kept alive the memory of Jesus and the women who witnessed the empty tomb)? Was there solidarity among all those who did not belong to the male elite? Can we even speak of a uniform group that shared an oral tradition?

For this specific study of oral genres, women, and the resurrection scene, it is imprecise to draw a clear-cut line (based on the fact that women are mentioned only by the Gospels) between the female tradition known to the Gospels and the male tradition known to Paul/Acts. What categories of women would keep the tradition alive in which these women were the first witnesses, but failed to be good disciples? One would expect that female storytellers would give a more positive picture of these named women, and not play on gender stereotypes. Somehow, most of the texts dealing with the empty tomb and the resurrection of Jesus represent masculine discourse and give women little or no attention, or associate women with female vices.

By use of social imagination we may fill in the gaps in these communication processes: Could perhaps some of these traditions reflect the point of view of literate male slaves and their fellow female slaves who made fun of the freeborn wives (i.e., characters who resembled their owners)? And when it comes to Paul or Acts, who was interested in remembering the resurrection scene with no central female witnesses—perhaps some offended women who were not mentioned by name according to tradition, or their literate children or grandchildren? Or are the extant texts the result of completely different negotiation processes?

My point is that we miss many nuances and complexities among early Christian groups and oral traditions if we limit our interest to gender and orality. The picture is far more complex, and intersectionality helps us ask the other question. Whatever relation there was between oral and written traditions, the groups surrounding these traditions were diverse and most likely included characters with various genders, social backgrounds, ethnicities, ages, and languages. I think these nuances are important to reconsider for those who are interested in storytelling, oral traditions, and early Christian memory, and highly relevant when focusing on women and the empty tomb.

6

Limited Access

Stereotyping the Voice in the Pastoral Epistles

INTRODUCTION

OF ALL THE VICES of the so-called opponents listed in the Pastoral Epistles, one of the most insidious, according to the Pastoral Paul, is related to how these opponents speak. Jennifer Glancy has argued that when these epistles construct the proper ways to speak and talk, they follow the standards of masculinity in antiquity.[1] This chapter will use memory theory and intersectionality and engage with discourses of speech and talk in the Pastorals, and in particular examine texts in which certain blameworthy ways of speaking and talking are constructed as unmasculine and therefore to be avoided. Which voices that were allowed and accepted will reveal much about the mechanisms of marginalization and exclusion.

Gender plays a major role in ancient discourses when speech and talk was categorized as proper or improper.[2] This part of the book employs intersectionality to argue that gender alone is insufficient when speech and talk are evaluated. What kind of patterns can we find in the Pastoral Epistles? I employ Matsuda's other question in order to re-imagine the possible social scenarios that underlay various passages related to speech and talk.

In chapter 5 I asked whose voices were heard when the empty tomb scene was remembered. Moving on from narrative accounts to a different genre—namely early Christian epistles, which probably stem from third-

1. Glancy, "Protocols of Masculinity in the Pastoral Epistles."
2. See Kartzow, "Female Gossipers and Their Reputation in the Pastoral Epistles."

generation Christian communities in Asia Minor—we are confronted with other types of memories. Silence and speech appear as powerful rhetorical devices that are used to make a certain point in the correspondence or to construct ideal or deviant human behavior. Through reading these epistles we only hear the voice of the Pastoral Paul, the Paul as he is remembered by a certain group some generations after Paul. We do not know how the readers or listeners contributed in the process and constructed identity out of this written memory.[3] For the Pastoral Paul, however, some characters and their way of speaking and talking were worth remembering, for the most part as a way of illustrating what he categorized as the opposite of sound teaching. When it comes to these discourses, stereotypes play a central role. This chapter will discuss four examples of stereotyping of the voice, while the next chapter will examine the stereotype of gossip and will read the Pastorals together with a Lukan parable.

BLAMEWORTHY SPEECH

On several occasions in the Pastoral Epistles, improper speech and talk are cited among the main characteristics of the Pastoral Paul's opponents or of those who behave wrongly.[4] I have found some striking examples, and I begin with those passages in which various categories of women are criticized.

Old wives' tales

In 1 Tim 4:7a the false teaching is said to be "old wives' tales" [γραώδεις μύθους].[5] The term γραώδης is not documented elsewhere in the New Testament, LXX, or the Apostolic Fathers, but in philosophical polemic it is used for fables that grown men would pay no credence to but that might entertain youngsters.[6] The etymological origin of this term shows how the combination of a certain age and a certain gender gave specific

---

3. Fatum, "Christ Domesticated."
4. A point strongly made in Glancy, "Protocols of Masculinity in the Pastoral Epistles."
5. See how γραώδης comes from "old woman" in LSJ and Roloff, *Der Erste Brief an Timotheus*, 243 and note.
6. Quinn and Wacker, *The First and Second Letters to Timothy*, 367. See also Mounce, *Pastoral Epistles*, 251.

connotations related to speech.⁷ Ideal men, on the contrary, should instead train themselves in godliness (1 Tim 4:7b). This brief verse represents in itself an interesting example of how ideal speech is contrasted by use of gendered imagination: the phrase "old wives' tales" gives negative and perhaps also humoristic associations and serves to castigate false teachers, while to train and practice are masculine virtues and represent the ideal behavior of the sound teachers. In many Bible translations, this expression is translated without showing any gender implication or referring to old age, with words such as "empty talk" or "profane myths."

Could those who told such "old wives' tales" also include slaves? Would old female slaves also be blamed for telling tales, or did this designation particularly target free women who had a background as wives and mothers and female householders? Or did gender become less important as women got older; supposedly, even free postmenopausal women were granted more freedom since they did not need the same male protection, as they were no longer thought to be in danger of bringing shame through sexual violation.⁸ Perhaps old age also reduced the difference between slave and free women?

Women, gossip, and slander

The connection between women and gossip/slander is made in several passages in the Pastoral Epistles. In 1 Tim 3:11 some female deacons are instructed to not be slanderers, and διάβολος is also used of older women (or women elders) in Titus: They are told not to be slanderers, but to be good domestic examples for the younger women (Titus 2:3). In 1 Tim 5:13 the young widows—in contrast to old widows, who are "real" widows—are instructed to not be gossips and busybodies who wander about the households and say things that they should not. All these three categories of gossipy women belong to the class of free women who should marry.

It is worth noticing that the three central passages that possibly attribute titles of some kind to free women ("deaconesses," female elders, and widows) all blame them for being gossipy. This may suggest that making accusations of deviant speech and talk was an effective device in order to

---

7. See Bremmer, who argues in regard to the telling of myths in the homes that "old women were not highly esteemed as a class in ancient Greece"; Bremmer, "Performing Myths," 126.

8. Hearon, *The Mary Magdalene Tradition*, 25.

reinscribe domestic female roles for free women, since it ridiculed and naturalized women.[9] In chapter 7 I will discuss gossip and widows in greater detail.

Another important intersectional observation concerns women, speech, and age. Old wives' tales obviously deal with ideas about old women, but also related to one of the slander-texts and in the case of widows, a certain distinction is made between women of different ages. While old wives and older women are connected to tales and slander respectively, in the case of widows it is the younger ones who are blamed, while the older ones seem to follow proper standards for speech.

Slaves should not talk back

So far we have seen that the Pastoral Paul associates a variety of women, perhaps including some slave women, with such inappropriate speech as tales, slander, and gossip. But not only gender regulated speech: in Titus slaves shall not talk back to or speak up against [ἀντιλέγω] their masters (Titus 2:9–10), while in 1 Tim slaves are also told to respect and obey their masters (1 Tim 6:1–2). Both these instructions employ social practices and roles that were stereotypically expected of slaves in antiquity. I think these two themes are related: one way that slaves could be obedient was to not talk back to or speak up against their masters.

According to Titus 2:9–10, slaves should not contradict or question the words of those who were above them in the social hierarchy. What the masters said should not be met with alternative tales from the slaves, as if those in power owned the discourse and should have the last word.[10]

Except for these two instructions given to slaves, the only comment on slavery in the Pastoral Epistles is the small fragment I classified in chapter 4 as having "destabilizing potential," namely the phrase "slave traders" that appears on the vice list of 1 Tim 1:10 together with negative figures such as fornicators, sodomites, and liars. To oppose the slave trade would have been a radical social statement at the time, in strong contrast to the conventional hierarchical language employed elsewhere in the Pastorals.

When the Pastoral Epistles mention slaves, there are no indications what gender these slaves are supposed to be, with the plural form

9. Kartzow, *Gossip and Gender*, 204.
10. As is listed as one possible meaning of ἀντιλέγω in LSJ.

being given in masculine grammatical gender. Inspired by Osiek and MacDonald, I consider "slaves" to mean both male and female slaves. One of the assumptions Osiek and MacDonald mention in their book is that "masculine plural titles should not always presume men to the exclusion of women." Hence, when various NT texts mention "apostles," "prophets," "teachers," "deacons," or "bishops," the plural masculine grammatical designation may include women.[11] Although "slave" can hardly be called a title, I find their method useful in order to make all kinds of women more visible, not only women in leadership positions. Accordingly, the instruction to slaves not to talk back may be included in the list of passages that use intersectional stereotypes related to gender and class to categorize slaves' way of speaking and talking.

Cretans are lairs, Jews tell myths

The letter to Titus contrasts ideal masculine speech not only by using gender, age, and social status, but by using ethnic reasoning as well.[12] A critical passage about the false teachers (where they are called rebellious, idle talkers, and deceivers, where "those of the circumcised" in particular are blamed, see chapter 4 in this book) includes a phrase that has been called the *Liar Paradox*. Titus 1:12–14 refers to a saying from Epimedes that "Cretans are always liars, beasts, lazy gluttons," and the Pastoral Paul adds, with convincing rhetorical power, "This testimony is true."[13] For this reason the letter argues that Titus must rebuke them sharply so that they do not pay attention to Jewish myths or commandments of those who reject the truth.

These verses employ ethnic reasoning in which a geographical location and its people are targeted by a racial stereotype, combined with a negative characterization of religious myths, in order to blame the other and promote the self. Christian truth is hence constructed by naming and blaming people of a different race or faith.[14]

This statement about Jews has played a role in the Christian history of anti-Semitism, and has been central for interpreters who see "anti-

---

11. Osiek and MacDonald, *A Woman's Place*, 6.
12. See the subtitle of Buell, *Why This New Race*.
13. See Marshall, "'I Left You in Crete'," 801–2.
14. On the strategy of "naming and blaming" in these letters, see Fatum, "Christ Domesticated," 185.

Judaic attitudes" in Titus.[15] But this attitude somehow intersects with the racial essentialism concerning the Cretans, who behave according to their nature—that is, they are liars.[16] Negative ideas about deviant racial, ethnic, or religious ways of speaking and talking seem to overlap in a rather problematic way.[17] I am surprised to see that some interpreters, who are sensitive to the anti-Judaic attitudes, explain and defend "Paul's" view of the Cretans, instead of challenging them. Some even suggest that Paul's instructions in Titus are a sign of the savagery and incivility of the native population of Crete.[18]

Scholars who try to reconstruct the social climate of ancient Crete sometimes tend to overlook the rhetorical situation of these letters. How can they emphasize the anti-Jewish attitudes without noticing how the image of the Cretan people is constructed according to similar stereotypes and represents ethnic/racial/religious essentialism? The Pastoral Epistles remember Paul as an "Apostle to the nations," but some "nations" seem to be more appreciated than others.

A follow-up question to both the category "Jew" and "Cretan" would concern who could be included in these terms. As asked in chapter 4: could women, slaves, or children, and all intersections of these categories, also be considered to belong to these groups?

INTERSECTIONAL CHALLENGES

All these different categories of people are blamed for improper speech and talk. By using age in relation to women and widows, the social status of slaves, the ethnic origin of liars, or religious faith of those who tell myths, it becomes clear that very few categories of people represent

---

15. Stegemann, "Anti-Semitic and Racial Prejudices in Titus 1:10–16," 293. See also Marshall, "'I Left You in Crete,'" 797. See also Schäfer, *Judeophobia*.

16. Solevåg and Kartzow, "Hvem bryr seg om Pastoralbrevene?" 264.

17. A similar point is made in Stegemann, "Anti-Semitic and Racial Prejudices in Titus 1:10–16," 293–94.

18. See for example Johnson, *Letters to Paul's Delegates*. He argues, related to the passage on women in Titus 2, that "Everything in the letter to this point has suggested that before their conversion, these Christians had been dominated by 'every sort of lawlessness,' were driven by 'godlessness and worldly desire,' and had not, in fact, been capable of living lives of prudence, justice, and godliness." Johnson finds it surprising that women need to be taught to love their husbands and children and asks: "is this a sign of the savageness and incivility of the native population, that responses ordinarily thought to be 'natural' should require teaching?" (240).

a recommendable way of speaking. None of these groups seem to have reached the ideal, masculine way of speaking and talking.

I think Matsuda's question is very helpful. It has shown that several central categories from intersectional thinking, such as gender, age, social status, ethnicity, and religion, intersect in order to construct structures of ideal speech in the Pastoral Epistles. These letters are overloaded with stereotypes related to speech and talk, reducing almost all possible categories of social positions into marginality.

We may nevertheless reflect further on possible social scenarios and theorize the gaps. What about persons who belonged to more than one category: for example, would all of the Pastoral Paul's instructions apply to a Jewish female slave from Crete, as if vice were added to vice? According to the Pastoral Paul, she would have several reasons for keeping her mouth shut, as she belonged to various groups who should not tell tales, talk back, or be gossipers, and coming from Crete she was also counted among the liars. Or is it primarily *male* slaves who should not talk back and *male free* citizens of Crete who are liars, and *Jewish free males* who tell the myths?

CONCLUSION: IN MEMORY OF WHOM?

Who needed such ideas about speech and talk in order to secure their own identity and privilege? Indeed, the Pastoral Epistles followed standards of masculinity in antiquity when proper ways of speaking and talking are constructed, but not only women seem to be left out of the ideal discourse, as blame was also apportioned to slaves of both genders, women of various ages and social statuses, Jews, and Cretans.

In the Pastoral Epistles, the patterns of ideal speech deal not only with gender—gender intersects with social status, age, ethnicity, and religion as well. When Paul is remembered in relation to proper speech, very few characters among the early Christians seem to behave according to the accepted standards. Who are allowed to talk? Who are allowed to break the silence? Whose voices are heard and remembered?

These hierarchical structures, in which only a few accepted and selected persons are given permission to speak, create a system that excludes several persons. Discriminating attitudes towards women of various categories, people from different ethnic backgrounds or faiths, or people from lower social positions are challenging to deal with for present-day interpreters. It is interesting that by paying attention to speech and talk, the hierarchical systems seem rather strict. Although these epistles contain a destabilizing potential in regard to other issues (see chapter 4), they see no need to moderate the power systems when dealing with whose voices should be heard and remembered.

Mieke Bal refers to how "self-evident ideas, a culture's stock of wisdom, include what we call stereotype."[19] In regard to speech and talk, the Pastoral Epistles represent a culture whose memory employs a stock of wisdom that has a limited interest in tolerance and dialogue.[20] The hierarchical structure functions as the rhetorical energy of the epistles, and the building blocks seem to be stereotypes. As modern readers, we are all aware of the dangerous dynamics of stereotypes dealing with race/religion, gender, or sexuality, which has caused so much suffering for individual human beings in our societies. Regrettably, the Bible has often been used to legitimate such destructive processes.

---

19. Bal, *Loving Yusuf*, 7–8.
20. This attitude is called "heterophobic prejudices" in Stegemann, "Anti-Semitic and Racial Prejudices in Titus 1:10–16," 285–86.

7

Negotiating Power Relations

Talkative Widows out of Place
(Luke 18:2–5 and 1 Tim 5:13–14)

INTRODUCTION

IN THE PREVIOUS CHAPTERS I have tried to find some patterns of speech in various early Christian texts, dealing in particular with "oral genres" in the Gospels and stereotyping of speech and talk in the Pastoral Epistles. I will now follow up by going more into detail in relation to one specific kind of speech: gossip. My hypothesis is that two passages that both deal with widows—the parable of the widow and the judge in Luke 18:1–8 and the so-called "widows' tale" in 1 Tim 5:3–16—can be connected in a new way that few have studied before. I suggest that these texts are involved in similar discourses, not only in that they mention widows but also because they employ the gendered stereotype that gossip belongs to women.[1] Though it has been argued that the parable of the widow and the judge is the only authentic parable that does not reflect traditional female roles,[2] I would suggest that it nevertheless produces meaning by use of conventional ideas about female speech.

The New Testament books that most frequently mention widows are the Gospel of Luke and the Pastoral Epistles.[3] When interpreters have compared widows in Luke and the Pastorals, it has been noted that the prophet-widow Anna in the beginning of Luke's gospel, who "prayed night and day" (Luke 2:37), may be a model for the "real widow" in 1 Tim

---

1. Walker, *The Woman's Encyclopedia of Myths and Secrets*. See also Spacks, *Gossip*.
2. Corley, *Feminist Myths of Chriastian Origins*, 58.
3. Price, *The Widow Traditions in Luke-Acts*.

5:5 who set her hope in God and "prayed night and day." Pious and praying widows seem to be a dominating motif in early Christian discourse, including the parable of the widow and the judge: in the frame narrative of the parable, the reason Jesus told the disciples this parable also pertains to patient and intense praying—they need to pray always and not lose heart (Luke 18:1).

However, the relation between the Lukan frame and the parable of the widow and the judge creates a strange logic. The parable features a judge who respected neither God nor man, and who only relented and granted justice to the persistent widow for the mysterious reason that he feared she would give him "a black eye." Is God compared with an unjust judge in this parable? Will he change his mind if we pray night and day?

There is no consensus about precisely what this parable tells,[4] and many interpreters have discussed the relationship between "the core" (vv. 2–5) and Luke's secondary commentary (vv. 1 and 6–8).[5] Since this parable has been so hard to understand, this widow has been stored away in the archive and almost forgotten. Part of this narrative gap and inconsequence may be explained if we read the parable separately from the Lukan frame and try to make sense of it on its own terms. Accordingly, instead of relating the parable to the Pastoral Epistles within the context of praying and widows, I will take a different point of departure by employing theories of gossip.

Gossip is not one of the topics upon which the hegemonic political and theoretical order rests, and that might in itself be a good reason to study this category when we are interested in the margins.[6] In my book on gossip and gender in the Pastoral Epistles, I tried to show how gossip could be a useful analytical category in order to unmask rhetoric and to suggest possible social scenarios that generated early Christian texts.[7]

---

4. Reid, "A Godly Widow Persistently Pursuing Justice," 25.

5. See Cotter, "The Parable of the Feisty Widow and the Threatened Judge (Luke 18:1–8)," 328. See also Reid, "A Godly Widow," 27–28. Herzog argues it is difficult to separate the parable from its Lukan context; see Herzog, *Parables as Subversive Speech*, 219. See also Annette Metz, "How a Woman Who Fought Back and Demanded Her Rights Became an Importunate Widow," 85. On the strange role of God as a anti-metaphor, see Scott, *Hear Then the Parable*, 175.

6. Leach, "Feminist Figurations," 232.

7. Kartzow, *Gossip and Gender*.

In this chapter I will use intersectionality and memory theory to fill in the gaps and ask new questions of the two text passages under investigation here. The ways in which widows and their speech and talk were remembered in early Christian texts may help uncover power relations and the destability of marginality. I start by discussing ideas about widows in antiquity by use of recent interpretations of ancient texts. Then I present some of my findings about ancient figurations of female gossipers, followed by a discussion of female gossipers in the Pastoral Epistles. I also present some other early Christian texts that associate widows and gossip, before finally reading the parable of the widow and the judge within a framework of gender and gossip.

WIDOWS IN ANTIQUITY

The category of "widow" in the ancient world was an ambiguous one. She was "sexually awakened" but lacked male protection.[8] She was suspect and her character and behavior were favorite themes for gossipers.[9] As a former wife, she belonged to the ideal class of women, but her status as a widow disturbed her role. It was significant whether she was old or young (cf. 1 Timothy 5). Economically she was most often dependent on her former husband's family. Her role vis-à-vis her children, if she had any, was complicated. Widowhood could mean remarriage and a new family-in-law, or she could be forced into prostitution in order to survive. For free women, the triad virgin, wife, and widow was the natural and expected life scenario of an ideal woman, but real-life experiences could be challenging for a widow, for example if her husband died when she was young.

The responsibility for helping widows and orphans is known from a variety of ancient sources.[10] Widows had a complex social role, however; as sexually experienced, but outside the control of a husband, they could be dangerous women.[11] Karel van der Toorn has pointed out that a widow in the ancient Near East represented a potential threat to the established order of the patriarchal society. A widow could be too independent, a potential seductress, or a witch—in short, a danger to public order. As an

---

8. Walcot, "On Widows and Their Reputation in Antiquity."
9. Kartzow, "Female Gossipers and Their Reputation in the Pastoral Epistles."
10. van der Toorn, "Torn between Vice and Virtue."
11. See Kartzow, "Female Gossipers and Their Reputation in the Pastoral Epistles."

independent woman her role in the public perception was ambiguous, as van der Toorn notes[12]: "On the one hand, she is a monument of devotion, wisdom, and chastity; on the other hand, she is known as an easy prey for religious fanatics, a prattler, and a woman of loose sexual habits."[13]

In antiquity, also in Christian texts, χήρα covers a wide spectrum of women, including virgins, women living apart from their husbands, divorced women, and women whose husbands were dead.[14] But, to ask the other question: Could only free women be widowed? Of course, a slave woman could also lose her partner, if she had any, and could also experience sorrow and suffering.[15] Although slave couples were not legally accepted as married, they may have lived together as families. In the two texts under consideration here, however, the ideal household discourse and the role of free women seem to constitute the social environment. When examining widows as a complex category of women, it is particularly useful to look at the intersections of several social classification systems (age, status, sexuality, family relations, economic position) in order to understand their vulnerable position, but also to grasp the variation among those classified as widows.

ANCIENT FIGURATIONS OF FEMALE GOSSIPERS

Several passages in the Pastoral Epistles mention gossip, as I pointed out in the last chapter. In my book on gossip and gender I examined several texts that associate women and gossip, as well as other texts dealing with gossip and masculinity, in order to place the Pastoral Epistles' texts on gossip in a broader rhetorical context. I also built on recent interdisciplinary research on gossip, which uses various definitions, taxonomies, and methods.[16]

---

12. Note how a similar point is made from a later period in Walcot, "On Widows and Their Reputation in Antiquity."

13. van der Toorn, "Torn between Vice and Virtue," 13.

14. In Tertullian, Ignatius, the lexicographer Hesychius, Philo, and LXX; see Stählin, "χήρα," 440–41. See also Brown's commentary in Meyers, *Women in Scripture*, 492. Dewey argues regarding 1 Timothy 5 that "'[w]idow' is an early title for a woman devoted to Christian ministry who was not dependent on a man"; Dewey, "1 Timothy," 448.

15. This way of employing the widow category to non-legal marriage-copies is discussed in Maseno and Kartzow, "Widows, Intersectionality and the Parable in Luke 18."

16. See Foster, "Research on Gossip."

In the ancient texts I investigated I found that female gossipers blur traditional boundaries between private and public. Since these space categories were gendered (private = female, public = male), gossip represented a threat to the cosmic principles that were intended to maintain social order and prevent chaos. Information and knowledge were distributed through gossip by persons who were not formally authorized, and in a society lacking other forms of media and news channels, the access to gossip could influence life and death. Female gossipers were therefore not merely silly little women concerned with domestic issues, as some ancient authors strive to convince their readers. Rather, their words crossed boundaries, and female gossipers initiated information flows that disturbed male order within the households and the city as a whole. Some women are portrayed as active users of the gossip network, to get what they want or to change the public discourse. Most ancient texts condemn or warn against this information flow, while some of their authors use female gossip to gain information or to establish moral standards.[17]

Most of the texts deal with topics from gossip's favorite realm, that of love and sexuality. There are, however, a few but interesting exceptions: Women are even labeled gossipers when the content of what they say is far removed from the typical realm of gossip. Some women who use gossip to interfere with politics and public matters are also labeled gossipers. In some of the texts, the *function and effect* of gossip seem to be more threatening than the actual content of what is said. Female gossip networks are presumed to be extremely efficient: rumors spread rapidly, from person to person and from group to group. This is dangerous and damaging because rumors, accusations, and information (whether false or true) are out of control within the gossip network.[18]

FEMALE GOSSIPERS IN THE PASTORAL EPISTLES

The frequent comments about gossip in the Pastoral Epistles are noteworthy.[19] I discussed some of these terms in the last chapter, where I scrutinized stereotypes of speech and talk in these epistles more broadly. Here I will highlight how interpreters explicitly have characterized these Greek terms as gossip.

---

17. See in particular Chapter 3 in Kartzow, *Gossip and Gender*.
18. See the table in ibid., 211.
19. As stated by Rohrbaugh, "Gossip in the New Testament," 256.

In the middle of a list in 1 Tim in which deacons are told to be serious and blameless, the focus abruptly shifts to certain women: "Women, likewise, must be serious, not slanderers, but temperate, faithful in all things" (1 Tim 3:11). Quinn and Wacker translate *diabolos*, as used on women in this context, with "devils of gossip."[20] Διάβολος is also used of older women (or women elders) [πρεσβῦτις]:[21] they are told not to be slanderers, but to be good domestic examples for the younger women (Titus 2:3). The epistles twice label the speech of women negatively by using the same Greek term.[22] Another devaluating characterization given of the false teaching is "old wives' tales" (1 Tim 4:7; see last chapter). This phrase uses a stereotypical expectation towards old women and their storytelling, but no further information about the content of these tales is reported.[23] Jouette Bassler interprets old wives' tales as "unreliable gossip."[24]

Perhaps the most polemical passage in these epistles deals with why young widows must not be enrolled among the widows, and one of the vices listed is most often translated as "gossip" (1 Tim 5:13): "And at the same time they [the young widows] learn to be idle, gadding about in the houses, not only idle but also gossipers and busybodies, saying what they should not."

These epistles adopt the common moral in which women are instructed not to be slanderers, babblers, gossips, and busybodies. Reading these verses together with the verse on "old wives' tales," I argue that we see a pattern related to gender and speech: women have a tendency to be involved in such a way of speaking, and the Pastoral Epistles therefore repeatedly instruct them to refrain from it.

20. Quinn and Wacker, *The First and Second Letters to Timothy*, 276. Also translated with "gossip" in Johnson, *The First and Second Letters to Timothy*, 299.

21. The various possible interpretations of this term were discussed in Solevåg and Kartzow, "Who Loves the Pastorals and Why?" Published in Norwegian: Solevåg and Kartzow, "Hvem bryr seg om Pastoralbrevene?"

22. For the rhetorician Lucian, *diabolos* is a threat to friendship: it is the hidden and secret talk, it is the opposite of truth, and finds its contrast in public discourse among educated men; no woman figures as an example. Slanderers, according to Lucian, obviously did not talk in a proper way, according to male standards. See Kartzow, *Gossip and Gender*, 47–48.

23. See more on old women who are depicted telling stories in Greco-Roman texts, Hearon, *The Mary Magdalene Tradition*, 25.

24. Bassler, *1 Timothy, 2 Timothy, Titus*, 84. Note also the close connection shown to be between *gossip* and *old wives' tales* in Walker, *The Woman's Encyclopedia of Myths and Secrets*, 350.

WIDOWS AND GOSSIP

One of the most "prominent" gossip texts in the Pastoral Epistles refers to widows, but this is not the only place where widows and gossip are associated. It is intriguing to find parallel ideas about widows and gossip in Christian texts written at the same time as, and perhaps even before, the Pastoral Epistles and the Gospel of Luke.

1. Ignatius of Antioch writes: "Let not the widows be wanderers about, nor fond of dainties, nor gadders from house to house; but let them be like Judith, noted for her seriousness; and like Anna, eminent for her sobriety."[25] He uses the scenario that widows are wanderers and are gadding about from house to house, with clear echoes in 1 Tim 5:13, and also referring to Anna in Luke 2:36–38.

2. According to Polycarp, widows are to be taught "to be discreet in the faith of the Lord, praying ceaselessly for all men, being far from all slander, evil speaking, false witness, love of money and all evil, knowing that they are an altar of God" (IV.3).[26] What they shall do in contrast is to pray, something that is reminiscent of the recommendations made by both Ignatius and the Pastoral Paul, with similarities to Anna in Luke 2.

3. The connection between gossip and widows as altars developed and changed content: according to the third century *Didascalia Apostolorum*, the widow should remember that she is the altar of God and should therefore remain at home, rather than wander about among the houses, since the altar of God does not move but remains in one place.[27] Carolyn Osiek sees this as a decline of a symbol; widows should not be wandering about among the houses, as the Pastoral Epistles also admonish.[28]

---

25. Ignatius, *Letter to the Philadelphians*, ANF 1.82. See Thurston, *The Widows*, 62. See also Standhartinger, „'Wie die verehrteste Judith und die besonnenste Hanna.' Traditionsgeschichtliche Beobachtungen zur Herkunft der Witwengruppen im entstehenden Christentum," 103–26.

26. The comparison of widow and altar has been discussed by several scholars; see Osiek, "The Widow as Altar." Thurston, "The Widow as the 'Altar of God.'"

27. *Didascalia Apostolorum*, 133–34, written in the third century in Greek, but surviving only in a Syriac version; see Thurston, "The Widow as the 'Altar of God,'" 284. See Methuen, "Widows, Bishops and the Struggle for Authority in the *Didascalia Apostolorum*." See also Osiek, "The Widow as Altar," 163 and note.

28. "The metaphor that compared the widow to the altar of God was once a powerful symbol expressing a spiritual and social relationship of one group of women to other

It is an open question why the combination of widows and gossip plays such a prominent role in early Christian memory. It is also noteworthy that the widow figures from the Pastoral Epistles and Luke are on several occasions combined and blended in new and creative ways. However, in the other ancient texts I studied in my book on gossip, widows do not represent a dominant group within the discourse of gossip. In fact, they are almost absent from the overall "non-Christian" gossip discourse in antiquity.[29]

In short, widows were marginalized in Christian texts by use of the stereotype of gossip. But why are precisely widows the focal point in Christian variations of the stereotype that gossip is female speech? Perhaps "widow" for early Christian groups was a name tag given to several categories of women? Perhaps the memory of gossipy widows was a commonplace *topos*? If so, it seems highly relevant to ask: Can the association of widows and gossip in early Christian discourse also play a role in other New Testament texts, such as Luke 18:2–5?

THE PARABLE OF THE WIDOW AND THE JUDGE

Several scholars of the historical Jesus have recently re-examined the parable of the widow and the judge in Luke 18:2–5.[30] As mentioned above, there is no consensus about precisely what this parable tells; the interpretation I present here does not aim to explain the connection between Luke's comments and the narrative, but seeks instead to suggest an alternative that may explain the socio-rhetorical logic of the narrative and investigate how that logic corresponds to everyday experience, as Annette Metz reflects upon.[31] The overall question to this narrative is: Why does

---

members of the Christian church," but ended up as a vehicle of oppression. Osiek, "The Widow as Altar," 168–69.

29. See Kartzow, *Gossip and Gender*, 211.

30. See Metz, "How a Woman Who Fought Back and Demanded Her Rights Became an Importunate Widow," 49. For a discussion of this parable, see also Maseno and Kartzow, "Widows, Intersectionality and the Parable in Luke 18." Note also that this parable is used as a basis for the collection of essays dealing with HIV/AIDS and gendered readings of the Bible; see esp. pp. 3–4 and 13–21 in *Grant me Justice! HIV/AIDS & Gender Readings of the Bible*, edited by Dube and Kanyoro.

31. Metz, "How a Woman Who Fought Back and Demanded Her Rights Became an Importunate Widow," 85.

the judge change his mind? Why does the widow suddenly receive justice, against all odds?[32]

The confrontation between a judge and a widow

A widow and a judge were both characters with special associations and roles in the religious landscape of first- and second-century Palestine. Judges were carriers of God's justice and law and were among the male urban elite, but the judge in the parable seems to be acting outside the bounds of society since he neither fears God nor has respect for any man.[33] He may represent the class interest of the widow's adversaries, as Herzog suggests.[34] The concerns of this widow, whatever aroused them, seem at first to be none of his business.[35] What kind of judge he is supposed to be, whether Roman, Jewish, or Christian, is also an open question.[36] The legal situation in Palestine during the time of Jesus was vague and complex, but recent research on the courts of the Greco-Roman world has provided some context for understanding this parable.[37]

The parable does not mention in what way the widow is bothering the judge (v. 5).[38] The widow is no longer meek and obedient, however, but appears active and aggressive,[39] or as Corley argues, "[h]er actions border upon harassment."[40] The judge gives in to her wishes, but schol-

---

32. Herzog, *Parables as Subversive Speech*, 219.

33. Scott, *Hear Then the Parable*, 178–80.

34. Herzog, *Parables as Subversive Speech*, 226.

35. The widow relates to him with no introductory words of honor, but in the imperative mood, as Luke reports it. That she approaches the judge on her own, going directly to him without company, is puzzling to scholars. See Scott, *Hear Then the Parable*, 183.

36. Price, *The Widow Traditions in Luke-Acts*, 197–98.

37. See in particular Cotter, "The Parable of the Feisty Widow and the Threatened Judge (Luke 18:1–8)," 328. Others would argue that this text focuses not so much on the legal matters as the confrontation between the widow and the judge; see Scott, *Hear Then the Parable*, 184.

38. See Reid, "A Godly Widow," 29–30. Regarding the widow, Metz notes that "she must at any rate have arranged meetings and sought out situations in which she could confront the judge. This implies many individual actions which go beyond the rules of social conduct which were applied to a widow who lived on her own." Metz, "How a Woman Who Fought Back and Demanded Her Rights Became an Importunate Widow," 64.

39. Herzog, *Parables as Subversive Speech*, 231.

40. Corley, *Feminist Myths of Chriastian Origins*, 58. A rather different role for the widow has also been suggested: "It is the widow who is cast in the image of God," according to Reid, "A Godly Widow," 31.

ars disagree to why he did so. Like other parable narratives, this one is open-ended and leaves it to the listeners and readers to puzzle over its meaning.[41]

Possible reasons for the judge to change his mind

When hearing parables, listeners must fill in the gaps in the narrative in order for it to produce meaning. How did the earliest readers or listeners make sense of this story, and how did it correspond to their ideas about speech and talk and widows? It is the judge's stated reason for changing his mind that in particular leaves interpreters with several possibilities and allows for a creative engagement with the parable. The Greek term ὑπωπιάζω, which is used to describe how the narrative develops, opens up for several interpretations.[42] I will in the following refer to some suggestions:

1. It might be that the judge is afraid that the widow will attack him physically by running into his eye or face, like in a boxing match, and give him a "black eye," the etymological meaning of the Greek term used. However, it seems unlikely that such a female character was expected to pose a physical threat of any kind, since a chief characteristic of a widow was her defenselessness and since the judge himself was of high social rank.[43] Some interpreters would argue that this is the irony of the parable: the powerless appears to win at the end.[44]

2. Another option is that the judge might be sick and tired of the widow since she repeatedly approaches him, just as Paul in Acts 16:16–18 healed the possessed slave girl after she pestered him for a long time (see next chapter). In the Lukan universe, female irrita-

---

41. Reid, "A Godly Widow," 30.

42. See this term in LSJ, Bauer, and *TDNT*. See also Scott, *Hear Then the Parable*, 185–86.

43. Ibid., 185. Cotter is of another opinion, arguing that the widow behaves contrary to convention: "she would not be seen as a meek and subservient sort of woman, but feisty and frustrated and unwilling to abide by the social rules that would keep her invisible and silent while this judge refuses her." He fears public ridicule by appearing in public with a black eye. Cotter, "The Parable of the Feisty Widow and the Threatened Judge (Luke 18:1–8)," 341–42.

44. Scott calls it "the great irony of this story" that he who neither fears God nor man comes to fear a widow; see Scott, *Hear Then the Parable*, 185–86.

tion generates male action. However, if the indifferent judge was irritated by this powerless person, he could have rejected her by other means and did not have to give in to her wishes. After all, a privileged man was not supposed to change his mind as a result of female annoyance.

3. A final explanation is that although he fears neither God nor man, the judge is afraid the widow will be able to influence his life in one way or the other. This is where I see the possible role of gendered gossip. Perhaps he fears that she will spread gossip and slander about him, which is one of the possible meanings of the term ὑπωπιάζω.[45] In an article from as early as 1971–1972, Duncan Derrett suggested that the judge was afraid the widow could be "spreading rumors about him" and ruin his reputation. However fearless an elite man could be, readers and listeners would have inferred that the judge was aware of the possible effect of the widow's gossip. She tests out his limits and wins; he fears neither God nor humans, but he cannot protect himself against female slander and gossip.[46]

I would follow up by suggesting that this parable gives an example of how powerful female gossip could be. Women in general—and, in an early Christian context, widows in particular—are seen as experts in gossip. The parable also shows that supposedly powerless and marginal characters such as widows did have means to control and influence their own situation. When the widow in the parable does not get her will, her loyalty to the judge is broken, and in her desperation she is in a position of using her strongest weapon to hurt him. Read this way, female gossip represents the parable's destabilizing potential.[47]

Gossip may be the key to understanding the narrative universe of the parable: of course the judge had to change his mind; otherwise the widow would use her gendered access to the gossip network. Information, whether true or false, would spread rapidly and without his control and potentially destroy his reputation. He knew she would be able to talk to her friends, neighbors, relatives, and slaves, who again would talk to other more influential people who inhabited the city. This gossip would not only circulate in the private female world but would spread rapidly

---

45. See Derrett, "Law in the New Testament," 189–91.
46. Herzog, *Parables as Subversive Speech*, 230–31.
47. Hornsby, "The Annoying Woman: Biblical Scholarship after Judith Butler," 83.

and hurt his masculinity, destroy his public reputation, and render him socially dead—hence his ultimate surrender to her request. I suggest that it was obvious for the first listeners of this parable that the widow had access to such instruments of power, since they lived in an oral world in which information was circulated through face-to-face communication. Accordingly, connecting this parable to the gossipy widows in the Pastoral Epistles and to the overall gossip discourse in antiquity may increase the plausibility of Duncan Derrett's forgotten interpretation.

CONCLUSION

Whatever relation there might have been between Luke and the Pastoral Epistles, I have argued that in regard to gossip they both employ a gendered stereotype. The Pastoral Epistles connect women and gossip and instruct them to refrain from it. These epistles share the assumption with other early Christian texts that widows are particularly prone to engage in gossip, and also the Lukan parable produces meaning by use of a similar stereotype. Female gossip thus seems to be strong, effective, dangerous, and forceful in both early Christian discourse and other ancient texts. The Pastoral Paul feels threatened by female gossip and warns against it, while the judge in Luke 18:2–5 takes the consequences of it. If the underlying logic was that the judge did change his mind due to female gossip, it may show how women who had marginalized public roles nevertheless had other channels through which they gained their will, against all odds.

By taking gossip into consideration we may obtain a more nuanced picture of early Christian groups. Women's speech was regulated and controlled, but as the parable perhaps shows, also women could use their speech to wield power and influence. Gossip seems to be extremely ambiguous and did operate on several levels: gossip was a gendered stereotype and a rhetorical device for controlling women and constructing them as silent subordinates, but simultaneously, gossip could be a tool for those who suffered from gender regulations. Gossip may be one of the means by which power may be exercised by benefitting from the uncontrolled and far-reaching effect of speech and talk. As I have suggested in this chapter, the parable in Luke 18 may accordingly be involved in the ancient gossip discourse.

8

Talking Pair

*Paul and the Fortune-telling Slave Girl
(Acts 16:16–18)*

INTRODUCTION

IN THIS FINAL CHAPTER dealing with the dynamics of speech and talk, I will focus on a small episode in which Paul encounters a possessed, fortune-telling slave girl in Philippi (Acts 16:16–18). This text passage seems currently to be part of the archive rather than the canon: Paul is remembered in Acts as a hero on a missionary travel, while she is a marginal character belonging to the archive, hardly remembered at all. This episode is perhaps among the most challenging representations of how early Christian male heroes met local inhabitants and low-status characters on their missionary travels. I will address the variety of ways in which speech and talk operate, and I will also add and discuss a new category to the intersectional thinking: that of health and disability. In addition I will employ memory theory and intersectionality to critically approach the conventional interpretative model of finding couples and double figures in Luke-Acts to suggest a new pair: that of Paul and the slave girl.

This passage is part of a longer section in Acts, dealing with Paul's missionary journey.[1] Arriving by boat to Philippi, Paul and his company remained in the city for some days. Among the different people they met was a woman named Lydia, a God-fearing seller of purple cloth, who was baptized along with her whole household. One day when Paul and his company were going out to pray, they met a slave girl who was possessed

---

1. For a critical discussion on how Philippi marks the first entrance of Christianity to Europe, see Staley, "Changing Woman," 114–16.

by a spirit of divination and who earned money for her owners through fortune-telling (vv. 16–18). She exasperated Paul by repeatedly crying out that Paul and his men were slaves of the Most High God and that they proclaimed a way of salvation. Paul exorcised the spirit, but her owners thereby lost their hope of making money and dragged Paul and his companion Silas into the marketplace, accusing them of disturbing the city.

A few preliminary observations: As described by Luke, the possessed slave girl is a talkative character in more than one way. First of all, she is a fortuneteller. However, her fortune-telling is interpreted differently by the various characters in the story: Paul is irritated by it and her owners profit from it. The owners needed this talent, regardless of whether she was possessed or out of her mind; Paul, on the other hand, interprets her talent as a possession of a competing spiritual power and heals her, just as he heals other sick or disabled people on his travels.

Second, her exclamations regarding Paul and his men could classify her among the female prophetesses in Luke-Acts. Together with the four unmarried daughters of Philip in Acts 21:9 and the widow Anna in Luke 2:36–38, she is among the very few female characters that are connected to prophecy. Unique for this female prophet is that what she says is reported in the narrative. In addition, her words correspond closely to the Christian message. In spite of this, she is effectively silenced when Paul "heals" her from what he considers to be a demonic possession.

My reason for classifying this slave girl and Paul as a pair is the content of what she says: she cries out that Paul and his men are slaves of God. I will use intersectionality to reflect upon what kind of "slave pair" they may be. She is an owned slave body who uses her prophetic ability in order to earn money for her owners, while Paul's "slavery" seems to have an entirely different meaning. The memory of him is that of the most prominent apostle of Acts, while she is left on the street—or stored away in the archive—after Paul has departed, no longer talented in fortune-telling. I want to challenge this memory situation by suggesting that they constitute a pair, taking the conventional model of pairing in Biblical scholarship as my point of departure.

THE PAIR MODEL

Scholarship on Luke-Acts has highlighted a variety of parallel stories, pairs, and contrast figures by use of several theoretical frameworks and methods. Table 2 gives an overview of suggestions related to Acts 16, mentioning also briefly some keywords of reason and theory:[2]

TABLE 2. Paired characters in Acts 16.

Paired character I	Paired character II	Reason for pairing	Theoretical orientations
Lydia	Cornelius (Acts 10)	Male and female conversion	Narrative structure, heterogender
Lydia	Jailer	Male and female heads of households, both baptized	Social history, "the semantic field of household," heterogender
Lydia	Mantic slave	Women in leadership roles vs. female slave; "good" and "bad" women; orthodoxy vs. heresy	Narrative structure, feminist interpretations, Pauline theological over pagan possession
Mantic slave	Crippled man (Acts 14)	Both characters are healed	Narrative structure, heterogender
Paul	Slave owners	Both fight over the control of the mantic slave	Ancient models of masculinity

What I find fascinating with all these suggestions is that pairs and couples are constructed along many different lines of sameness and difference. Turid Karlsen Seim asks in her study of patterns of gender in Luke-Acts how duality and/or parallelism are to be determined, and argues that the interpreters themselves make their own significant contributions to the discovery or creation of parallels.[3] This point seems crucial; categorizations and classifications change a lot over time;[4] what looks like "same" to us might have been considered "different" to Luke and his audience. I have elsewhere challenged this complexity of pairing by using Plutarch's

---

2. I discuss these pairs and their contexts in more depth in Kartzow, "The Complexity of Pairing."

3. Note that she is interested in pairs of narratives, statements, and episodes and not primarily characters as I am; see Seim, *The Double Message*, 13–14.

4. "Roman categories rarely map straightforwardly onto modern ones," as argued in Edwards, *The Politics of Immorality in Ancient Rome*, 4.

Parallel Lives, and suggested that interpreters should be more critical of what they see as Luke's techniques and what comes from our own notions of what it takes to construct pairs.[5] By employing Matsuda's method of asking the other question, I will in this chapter challenge some of the criteria taken for granted in the conventional models of pairing in Biblical scholarship. These deconstructed pairs will constitute a useful background for following my argumentation when I suggest the new pairing of Paul and the possessed slave-girl.

HETEROGENDER AND PAIRING

Intersectionality helps deconstruct gender by being critical to all kinds of self-evident and uniform categorization. What has been called heterogender—the term used to emphasize that heterosexuality and male-female dualism are taken for granted—is particularly striking when pairing the mantic slave and the crippled man in Acts 14.[6] In feminist theory this tendency to pair male and female has also been classified as "compulsory heterosexuality."[7] It is taken for granted that a man and a woman belong together since they are sexually attracted to each other and could potentially make up a pair. In these two very different stories in Acts a man and a woman are both healed, the rationale for why interpreters who are interested in Luke's redaction see them as a pair.[8] The gender opposition and expected difference between a man and a woman qualify the crippled man and the mantic slave girl to be a pair.

I will argue, however, that by emphasizing gender dichotomy in this Lukan pair, interpreters downplay important differences that most likely existed between such persons in the ancient world. Issues related to social class and the consequence of disability need to be taken into account. Position and economy determined such persons' lives in very different ways. In fact, the crippled man is the one who suffers from disability before being healed, while the slave girl is probably deprived of her profession after Paul "heals" her. Related to speech and talk, he is given back his

---

5. Kartzow, "The Complexity of Pairing."

6. See also chapter 3 above about how the story of Joseph and Aseneth was interpreted by use of hetero-gender theories.

7. Gamble, *The Routledge Companion to Feminism and Postfeminism*, 249.

8. D'Angelo, "Women in Luke-Acts," 445–46.

role as a proper man with a voice worth listening to in the male public space, while she loses her voice after encountering the Christian healer.

Another effect is how this pairing essentializes those who are healed, as if being cured is the same for all. A cured free male and a "cured" female slave perhaps share little in common that would qualify them to be a pair in late antiquity. She is in fact someone's property, and her condition influences not only her own well-being, but also her value to her owners. Ancient thinkers probably did not view such characters as a pair, since their complementary gender was overruled by other issues, such as class and difference in disability. Interpreters who exclusively focus on gender dichotomy risk being blind to this complexity. The crippled man and the mantic slave may look like a pair to some modern readers, since most pairs are comprised of one man and one woman. However, such a pair is not discovered in the Lukan text but created by interpreters, to use Karlsen Seim's clarifying terms.

THE DIVIDED FEMALE: SILENT VIRTUE AND TALKING VICE

Acts 16 has been important for feminist scholarship, not due to the fortune-telling slave girl but to Lydia. For a Christian theological reading Lydia is also the ideal woman of Acts 16. As they are presented in the narrative, the mantic slave girl has been seen as a contrast figure to Lydia.[9] The well-to-do cloth merchant offers hospitality to Paul, whereas the slave girl harasses him.[10] Lydia becomes part of the Christian community as a potentially female leader of a local group, while no conversion or baptism are heard of in the case of the mantic slave. Unlike Lydia, the slave girl is not considered to be part of the exclusive group of early Christian women in Philippi.[11]

For many years New Testament feminist scholarship focused in particular on women in leadership roles, seeing Acts 16 as a text about Lydia and the women congregating with her. By emphasizing women as prominent characters and by challenging male dominance, a more nuanced picture was drawn of early Christian discourse. However, the task of finding foremothers in leadership roles led some interpreters to overlook the female slave and her prophesying when reading Acts 16. In chapter 1

---

9. Matthews, "Elite Women, Public Religion, and Christian Propaganda in Acts 16," 112.

10. Ibid., 127.

11. See for example "The Philippian Episode" in Portefaix, *Sisters Rejoice*, 169–72.

I criticized a similar tendency in the interpretation history of the parable in Luke 12:35–48, where female slaves who were beaten have not been considered important enough when early Christian women were studied. By help of intersectionality, one-dimensional feminist readings only concerned with gender may be challenged for being insensitive to "class issues."[12] By choosing other research criteria than female leadership, and by emphasizing speech and slave status, the mantic slave girl can be given a role in early Christian women's history, side by side with Lydia.

This interpretation uses the ambiguity of the story itself, and challenges her marginality as a character stored away in the archive. In one sense, Paul treats her badly, but the text remembers her prophetic words. By paying attention to the dynamics of speech and talk by use of memory theory and intersectionality, the marginal role of the possessed slave girl is destabilized.

A PAIR OF TALKING SLAVES

In order to stress how interpreters of Acts are responsible for the pairs we find, and how we consciously or unconsciously connect people in relations based on sameness and difference, I want to introduce a new pair, building on Luke's use of metaphorical language. The new pair I suggest has been bypassed or never discovered/created by interpreters. This seems a bit strange, since almost all other characters in Acts 16 have been paired—or is this pair simply too speculative?

In this section I will combine the process of pairing with an intersectional approach that takes the flexible usage of slavery language into consideration. By emphasizing several categories working together and mutually constructing each other, the mantic slave girl and the apostle Paul—freeborn, but a slave of God—may work as a pair. The intersection of gender, sexuality, ethnicity, and class may explain the social fabric of Acts 16 as a whole, demonstrated by focusing on this pair. The compact usage of slavery language in this passage, both as social description and on a metaphorical level, calls attention to how early Christian ideology depends on certain power systems in which gender and class intersect in

---

12. But see the astute observation that this slave girl is "quadruple marginalized," related to gender, class, possession, and economy; C. J. Martin, "The Acts of the Apostles," 784.

complex ways. The ethical responsibility of interpreters challenges us to inquire into the social reality that metaphors re-inscribe and depend on.

Both the slave girl and Paul/Silas are described through slavery language, although the function of their "slavery" differs: she is said to be a παιδίσκη, and the meaning of this term may variously be young female, servant, slave, or prostitute.[13] As I discussed in chapter 1, the male and female slaves who were beaten by the slave manager were characterized by a term with a similar etymology. Since also the possessed girl's masters are mentioned [τοῖς κυρίοις αὐτῆς] she is meant to be a slave. Due to her talent in fortune-telling she earned money for her owners (also plural in v. 19) through her "profession."

The fact that more than one person is referred to as her owner may indicate that she was shared property, not belonging to one household or family but several. Due to inheritance or economic transactions a slave could have many owners and thereby be more vulnerable than household slaves.[14] The plural may imply that she was a promising investment for several persons, although I think Malina and Pilch are too influenced by heterogender in their recent commentary and too eager to pair when they speculate that the girl's owners are "plausibl[y] a man and woman, a couple."[15]

However, it is not her but Paul and his men who in Acts 16 are referred to by the most common term for slave [δοῦλος].[16] The slave girl follows them, exclaiming that they are slaves of the Most High God [Οὗτοι οἱ ἄνθρωποι δοῦλοι τοῦ θεοῦ τοῦ ὑψίστου εἰσίν] who proclaim a way of salvation.[17] Paul and his men are obviously not slaves in the same way as she is: they were not owned bodies available for many other persons, considered to be part of shared property, required to "make money" for others, and subject to being sold or sent away.[18] Such life conditions probably determined her life, and the owners' anger towards Paul for healing

---

13. According to Matthews, who builds on LSJ; see "Elite Women, Public Religion, and Christian Propaganda in Acts 16," 127 and note.

14. Glancy, *Slavery in Early Christianity*, 11, 73–74.

15. Malina and Pilch, *Social-Science Commentary on the Book of Acts*, 116.

16. Note that also Titus 1:1 calls Paul a slave of God. For the Jewish background of this metaphorical use, see Bartchy, "Slavery/New Testament," 72.

17. Scholars discuss whether this way of entitling God was common in Judaism or hinted rather at Zeus; see overview in Pervo, *Acts*, 405–6 and note 50.

18. See such characteristics of slavery, discussed elsewhere in this book, especially in chapters 1, 4 9, and 11.

her may show how dependent freeborn persons could be on a slave's contribution to the economy.

In contrast, Paul and his men are slaves of God, a much used metaphor in early Christian literature.[19] Early Christian thinkers used the image of slavery in order to describe their relation to God, Jesus, and their fellow Christians. The metaphorical use of slavery language depends on the reality of slavery to make sense, thereby re-inscribing the relations of slavery, as several scholars have pointed out.[20] When interpreters offer a one-dimensional interest in slavery language as theological terminology only, they may overlook real slavery in Acts 16.

Almost ironically, Luke has her, a female slave, articulate important aspects of Christian identity by use of slavery language.[21] Reading Acts as a religious text about the early Christian male heroes, this particular slave—an owned female body, who had her destiny in other people's hands—is a marginal character. But religious ideas are closely connected to social reality: if we only see slavery as a metaphor for (free persons') relation to God or Christ, we may overlook glimpses of slave reality in this passage.[22]

THE TRUTH-TELLING SLAVE GIRL

The slave girl is not named, but the evil spirit that possesses her is: πνεῦμα πύθωνα.[23] Neither is she given any ethnicity, nationality, nor family.[24] The unexpected element is that she, located at the bottom of several hieratical

---

19. Glancy, *Slavery in Early Christianity*, 97. See also D. B. Martin, *Slavery as Salvation*. Note also that Abrahamsen has, by use of epigraphic material, suggested that servant/slave was a position held by church officials at Philippi, both men and women; see "Women at Philippi," 26.

20. On the metaphorical usage of slavery in Christian discourse, see Glancy, *Slavery in Early Christianity*, 92–101 and Castelli, "Romans," 294.

21. In a footnote Pervo notes: "There is irony: a slave recognizes the missionaries as slaves of God." Pervo, *Acts*, 406.

22. These issues have in particular been addressed in scholarship on Philemon, see Barclay, "Paul, Philemon and the Dilemma of Christian Slave-Ownership". See also the overview in Byron, *Recent Research on Paul and Slavery*, 116–37.

23. Seim, *The Double Message*, 172–73.

24. These are typical traits for slaves; see, e.g., C. Martin, "Womanist Interpretations of the New Testament"; Glancy, *Slavery in Early Christianity*; and Byron, *Recent Research on Paul and Slavery*.

systems, is pestering them with nothing but the truth![25] It is striking that the text itself somehow constructs its own illogical logic, since what the slave girl says represents the Lukan narrative's own point of view. It is hard to distinguish between the Python spirit and the Holy Spirit when it bears witness to the same truth.[26] I see this as the text's destabilizing potential that invites interpreters to be creative and responsible.[27]

Although it is unfair, Paul is also punishing her and indirectly blaming her, because her owners used her talent to earn money.[28] However, in the marketplace Paul and Silas were charged of generating a conflict between Jewish and Roman customs. Pervo concisely notes that this "incident is quite exciting but without much logic."[29] Was it a Jewish custom to cure female slaves? Why this strong reaction? The text gives no answer to that; for some reason Paul wanted to heal someone who spoke the truth about God and God's men even though he risked provoking public anger.

CONCLUSION: HEALED OR SILENCED? THE POTENTIAL FUTURE FOR THE SLAVE-GIRL

Paul and the other followers of Christ are the protagonists in Acts, while the mantic slave girl plays a rather marginal role. Nevertheless, if we want to retrieve her story from the archive and let it be part of canon, we must take what we know about her and re-imagine how it may have influenced such a person to be in touch with early Christian missionaries. To see Paul and this fortune-telling girl as a pair may help bring her forth from the margins of early Christian memory, although her actual role in Acts is not a prominent one.

---

25. Seim, *The Double Message*, 173. Also the Church Fathers noticed that she spoke the truth, and did not accuse her of blasphemy. Rather, they blamed the spirit, and argued that Paul had to free her from it although the testimony was true. The spirit could persuade many others to pay attention to all the lies that came along with this testimony, and lead attention away from the Christian message; see, e.g., Origen, Bede, and Chrysostom. Oden, *Ancient Christian Commentary on Scripture: Acts*, 202–3.

26. Seim, *The Double Message*, 173. See also another unclean spirit who testifies to the truth, in Luke 4:31–37.

27. Hornsby, "The Annoying Woman," 83.

28. See also the story of Simon Magus (Acts 8:17–24) and Seim, *The Double Message*, 174.

29. Pervo, *Acts*, 406.

Female slaves had both their class and gender as a social handicap, and being the only female prophetess whose words are reported in Acts, the possessed slave is classified among those who belonged to a primitive and dangerous religion. Apparently, there is no room for prophesying female slaves in the new Christian community that Paul is establishing on his mission to Philippi. The mantic slave girl returns to her senses, as Dennis MacDonald observes,[30] but in the ancient Mediterranean society, what kind of life would such a character return to when she had lost her talent in fortune-telling? I find O'Toole's commentary in the Anchor Bible Dictionary too sympathetic to Luke and too optimistic regarding the reality of ancient slavery when he argues that "she should be numbered among the disadvantaged of the sort who are the particular objects of Jesus' salvation."[31]

What kind of salvation is she offered? Was she in any way healed and returned to her proper self? Because of her slave status, this healing represented primarily a change that was problematic for her owners and therefore threatening to her continued existence. Paul frees her from being possessed, for him representing spiritual slavery, but he does not free her from her angry owners. They blame the Christian men for eliminating their income—understandable within the ancient economic system—but how would they punish her? From being a slave who earned money for her owners by fortune-telling on the street, a possible way to continue would be to remain on the street, but now selling her body. If following after Paul and his men and using her prophetic gifts in their service resulted in a future as a prostitute, Christian healing, preformed by Paul, the slave of God, did not necessarily bring liberation and freedom to the mantic slave. She had lost her talent in telling fortunes, but as a consequence of this silencing she probably also lost her profession, her privileges, and her future. After being healed, the slave girl can no longer provide her owners with income, nor is it stated in Acts that Paul welcomed her into the early Christian movement. Instead of liberating the mantic girl from slavery, Luke's Paul has her losing her profession. The story has no happy ending for her, and if such a person ever existed she probably faced a future more troublesome than her past. Interpreters are confronted with an ethical challenge when a New Testament text, instead of challenging

30. D. R. MacDonald, "Lydia and Her Sisters as Lukan Fictions," 110.
31. O'Toole, "Slave Girl at Philippi," 58.

the gendered slave-holding system, uses it to construct Christian identity and memory.

So why bother to dwell with the destiny of this female slave? To ask about the future of a likely fictional character may seem like a project more fit for novelists than for scholars. However, although this episode is not among the most famous ones, it is part of the written memory of religions and cultures, so I would make a case for why a potentially fictional and imagined future makes a difference. Even if she is purely fiction, there are consequences for the social and cultural logic with which Luke operates here. Was there no room for female slaves in this early Christian community? Were prophesying women excluded? Were prophesying slaves excluded?

Acts 2:18 recalls some powerful words from the prophet Joel, who declared that in the last days even male and female slaves will be given the spirit and shall prophesize. When it comes to the story of the fortune-telling slave girl, however, these liberating words seem to be more like a dream than a fulfilled vision.

PART THREE

Overlapping Relationships

It is in the various relations between human beings that identity and hierarchy are negotiated. One of the benefits of intersectionality is that it emphasizes the relational nature of identity and highlights interaction between the categories as a separate object for analysis. In Part Three I highlight two New Testament texts that have not only been given much attention by Biblical scholars, but have also played central roles in current discussions of hierarchy and freedom in family, church, and society. Gal 3:28 is the main liberation credo for all those who want to proclaim liberation related to ethnicity, class, and gender, while the household codes show that early Christian hierarchies were constructed with similar arguments as other groups in antiquity, following the same patterns of dominance related to gender, class, and age/generation. I use intersectionality and memory theory to bring these two texts with their lists of relationship pairs into the conversation. By asking the other question, a complex web of power relations appears. What about those who belonged to more than one relationship pair in these lists, for example a foreign male slave child? I draw on a Greek papyrus fragment and on recent research on the ancient family in order to broaden the perspectives and emphasize marginalized identities.

9

Conceptualizing Power Structures

Galatians 3:28 and the Colossian Household Codes

INTRODUCTION

SOCIAL RELATIONS AND THEIR ideological underpinnings in the world of the New Testament were characterized by differentiations and hierarchies. The role of Biblical writings vis-à-vis these hierarchies, supporting or questioning them, has been much discussed. In this chapter I am not asking whether early Christianity erased social hierarchies, a question that, according to Carolyn Osiek and Margaret MacDonald, "is part of a larger one about how if at all Christian faith made a difference in these relationships."[1] Rather, it seems as if early Christian literature employs hierarchies in creative and selective ways, variously renegotiating social structures known from broader society, copying such structures, or coming up with alternative ideas. My primary interest is to investigate how these hierarchies and relationships were shaped discursively and what socio-rhetorical logic they employ.[2]

In what follows, I bring together the discussions regarding ethnicity, class, gender, and age in Gal 3:28 and the Colossian household codes[3] and look at the relationship *between* the various categories, suggesting a

---

1. Osiek and MacDonald, *A Woman's Place*, 152.

2. I thank in particular Buell, Glancy, and Moxnes for making useful comments on this chapter; see Kartzow, "'Asking the Other Question.'"

3. To name these categories is challenging and is simplified in this chapter for practical reasons. The category "ethnicity," meant to determine the "Jew/Greek pair" in Gal 3:28, could just as well be called "religion" or "race." Likewise, "age" to describe the relation between parents and children in the household codes could also be "generation" or "family position." "Class" issues are often discussed under headlines such as "social

theoretical vocabulary that speaks about hierarchy and social categories in a more complex way.[4] Instead of focusing on one of these relationship pairs in isolation, as is most common in commentaries,[5] I will examine how the categories intersect and mutually construct each other through the method of "asking the other question."

Gal 3:28, proclaiming that "[t]here is neither Jew nor Greek, there is neither slave nor free, there is neither male nor female; for you are all one in Christ Jesus," has been called the Magna Carta of the New Testament, or a credo for those who search for liberating powers in the Pauline letters.[6] In scholarly discussions of equality and hierarchy, Gal 3:28 is often pitted against the household codes in other letters using a model of pure origins and decline: the household codes represented "a reaction against earlier freedom and innovation."[7] Although second- and third-generation Christians took over contemporary patterns of power and dominance, the more authentic Pauline statement in Gal 3:28 functions to reduce or eliminate the hierarchical structure of the household codes, since the first believers were all one in Christ Jesus.[8] My approach is another one: by means of intersectionality and the first-century Greek papyrus fragment *Acta Isidori*, I suggest that Gal 3:28 and the household codes belong to different gender discourses. Within their own specific contexts, both texts take part in negotiations over status, gender, sexuality, and reproduction, categories that all seem to be crucial when identities were contested and hierarchies constructed.

---

status" or "position," since "class" is seen as too anachronistic for ancient sources. See the discussion in the introduction.

4. For instance, when Meeks argues that "[t]he distinction in status between slave and free (or freed) could override others, such as the hierarchy of the sexes," I will rather look at how these hierarchies overlap, showing that "the hierarchy of the sexes" did not work in isolation, but constructed complex and intersecting hierarchies among slaves and free. See Meeks, *The First Urban Christians*, 20.

5. To mention only a few examples, see Betz, *Galatians*, 190–200; Martyn, *Galatians*, 376–77; and M. Y. MacDonald, *Colossians and Ephesians*, 152–59.

6. For a recent discussion on "gender egalitarianism," see Beavis, "Christian Origins, Egalitarianism, and Utopia," 27–49.

7. Osiek and Balch, *Families in the New Testament World*, 178.

8. Discussed in Meeks, "The 'Haustafeln' and American Slavery," 245.

HIERARCHY AND INTERSECTIONALITY

Although ideas about social categories and hierarchy change over time,[9] theoretical reflections about hierarchy may nevertheless enable interpreters to pose new questions to Biblical texts. This process does not necessarily bring us closer to the ancient authors' intentions with their texts, but may provide some tools to comprehend more of the complexity in their rhetorical universe.

According to the Oxford Dictionary of English, hierarchy is "a system in which members of an organization or society are ranked according to relative status or authority." How, then, are such systems employed in early Christian discourses, and in what way did hierarchies help construct Christian identity? Texts like Gal 3:28 and Col 3:18–4:1 suggest that discourses about identity and hierarchy were rather complex. Ancient individuals probably experienced challenging dilemmas over status and position. A person could be at the bottom of one hierarchy and the top of another. Cross-cutting ties, multiple loyalties, and diverse combinations of identities may describe the Roman Empire at the advent of Christianity. Identity construction often seems to be a work in progress.[10]

CATEGORIES, HIERARCHIES, AND SYSTEMS OF OPPRESSION IN ANTIQUITY: A FRAGMENT

To my knowledge the text fragment *Acta Isidori* has not previously been used in dialogue with New Testament texts dealing with issues of hierarchy and identity. Although reflecting an Egyptian context re-imagined in Rome, it nevertheless has something to contribute to the intersectional reading of Gal 3:28 and the household codes, since it employs similar categories.

The *Acta Isidori*, an anonymous papyrus fragment in Greek from presumably sometime between 40 and 55 CE,[11] gives a unique glimpse into how hierarchies may interact and how classifications related to gen-

---

9. On the relation between "Roman categories" and "modern ones," see Edwards, *The Politics of Immorality in Ancient Rome*, 4.

10. See Knust, *Abandoned to Lust*, 85. Conway, *Behold the Man*, 68–69. Buell notes that even ethnicity was subject to negotiation and change; see Buell, *Why This New Race*, e.g., 168.

11. The complex issue of dating is discussed in Musurillo, *The Acts of the Pagan Martyrs*, 118–23.

der, sexuality, social position, and ethnicity/religion mutually construct each other. Scholars admit it is hard to identify situations or persons mentioned in the text. The *Acta Isidori* belongs to documents that are not official protocols of the Roman authorities, but may be classified as "popular stories/fiction" or "historical novels."[12]

By describing a "trial" in the imperial garden of Rome, the fragment portrays Jews as representing the interests of the Romans in the power struggle against the Alexandrian Greeks. In this trial, the emperor Claudius accuses Isidorus of having killed many of his friends, but Isidorus replies that he only did so to fulfill the wish of Claudius' predecessor. The dialogue reflects the tension and mutual dislike between Rome and its Alexandrian Greek subjects, who, according to Schäfer, disliked the Jews and those who defended them.[13] In the rather bizarre final conversation between the emperor and Isidorus, the emperor is blamed for supporting the Jews in Alexandria, and the two men start to accuse each other:

> Claudius Caesar: "Isidorus, are you really the son of an actress?"
>
> Isidorus: "I am neither slave nor actress's son, but gymnasiarch of the glorious city of Alexandria. But you are the cast-off son of the Jewish Salome!"[14]

In this small exchange in the presence of senators and among "men of consular rank,"[15] several identity markers are used to blame the other part: 1) son of an actress, 2) slave, and 3) the cast-off son of the Jewish Salome. Claudius seems to be forming a question based on rumors, or he merely uses it as a standard insult: your mother is a questionable woman.[16] An actress or musician could be both a slave owned by someone who wanted her to work as an actress, or she could be a freed or freeborn

12. Schäfer, *Judeophobia*, 152–53.

13. Ibid., 155.

14. See *Acta Isidori*, 4, col. 3, 7–12, in Musurillo, ed. *The Acts of the Pagan Martyrs. Acta Alexandrinorum*, 19 and 25. Reconstructed Greek text (from TLG): Κλαύδιος Καῖσαρ·ἀσφαλῶς [ἐ]κ μουσικῆς εἶ, Ἰσίδωρε; Ἰσίδωρος·[ἐγ]ὼ μὲν οὔκ εἰμι δοῦλος οὐδὲ μουσικῆς [υἱ]ός, ἀλλὰ διασήμου πόλεως [Ἀ]λεξαν- [δρ]εί[ας] γυμνασίαρχος. σὺ δὲ ἐκ Σαλώμη[ς] [τ]ῆς Ἰουδα[ίας υ]ἱὸς [ἀπό]βλητος.

15. Schäfer, *Judeophobia*, 153.

16. According to Hunter, who has studied the function of gossip in law courts in classical Athens, "there is no individual who inspired more gossip that could be used against a man than his mother." Hunter, "Gossip and the Politics of Reputation in Classical Athens," 299–325, esp. 317.

woman working as an actress for a living. It has been argued that an important role that women could have outside the household in the Hebrew Bible was that of female musicians,[17] but in regard to this fragment I agree with Peter Schäfer that the *Acta Isidori* uses this designation in a far more derogatory way: "'Girl musician,' of course, means prostitute."[18] With this interpretation, Isidorus' mother is a loose woman, whose body is available for those who can pay. Her sexual reputation would normally place her at the bottom of the female hierarchy.

In order to answer this insulting question raised by the emperor about his mother being an actress/musician or prostitute, Isidorus starts by denying that he is a slave. This may seem strange: he was not accused of being a slave himself.[19] Perhaps he needed to emphasize his own social status since the son of an actress/musician or prostitute was not considered to be a free man, given that his father would be unknown? Or perhaps he hears in the question that his mother is considered a slave, and negotiates the fact that slave mothers were normally not legally acknowledged since their children became the owner's property? Roman law for Egypt specified that the status of children followed their mothers, that is, children of female slaves were automatically born as slaves.[20]

To have a mother with a questionable reputation influenced a man's social status, in perception if not also legally. Isidorus defends himself by countering that he is an elite man of the city of Alexandria, a man who deserves respect. In this conversation Isidorus is not so much asking the other question as *giving the other answer*, to play with Metsuda's methodology. He is actually asked about his mother, but his immediate reply deals with his own status: he is not a slave. The logic of this exchange points to how categories dealing with motherhood, origin, and class (parenthood) intersected.

The third identity marker used in this encounter also deals with mothers, and this time her ethnicity or religious heritage is intimidated by using the term *judaios*. But what does it indicate to be a "cast-off son

---

17. Meyers, "Mowinkel Lecture" (Oslo, 2008).

18. Schäfer, *Judeophobia*, 155.

19. See Catharine Edwards' discussion of the stigma attached to actors. She points out that "[t]he legal disabilities imposed on actors were severe, effectively assimilating them to slaves in important respects." In Edwards, *The Politics of Immorality in Ancient Rome*, 123.

20. See Lewis and Hanson, *On Government and Law in Roman Egypt*, 144.

of the Jewish Salome"? To be an illegitimate son, as Schäfer translates this term, was obviously a problem for citizens, but it was not the mother but the father who normally had the power to establish whether a freeborn child was legitimate or not. And which Salome is this supposed to be: Herod's sister; the daughter of Herod the Great by Elpis; the daughter of Herodias and Herod;[21] or, as Tal Ilan suggests, any Jewish woman, since Salome was one of the most common Jewish names at the time?[22] Although obviously used metaphorically, we need to ask again what kind of category "Jewish" is meant to be: ethnic, national, or religious?[23] In this contest over the status of mothers and sons, it is not spelled out which position is meant to be lowest in the hierarchy: to be the son of a prostitute, to be the cast-off son of the Jewish Salome, or to be a slave.

Many questions remain open, but this fragment shows some ways in which identity and position are discussed. Elite men used an opponent's maternal background and position as rhetorical devices. Both mothers in the *Acta Isidori* are constructed as questionable: the first one as being a loose woman or a slave, the second one as being Jewish and producing cast-off children. In this contest between men in regard to whose mother is the most inferior, sexual conduct, ethical and religious background, occupation, and social status all become relevant. This labyrinth of identity markers and hierarchies illustrates how complex the social systems could be and how various categories intersected.

NEGOTIATING IN CHRIST: AN INTERSECTIONAL APPROACH TO EARLY CHRISTIAN HIERARCHIES

I now turn to the New Testament and an intersectional approach to Gal 3:28 in order to illuminate the hierarchical reasoning in Colossians 3–4. Although the genre, dating, and authorship of these texts differ, their ways of structuring relationships follow a similar pattern, and both are used in present-day discussions about hierarchy and equality. Both texts present three relationship pairs[24] by use of two seemingly complementary

---

21. Various options listed in Musurillo, *The Acts of the Pagan Martyrs. Acta Alexandrinorum*, 128–29.

22. Ilan, *Integrating Women into Second Temple History*, 120–21, note 89. See also Ilan, *Lexicon of Jewish Names in Late Antiquity*.

23. See in particular chapters 3, 4, and 7 above.

24. The relation between husband-wife, master-slave, and parent-child is called "different relationship pairs" in M. Y. MacDonald, "A Place of Belonging," 278–79.

elements in each category. I am particularly interested in the possible *relation between the various relationship pairs* in each text, and also to highlight marginal social positions.

Intersections of "race, class, and gender" in Gal 3:28

Gal 3:28 reflects a complex web of social categories,[25] and what Paul is arguing here is disputed.[26] One possible interpretation is that the existing social hierarchy is of less importance in baptism, since all are one in Christ Jesus. Using categories that in social life expressed relatedness in a rather fixed and given hierarchical structure—e.g., free over slave and male over female—Paul seems to construct a different reality.[27] The effect of this argument, however, may be that he also emphasizes that although all are one "in Christ Jesus," they are separate, different, and unequal in all other areas of life.[28] In this perspective, Paul does not challenge the social hierarchy of his society, but rather uses it with a twist in order to construct a new spiritual world order.

In contrast to the parallel texts in 1 Cor 12:13 and Col 3:11, Gal 3:28 mentions "male and female." Scholars have for decades discussed whether or not this verse is "good news" for women,[29] but when using intersectionality I am more concerned about *what kind of women* who were potentially included in this category.

In the interpretative tradition of Gal 3:28, nationality/ethnicity, class, and gender are often seen as three separate categories.[30] If the categories

---

25. See for example, Briggs, "Slavery and Gender," esp. 175.

26. In particular, much work has been done arguing that this verse shows pre-Pauline gender-inclusive attitudes, fundamental to reimaging the first Christians as a "Discipleship of Equals." See in particular the groundbreaking contributions of Schüssler Fiorenza, for example *Discipleship of Equals*. Fatum, on the other hand, came to another conclusion in "Images of God and Glory of Man," 56–139.

27. Betz writes: "Surprisingly, v. 28 leads to the field of political and social ideals and practices. The first part (v. 28a–c) contains three parallel statements in the present tense, which define the religious, cultural, and social consequences of the Christian initiation." Betz, *Galatians*, 189.

28. If Gal 3:28 is read in light of what is said later in the letter about the non-Jewish slave mother Hagar (Gal 4:21–31), it becomes clear that "all are one in Christ Jesus" should not be taken at face value. See chapter 11 in this book.

29. See Beavis, "Christian Origins, Egalitarianism, and Utopia," 37 and 39.

30. In Betz, *Galatians*, 192–95, the second relationship pair in Gal 3:28b is translated as "neither slave nor freeman." In his analysis of this relationship pair, he does not discuss gender, thereby overlooking the important difference between male and female slaves.

in Galatians are combined in new ways, a more complicated structure appears.³¹ Using Matsuda's methodology, we may ask: what gender or social class could Jews or Greeks have?

1. Jewish slave male
2. Jewish slave female
3. Jewish free male
4. Jewish free female
5. Greek slave male
6. Greek slave female
7. Greek free male
8. Greek free female

These eight hypothetical combinations allow me to pose new questions to this passage. For example: If enslavement, at least legally, severed ties to an *ethnos* and *genos*, as I discussed in chapter 4, did it make sense to consider a slave either Jewish or Greek?³² The relation between slavery and ethnicity/religion was rather complex.

Free is above slave and male is above female in the ancient Mediterranean world, but it is not given who is privileged and who is subordinated in the relation between Jew and Greek.³³ In contrast to the *Acta Isidori*, however, "Jew" is not meant by Paul to be a derogatory term, and neither is Greek. Are the terms "Jew" or "Greek" to be understood for males and females alike to belong to an ethnic, religious, or racial category? Jew and Greek are not necessarily mutually exclusive, since there

---

See however Schüssler Fiorenza, *Rhetoric and Ethic*, 155–56, where she writes: "In order to understand and translate Gal 3:28–29, one needs to ask, for instance, whether the expressions 'Jew/Greek, slave/free' mean only men or whether they include wo/men so that wo/men as a matter of course belong to these groups."

31. Note, however, that while the two first relationship pairs connect the dual elements by use of οὐδὲ, male and female are connected by use of καὶ. If the ethnicity category as well as the class category are meant to be complementary, what does the "and" mean in the last relation? Could a person be either Jew or Greek, either slave or free, but *both* male and female? See suggestions to queer interpretations of this verse in D. B. Martin, *Sex and the Single Savior*, 77–90.

32. See Buell, *Why This New Race*. See also Buell, "God's Own People."

33. See Briggs, "Slavery and Gender," 182. She makes this point reflecting on how Jews were frequently persecuted and despised.

were several Greek-speaking Jews in the ancient Mediterranean world. Cynthia Baker has recently argued that the relation between "Jews" in antiquity has been "disregarded or unacknowledged as bearers or transmitters of other ethnic identities," and she suggests that we consider "Jews as a 'multiethnic' phenomenon."[34]

Could slaves be included in the gender relationship pair? Galatians' way of expressing gender employs terms that focus on the male and female [ἄρσεν καὶ θῆλυ], terms also used to determine animals' bodies, referring not only to "social" difference but also to a "biological" one, to use Betz' distinction.[35] Some interpreters have seen this expression as referring to patriarchal marriage, since the sex distinction achieved its highest purpose in marriage.[36] However, the terms used to express gender here are not "husband and wife." Another context in which it made sense to talk about the relationship pair of male and female dealt with reproduction, involving also slaves who normally could not marry.[37] I will return to this complex discussion when dealing with the intersection between gender, class, and parenthood in the household codes.

Intersectionality and the Household Codes

The household codes in Colossians have a similar threefold structure, though the purpose is not to negotiate hierarchy but to uphold and strengthen it. One of the leading scholars on the household codes, Margaret MacDonald, argues in a recent article that there are several unresolved questions related to these codes, mentioning in particular that we have to "[r]ecogniz[e] . . . the household codes as familial ideology that has a complex relationship to the life of real people."[38] She argues that more work needs to be done regarding the role of sexual behavior

---

34. Baker, "'From Every Nation under Heaven,'" 84–85, 99.

35. Betz, *Galatians*, 195. He writes: "In contrast to the preceding statements, this one names the sexes in the neuter, which indicates that not only the *social* difference between man and woman ('roles') are involved but the *biological* distinction." See also the LSJ.

36. The late Krister Stendahl pointed out that "male and female" seems to allude to Gen 1:27, emphasizing men and women's role in procreation, understood as referring to marriage; see the discussion in Schüssler Fiorenza, *Rhetoric and Ethic*, 156–57. See also Briggs, "Slavery and Gender," 178–79.

37. See Briggs, "Slavery and Gender," 179.

38. M. Y. MacDonald, "Beyond Identification of the Topos of Household Management," 84.

in exercising control of slaves, in relation to "the symbolic reversals of power inherent in baptismal proclamations, promises of inheritance to slaves, and language of collaboration with Paul which involves being a 'fellow slave.'"[39]

Before I present the eight hypothetical categories decoded from the household codes, I will use some insights from the intersectional analysis of Gal 3:28 to investigate each relationship pair. Col 3:18—4:1, by means of several imperatives, presents how the two parts in each pair should relate to one another. Three groups are instructed to obey their superiors: wives their husbands, children their parents and slaves their "earthly" masters. In addition to these three relations, husbands are instructed to "love their wives and never treat them harshly," masters shall treat their slaves "justly and fairly," while the moderating signs given for the relation between children and parents commands *fathers* not to provoke their children.

By accepting their position in the system, wives do what is fitting and children do their acceptable duty in the Lord. While Galatians argues that all are one *in Christ Jesus*, constructing a different spiritual reality, Colossians emphasizes that to keep one's place in the hierarchy is to act *in the Lord*. The early Christian household codes probably employ the Stoic system, building on three basic relations: husband-wife, master-slave, and parents-children (the Jew/Greek pair is not mentioned in Colossians).[40] These relationship pairs have often been interpreted as being separate, but how did the various power relations intersect?

In contrast to how Gal 3:28c talks about gender as male and female, the terms used to describe dual gender positions in Colossians, i.e., wives and husbands [γυνή and ἀνήρ], signify a certain status, since only free persons had legal access to marriage, as I discussed under "Family matters" in chapter 1.[41] Also legal parenthood depended in general on class, and children of enslaved mothers became the owner's property.[42] However, different terms are used for parents [γονεύς] (v. 20) and fathers [πατήρ] (v. 21). *Goneus* in plural, can, according to LSJ, stand for "begetter," "father," or "parents," indicating that mothers may be included in this

39. Ibid., 85.

40. See also other "household codes" in Ephesians, 1 Peter, and the Pastorals, discussed in M. Y. MacDonald, "A Place of Belonging," 278ff. See also Meeks, "The 'Haustafeln' and American Slavery," 335–40.

41. See also Harrill, *The Manumission of Slaves in Early Christianity*, 55.

42. Glancy, *Slavery in Early Christianity*. See in particular 26, 73–74.

term, in contrast to the male category *pater*.⁴³ Accordingly, if fathers and mothers together constitute parents, we may ask the other question: did slave mothers (and fathers when known) also count as parents? The status and position of mothers, as in the case of the *Acta Isidori* fragment and in the Pastoral Epistles motherhood ideology, seem to be crucial when constructing identity and organizing hierarchy.

Although slaves did not have legal access to either marriage or parenthood, they may nevertheless have formed couples and relationships.⁴⁴ Suzanne Dixon mentions so-called "irregular unions" as an alternative to marriage, such as slave partnerships and concubinage.⁴⁵ An intersectional analysis must not confuse ideology with lived experience:⁴⁶ although slaves were denied family roles according to law, slaves probably had access to various degrees of "family life." They probably formed long-term relationships, whether male and female or same-sex. By being the reproductive mothers (and fathers when known) to slave children, slaves were at least biological parents although not legally recognized as such. The question to the Colossian household codes, then, will be whether slave couples and biological mothers and fathers were included in the first and second relationship pair or not. In all its variety, we have to ask whether household management in the *ekklesia* follows legal standards within the Roman Empire, or whether slaves could be considered husbands and wives and parents.

The Colossian household codes require obedience to parents from children, but who functioned as the parents to a slave child: the owner(s), the biological mothers, various potential fathers, or others? Or is this requirement only directed to free children with legal parents, while slave children counted as slaves only and should accordingly primarily obey their owners? In this labyrinthine power structure, also a time aspect has to be added: free male children had to obey their parents, but in the future they would be on the top of all three categories as husbands, slave-owners, and fathers.

---

43. See the parallel text in Eph 6:1, which has fathers and mothers, echoing the Hebrew Bible (Deut 5:16 and Ex 20:12).

44. See D. B. Martin, "Slave Families and Slaves in Families," 207–30.

45. Dixon, *The Roman Family*, 90–94.

46. As pointed out by several scholars; see for example the section entitled "Rhetoric and reality" in Edwards, *The Politics of Immorality in Ancient Rome*, 9–12.

By means of intersectionality and Gal 3:28 I have tried to single out possible profiles and dilemmas within each hypothetical category. The household codes can be separated into rather unstable and complicated subgroups, with several uncertain elements:

1. Ruling and loving husband; slaveholder; parent
2. Obedient wife; slaveholder; parent
3. Obedient male slave; potentially biological father, but without social claims to paternity; potentially partner to other slave, but without legal recognition of "husbandhood" while enslaved
4. Obedient female slave (also obedient to male slave partner/ "husband"?); biological mother, but someone else owned her child; no access to wifehood, but could be manumitted due to several childbirths or to marrying a free man
5. Male child; freeborn; son, obedient to parents
6. Female child; freeborn; daughter, obedient to parents and future husband
7. Male child; slave; "son" of a slave mother, no legal father (but owned by someone else), obedient to owner and/or parents
8. Female child; slave; "daughter" of a slave mother, no legal father (but owned by someone else), obedient to owner and/or parents

INTERSECTIONAL CHALLENGES

In this last section I will emphasize some interpretative dilemmas when Gal 3:28 is used to illuminate the Colossian household codes by means of intersectionality. I find the relation between the social status pair (slave-free) and gender particularly interesting, but as a consequence of this discussion, the role of ethnicity/religion and of the relation between parents and children becomes rather complex. All these categories seem to be tightly connected, as also the conversation in *Acta Isidori* shows.

Slaves as persons, bodies, and things

In Gal 3:28 the terms used to determine gender may include slaves, while that is not the case with the household codes. Colossians 3–4 may echo the ancient idea that slaves were not human beings, and accordingly their gender (as well as ethnicity and age/generation) was irrelevant. Nevertheless, although slaves at times were considered things and not persons, male and female slave bodies served different roles and functions.[47]

The ongoing discussion of whether slaves were considered to have gender at all may be clarifying.[48] In the overall discourse of slavery in antiquity, several scholars have pointed out that "[s]laves of both genders were supposed to be only the passive objects of their master's will and desire."[49] The distinction between male and female was important only for free persons, for slaves it was irrelevant.[50] To some extent slaves were without gender and their sex did not matter.[51] Lin Foxhall has noted that male slaves, although belonging to a "subaltern" category of men, were still men, not women.[52] A male slave was physically born with a penis, but "symbolically, no slave had a phallus."[53] They did not take part in the masculine discourse; they were not in control of themselves but were owned property.[54] As bodies owned by others, they had no role in the ongoing struggle that freeborn, elite men participated in to negotiate and defend masculine values.[55] Osiek and MacDonald argue that if ancient thinkers had to categorize female slaves as either women or slaves, they would be considered slaves, not women. If a female slave was not a woman, she would not be met with the social expectations of women in the culture and did not have feminine traits ascribed to her.[56]

It might be useful to speak of the difference between men and women in antiquity in terms of the categories "sex and gender," where sex represents the natural and biologically given, and gender represents

---

47. See Glancy, *Slavery in Early Christianity*, 17–26.

48. This question has a long history, and has been addressed both with reference to the history and legacy of modern slavery as well as ancient slave systems. See in particular the discussion in Spelman, *Inessential Woman*. See also the various resources at Brooten, "Feminist Sexual Ethics Project."

49. Butler, "Notes on a *Membrum Disiectum*," 48.

50. Spelman, *Inessential Woman*, 42.

51. Ibid., 55.

52. Foxhall, "Introduction," 5.

53. Glancy, *Slavery in Early Christianity*, 25. See also Joshel and Murnaghan, *Women and Slaves in Greco-Roman Culture*, 10.

54. Joshel and Murnaghan, *Women and Slaves in Greco-Roman Culture*, 9.

55. Gleason, *Making Men*.

56. Osiek and MacDonald, *A Woman's Place*, 96.

the cultural ideas, gender roles, and how sex is interpreted.[57] This way of thinking about men and women has long been criticized within gender research, among other reasons because the natural sex can only be comprehended through cultural intermediaries such as language, and since it is difficult to draw a distinctive line between what is sex and what is gender.[58] Nevertheless, to understand ancient ideas about humans born with different bodies, and how they were interpreted, this distinction may be helpful.[59]

Sex is what slaves and free persons had in common. All female persons possibly shared reproductive functions, the potential bodily function of nursing babies, and if they reached a certain age they experienced menopause.[60] Regardless of whether Isidorus' mother was a slave or not, she counts as a mother. There were huge differences, however, when it came to how bodily functions and potentials were interpreted and how they determined the destiny of various female persons. Only freeborn women were considered part of the ideal gender system: they could marry and were expected to follow proper standards for women, keep their bodies intact until their husbands needed them for producing legitimate children, and follow the orders of the head of the household in which they lived, either their own husband or another male relative. These gender roles were obviously not applied to female slaves. The crucial question here is whether slave mothers shared more than their sex with free mothers. Did slave mothers' role in reproduction and wet nursing give them status and privilege, for example by requiring their children to be obedient to them, as free children should be to their parents? I asked related questions in chapter 4, where I wondered whether also female slaves were thought to be "saved through childbirth," as mentioned in 1 Tim 2:15.

What did male slaves and free men have in common? They shared a sex, which means they had male genitals, although only free men had

---

57. See Osiek, "Female Slaves, *Porneia*, and the Limits of Obedience," 255–56. See also the repeated phrase "gender, sex, and sexuality" in Vander Stichele and Penner, *Contextualizing Gender in Early Christian Discourse*, esp. 4.

58. See for example Chapter 1, "What is a Woman? Sex, Gender and the Body in Feminist Theory."

59. Joshel and Murnaghan, *Women and Slaves in Greco-Roman Culture*, 12.

60. Perhaps old free women, who were "no longer thought to be in danger of bringing shame through sexual violation," could have some more freedom and relate in different ways to slaves, like young children perhaps also could? See Hearon, *The Mary Magdalene Tradition*, 25.

a phallus. What they also had in common was that none of them could know for sure if they really had biological offspring. Who actually was the father of a child could not be confirmed with DNA tests like today, meaning that biological fatherhood could be sensitive to rumors and always surrounded by doubt and insecurity.[61] After a child was born of a free mother and wife, her husband had the right to either acknowledge the child or reject it, in which case it would be exposed.[62] Male slaves obviously had no such legal right. In addition, in contrast to female slaves who actually gave birth, a male slave's paternity was hard to establish. Those who were most far away from parenthood in the households seem to be male slaves, due both to social class and reproductive sex.

There were different gender roles for male and female slaves, indicating that their sexual differences were interpreted according to some sort of gender norms. Although they were outside the gender system that was operative for free persons, it might be imprecise to consider slaves only as having/being sex. They did indeed have gender roles, with for example female slaves being hired as wet nurses or expected to produce babies to increase their owners' property. I suggest that slaves belonged to a gender system, although not the same gender system as free persons. Unfortunately, few if any sources are concerned with describing how male and female slaves related to each other, but we can ask the other question(s): Did slaves copy gender roles of free persons, or were status and authority distributed differently in the hierarchical structures among slaves? Since a slave woman, being sexual available to her owner(s) and others, could have several potential fathers to her child(ren), how did it influence slave "families" that biological fatherhood was hard to determine most of the time?

Returning to the New Testament texts, we realize that Galatians and Colossians refer to gender in terms that are drawn from different gender discourses. In Gal 3:28 it is the bodies that classify persons as either male or female. Animals and human beings alike are male and female. It is their sex that determines their gender, so to speak. In Colossians 3–4, conversely, gender is talked about in terms that have a meaning for free persons only. It is not enough to have a female body if you want to have the "privilege" of being a wife subject to a husband. Gender identification

---

61. On the social function of rumor and gossip, see Kartzow, *Gossip and Gender*, 160–66.

62. Dixon, *The Roman Family*, 122.

is also a question of social status. Perhaps the category of "parents" in the relationship pair of Col 3:21 represents a middle position in which at least slave mothers, who had the biological process in common with free women and whose pregnancy was visible and whose motherhood was beyond doubt, could be included among parents.

Children: Gender, class, and race/religion

It was class and not biological sex that regulated access to marriage, but a more open question is whether it was legal or biological motherhood (and fatherhood when known) that regulated access to the parent category. In what way was also the category of children determined by class and gender? Asking the other question helps us search for how different identity markers influence the way children were categorized.[63] If only freeborn women produced legitimate children, what kind of gender system, if any, was operative for slave children?

When various ancient sources mention children, we have to question whether they have all children in mind, including exposed children, adopted children, step-children, and other children in the community, or only legitimate children born by free or freed mothers who were acknowledged by their fathers. Did slave children whose parents were unknown, dead, or living somewhere else count as children in the parents-children relationship pair in Col 3:18, or were they considered only slaves? We can also ask whether the children mentioned in the household codes necessarily were young or whether a (free) person was considered "a child" as long as his or her parents (father) lived.[64]

Although Gal 3:28 and Colossians 3–4 share an interest in gender and class, they do not share the third relationship pair. Nevertheless, as shown by the small conversation in the *Acta Isidori* as well as several other ancient texts, proper family and household relations (for example be-

---

63. The recent anthology *The Child in the Bible* adds the aspect of "the child" to biblical scholarship. It is argued that "just as in the case of using the lens of 'gender,' 'race,' or 'class' as categories of analysis, the lens of 'the child' reveals unexplored or neglected aspects of a text...."; see "Introduction" in Bunge et al., *The Child in the Bible*, xviii. I will suggest that we gain more from using an intersectional approach and asking the other question(s) than applying one "lens" only, since children also were of various genders, races, and classes.

64. For a discussion of the terminological and social similarities between children and slaves, see chapter 1.

tween mothers and sons) were also related to ethnic or religious status.[65] This generates two new sets of questions: What age or parental status were the Jew/Greek, slave/free, and male/female in Gal 3:28 supposed to have, or did this not matter?[66] And finally, although the household codes are not concerned with ethnicity/nationality/religion, we may still wonder whether it made a difference if the wife or husband, the female or male slave, or the mother or father or child (of all combinations) was Jewish or Greek or Roman or something else.

CONCLUSION

A colleague once said that good Biblical research is to ask good questions, and in this book and especially in this chapter, a particular way of *asking the other questions* has been the methodological starting point. I admit I have asked more questions than I have suggested answers, but this is in fact according to the procedure mentioned in the introduction to this book, that of presenting problems and questions for debate.

Such questions may challenge approaches that emerge from one particular perspective. Such questions may also help us face some of our own blind spots and highlight ambivalence and open-ended conclusions. Such questions may also be useful in the process of unpacking the discourses and suggesting alternative interpretations.

Hierarchical reasoning seems to be an important element in shaping early Christianity. We need to ask not only if early Christian texts employed or erased hierarchies, but how hierarchical structures worked in different contexts. Intersectionality helps us focus on those who were at the bottom of various hierarchies, assuming they made a difference although silenced in texts. When Gal 3:28 is read to illuminate Col 3:18—4:1, it seems insufficient to use gender as the only analytical category. The different ways these two texts talk about men and women can only be understood by emphasizing how gender intersects with the status of free and slave. Since these texts are involved in different gender discourses, Gal 3:28 cannot easily function to counter or delegitimize the power structure of the household codes, as has been common in Biblical scholarship.

---

65. See also the very interesting discussion in Joshel and Murnaghan, eds., *Women and Slaves in Greco-Roman Culture*, 1.

66. How is Gal 3:28 related to for example Gal 4:1, in which an heir, as long as he is a child, is said to be no better than a slave?

In *Acta Isidori* the issues of motherhood seem significant. If gender is expressed by the use of inclusive terms of parenthood, there might be an ambiguity related to the role of slaves. Procreation was indeed part of the hierarchical fabric of the empire: to produce legitimate offspring was a duty for free men and women, and childlessness could be a scandal for a wife. But also slaves, left out of this ideal discourse, produced children. I have suggested that slave mothers in particular could get access to certain privileges, for instance as not only being included among slaves in the household codes, but also considered parents. But was slave motherhood really a privilege? Motherhood represented a high risk for all women; romantic views of motherhood do not account for experienced realities.

When asking "the other question" of these texts, the old-fashioned distinction between sex and gender appears to be useful. Bodies in antiquity were not only considered to be male and female; they were also categorized according to class and ethnic/religious background. A striking example, relevant to the interpretation of the household codes in Colossians, is how all persons born with male bodies shared the insecurity related to biological fatherhood, although free and slave males had very different legal roles related to children. While free men had legal wives and could either accept or reject the children born by these wives, male slaves were excluded from fatherhood, due to their sex (that it, it was hard to establish the identity of the biological father) and class (that is, a slave had no legal right over his offspring). Female slaves who gave birth to children, although they had no legal rights over them, were perhaps closer to parenthood than male slaves. Intersectionality makes it clear that not all men were better off than all women; in fact, focusing on reproduction, slaves' positions in the households, and gender hierarchies among slaves reveals that status and position may have been distributed and negotiated in several different ways. In the household codes, parenthood seems to be a role of authority. Perhaps female slaves who also were mothers had certain privileges, corresponding to how they could deserve manumission after a certain number of childbirths? If so, female slaves who were childless end up as an even weaker group.

Early Christian memory was shaped by hierarchical reasoning, and alternative ways of imagining community or equality had to negotiate hierarchies. Therefore, intersectionality seems to be a very useful tool when studying Biblical texts. An intersectional approach reveals a web of social categories, giving us a glimpse into the cultural complexity of antiquity.

Such an approach also challenges interpreters to take the cultural complexity of our own era seriously.

A recent documentary film argues that today millions of people are living in conditions of slavery, although slavery is illegal in all countries.[67] These people are caught in structures in which a number of social categories work together and mutually construct each other. The stories of unpaid house slaves, debt slaves, child soldiers, child prostitutes, and victims of trafficking bear witness to how our global economy creates and upholds hierarchies that have similar features as slavery in antiquity. Engagement with New Testament texts may not only work to support structures of control and dominance, but also to critique the ways in which status and authority are distributed today. "In Christ Jesus" and "in the Lord" suggest alternative visions that may challenge complex hierarchies and support struggles for change. In order to understand how systems of privilege and oppression operate, we must examine the various intersections of ethnicity, class, gender, and age. To ask the other question may be a good place to start.

---

67. Robsahm, "Modern Slavery."

PART FOUR

Beyond Intersectionality
Thrice Vulnerable but Named

THIS FINAL PART TOUCHES upon the blurred line between historical reconstructions and imaginations. Creative suggestions and undocumented information will occur more frequently in this last part than in the previous chapters. I present two named women in early Christian memory, Blandina and Hagar, and also reflect on other possible female slaves. Early Christian discourse did not operate in a social or cultural vacuum, but in a concrete historical situation in which specific norms, values, and practices dominated the discourse. By adjusting, negotiating, and dissenting, early Christian thinkers managed to lay the foundation for a new movement. The analytical tools chosen in this book allow us to ask new questions, not only to the archive but also to the recovered memory. Such tools may help us to theorize the gaps in the sources. Our texts represent for the most part the memory of those in power, that is, those who won the struggle over what to remember. For some reason Blandina, a named female slave, ended up representing ideal behavior for both men and women. Hagar, in all her complexity, remains "the other woman" in early Christian discourse, but in later interpretations she has left this place of marginality and may help us move beyond intersectional oppression. To remember a person by a stable and unchangeable name gives him or her a lasting social identity and gives that person place and time in history, also when the individual life comes to an end. But why name slaves and why name female slaves? Why are so few male slaves mentioned by name in early Christian texts? Slaves were supposed to be cut off from all ties of ethnicity, religion, family, and origin. By naming female slaves, early Christian texts deal with fluidity and ambiguity inherent in all memory processes, and engage elements that may destabilize the margins.

10

Negotiating Hierarchy

The Ideal Slave/Woman Blandina

INTRODUCTION

THE WAYS IN WHICH early Christian hierarchies are used in the memory process to construct identity and shape social relations are the main interest of this chapter. Interpreters have studied hierarchies for various—and sometimes opposite—reasons: to legitimate church order and family patterns or to challenge power structures in contexts of oppression and discrimination.

In earlier chapters I have discussed how different New Testament texts negotiate and adjust hierarchical structures in creative and selective ways, at times renegotiating social structures known from the broader society, at times copying them with a twist, at times coming up with alternative ideas. The main focus of this chapter is to examine how these hierarchical structures are remembered, adjusted, and negotiated in another early Christian text, *The Martyrdom of Lyon*.

The text mentions a female slave, at the bottom of at least three hierarchical systems related to gender, class, and sexuality. But in contrast to most female slaves, she is given a name—Blandina—and also a position that is unusual for slaves. The naming of women was also discussed in chapter 5, where I emphasized the different names given to the women at the empty tomb. To remember a person by a stable and unchangeable name gives him or her a lasting social identity.[1] To be called by her own name gives Blandina, an enslaved woman, a sense of continuity with her mother and father who perhaps once named her out of love.[2] Slaves were

---

1. Walton, *Skaff deg eit liv!*, 192.
2. Nazer, "Epilogue," 310–11.

normally supposed to be cut off from all ties of ethnicity, religion, family, and origin and were even often re-named.³ By naming female slaves, early Christian texts have the potential to destabilize the margins.

In Galatians Paul proclaims "There is neither Jew nor Greek, there is neither slave nor free, there is neither male nor female; for you are all one in Christ Jesus"; in contrast, the household codes have been ascribed to the patriarchal surroundings in which the early Christians had to adjust to contemporary standards. In the hierarchical structures underlying Gal 3:28 and Colossians 3–4, the position that seems most marginal in relation to both gender and class is that of female slaves. Though a female slave, however, Blandina does not fit into the picture of being a marginal character.

REMEMBERED AND RENEGOTIATED HIERARCHIES: *THE MARTYRS OF LYONS*

The various practices of hierarchical reasoning found in the New Testament are used to construct meaning and identity. These ideas also had an afterlife and were remembered, rearticulated, and negotiated, and continue to create new meanings in new contexts.

The fourth-century Church historian Eusebius is the only source to the document called *The Martyrs of Lyons*, formulated as a letter written by the communities in Lyons and Vienna, in Gaul, to the churches of Asia and Phrygia. The letter offers a brutal portrait of an anti-Christian uprising in Gaul that reportedly took place in the summer of 177 CE.⁴ It can be read as an early representation of how Europeans treated strangers who came from the far East or South, believed in other gods, and were mocked and punished for their strangeness and otherness.

Much has been said about this document in order to localize it within time and place, but the fact that it was written down after several generations and referred to an earlier event, or perhaps earlier lost documents, show that it must have survived as a tale or a story, remembered for generations.

---

3. Hezser, *Jewish Slavery in Antiquity*, 19–20. Could Blandina be her new name as a slave?

4. Musurillo, ed. *The Acts of the Christian Martyrs*, xx.

SANCTUS' DEFENSE

One of the four martyrs portrayed in this document is Sanctus. In order to describe his resolute character and his refusal to give in to the interrogators and "say something that he should not," the argument builds on several categories, related to each other in a rather fascinating order:

> [Sanctus] resisted them with such determination that he would not even tell them his own name, his race [*ethnos*], or the city he was from, whether he was slave or a freedman. To all of their question he answered in Latin: "I am a Christian!"[5]

In the next sentence his steadfast refusal is partly repeated, but by use of slightly different categories: now it is his "name, birthplace, nationality [*genos*] or anything else" he will not reveal.

This passage can be read as a discussion about which categories that are relevant in order to construct identity. The interrogators are interested in the usual identity markers in order to place Sanctus in hierarchies and structures of power. What is his name and background? What is his ethnicity and nationality? Is he a slave or a freedman? Such categories could help them classify him, identify him, and perhaps treat him accordingly; we recall that categories are used to blame the opponent in *Acta Isidori* (see last chapter).

Instead of answering all these questions, however, Sanctus (like Isidorus before him) gives the other answer. Only one category counts for him, and that is his religion: "I am a Christian" are the only words he utters. He is not willing to follow the interrogators' classification system, since it is of no importance for a man who belongs to the Christians. His answer can be read as a realization of the baptismal formula in Gal 3:28: "For all of you are one in Christ Jesus" is remembered and rearticulated when Sanctus refuses to identify his name, origin, ethnicity, or class and chooses to mention his Christian identity alone.

THE INTRODUCTION OF BLANDINA

Also other power structures and hierarchies—ones that seem almost contradictory—are reflected in this text. The first introduction of the four martyrs is a telling example. The first three are introduced as Sanctus, the deacon of Vienna; Maturus, newly baptized but nevertheless a noble

---

5. *The Martyrs of Lyon* 20, in ibid.

athlete; and Attalus, from a Pergamon family. Their personal identities and backgrounds are specifically referred to; all three are presented as important and qualified Christians, and for Sanctus and Attalus also their geographical location is mentioned.

A fourth person is then presented: Blandina. Only her name is mentioned, and the text later reveals she is the slave of another woman. Blandina is thus presented in an entirely different manner, and she serves to demonstrate God's generosity:

> [Through Blandina] Christ proved that the things that men think cheap, ugly, and contemptuous are deemed worthy of glory before God . . . (17)

In this introduction Christian thought is constructed by use of hierarchies in which a female slave can be found at the bottom, an ideology that might be built on the memory of the household codes in Colossians 3–4, the parable in Luke 12, or the intersections of stereotypes and prejudices related to gender, class and race in the Pastoral Epistles. Blandina's role as cheap and ugly is to be an object upon whom Christ's mercy can be demonstrated. She is chosen and found worthy so that the order of God can win over the order of men.

Although this is how she is introduced, it is striking that in the rest of the text her love to God is praised for not only being outward but also "demonstrated in achievement." Although she is a female slave, Blandina is also called a woman, and she is compared to other women: after her martyrdom her persecutors "admitted that no woman had ever suffered so much in their experience."[6] Blandina is also compared to her mistress, and Blandina endures most pain (17). She is also blessed like a noble athlete (19).

Although she is a female slave, ugly, and an object on whom God's glory is demonstrated, her character shows that hierarchies in which gender and class often operate in fixed orders do not always determine who is the most ideal Christian heroes of the past. Her prominent position may also be seen as a realization of the vision of Gal 3:28.

---

6. *The Martyrs of Lyons*, 56.

CONCEPTUALIZING BLANDINA

Somehow Blandina is a boundary-crossing and ambiguous character, hard to classify in fixed categories. Jennifer Glancy says about Blandina that "in the intensity of her slavelike suffering she represents Christ."[7] Virginia Burrus ascribes Blandina a "culturally 'queer' identity."[8] Blandina is presented as a slave, a personification of what is cheap and ugly, but she is nevertheless called a woman and is even better than other women. She is also constructed by use of masculine virtue in her endurance of suffering, and blessed like a noble athlete. She is a bender of both class and gender, although some modern commentators, who otherwise have paid attention to many interesting nuances in the story of Blandina, overlook the complex issues related to what it may have indicated that she is not only a female martyr, but also a slave.

Gillian Clark, for example, creatively discusses the late antique debate on martyrdom and death and how the martyrs' bodies were "torn, broken, dismembered and burned." As two examples she mentions the respectable Perpetua and the slave Blandina.[9] They may both be relevant examples, but there are huge differences in how a free wife's body and a female slave's body could control and protect their physical integrity. The open body of a female slave was an object for a variety of penetrations, such as violence or rape. A wife's body should be protected and isolated, except when needed for her husband's procreation. Perpetua and Blandina hardly function as equal examples of martyred bodies, since a slave was part of the owner's property and had a different bodily biography.

For Elizabeth Castelli, who is interested in martyrdom and memory, Perpetua and Blandina are both explicitly treated as women martyrs. She argues that "the capacity of Christian women to be transformed into masculine heroes becomes almost a cliché" and categorizes this as "gender-bending." Her argument is convincing, and she uses it to explain how this "becomes one of the critical aspects of the paradoxical appropriation of Roman spectacle in the midst of Christian critique."[10] I fully agree with her conclusion, but if slaves are outside the gender system, in what way can a female slave in the same way as a freeborn woman be the subject

---

7. Glancy, *Corporal Knowledge*, 60.
8. Burrus, *Saving Shame*, 24.
9. G. Clark, "Bodies and Blood," 99.
10. Castelli, *Martyrdom and Memory*, 126.

(or object) of gender-bending? As mentioned earlier, several scholars have pointed out that in the ancient discourse of gender and slavery, the distinction between male and female was relevant primarily for free persons, not for slaves.[11] If ancient thinkers had to categorize female slaves as either women or slaves, they would be considered slaves, not women.[12]

Interpreters overlook the importance of class when they put the slave Blandina and the noble and slave-holding woman Perpetua from another martyr act side by side as examples of women martyrs, thereby running the risk of presenting gender as a homogenous category in antiquity. Suffering and death for a female slave had a different discursive meaning than for a noble woman, at least in perception. If Blandina should be compared with a character from the martyrdom of Perpetua, Perpetua's female slave Felicitas would be a more relevant example.[13]

THE RECOVERED MEMORY OF BLANDINA AND CLAUDIA

The interpretative habit of seeing similarities between the few named women we find in early Christian texts inspired me to look for connections between Blandina and other named but otherwise unidentified women in the New Testament; women mentioned in passing are more common, but revealing the name of such characters is rare.[14] I have in particular focused on Claudia in 2 Tim 4:21, who is also last in a list of four named but otherwise unidentified persons (along with Eubulus, Pudens, and Linus, she is mentioned as sending greetings to Timothy). Interpreters have suggested that she could have been a wife, a mother, or a widow related to the three men mentioned, or an otherwise unknown female church leader.[15] All her suggested roles connect her to other men, in heterosexual relations or as a mother. I would argue that in lack of proof to the contrary, we should also consider that she could have been a slave, and Blandina certainly shows us that female slaves could in fact be named and listed among influential men. If the Pastoral Paul did send

---

11. See for example Spelman, *Inessential Woman*, 42.
12. Osiek and MacDonald, *A Woman's Place*, 96.
13. See Solevåg, "Birthing Salvation," 231.

14. See a related attempt to play with female names in biblical interpretation in Standhartinger, "The Epistle to the Congregation in Colossae and the Invention of the 'Household Code.'"

15. Quinn and Wacker, *The First and Second Letters to Timothy*, 834–37.

greetings from a female slave, we would have yet another illustration of how unstable and negotiable hierarchies could be.

If we imagine that Claudia was a slave, how would such a character be integrated in the community? Perhaps she had a female owner like Blandina? Or perhaps some of the three men mentioned owned her (with sexual control over her body?), or perhaps she was the concubine or freed wife to one of them? Then she would be impressive as being a woman who overcome not only the instructions not to teach or say anything and be saved through childbirth (1 Tim 2:9-15), but also to obey her owners and not talk back (1 Tim 6:1-2; Titus 2: 9-10).[16] Was it really possible to live under such conditions and still be able to be worthy to be mentioned by Paul as someone with a name who sends greetings? If such a female slave ever existed, in real life or in the literary world of the pastoral Paul, the recovered memory of her bears witness to the great variety of early Christianity. I discussed text passages from the Pastoral Epistles with some destabilizing potential in chapter 4, and if the list of greetings includes a female slave, she may be a character of the archive with potential to overcome marginality.

To think and write about Claudia is one possible contribution to recovering the memory of marginalized persons, not to accept that we forget all those early Christian people whose memory did not reached the active canon. By asking about her social status we challenge "the power structures that are embedded and preserved in the archives we have inherited."[17] This approach touches upon the blurred line between historical reconstructions and imaginations and uses intersectionality and memory theory to theorize the gaps in the sources. The memory of Blandina is used to suggest that Claudia might have been another marginalized female slave who for some reason was worthy of being named.

CONCLUSION

To construct hierarchies in which people are categorized and put in their place are activities with strong Biblical traditions. However, early Christian texts are engaged in renegotiations as much as they apply given systems. New Testament texts operate on different levels in presenting a memory that can contribute to identity construction. Hierarchies are

16. See the discussion of these texts from the Pastoral Epistles in chapters 4 and 6 above.

17. Rowley and Wolthers, "Lost and Found," 9.

never innocent systems, but are dependent on power and access to various types of capital. It is far from coincidental who is above the others in systems of oppression.

In the case of Blandina, the attitudes towards women and slaves from the household codes are revitalized, but simultaneously the vision of Gal 3:28 is fulfilled. Ideas and power structures that for us might seem contradictory may be integrated and produce meaning in the creative process of remembering the past within another context. In the story of Blandina from the martyr acts, she is given the fixed role of a female slave, but she overcomes this role in the arena. That such a person has become part of early Christian memory challenges us to ask questions also in regard to other marginal women, such as Claudia in 2 Tim 4:21.

Blandina is a highly interesting character, and the memory of her queer person may support two hypotheses with great potential for further reflections: identity is a work in progress, and there are multiple possibilities embedded in most social settings, even at the bottom of the hierarchy.

11

The Memory of Hagar

A Model for Overcoming Marginality

INTRODUCTION

IDENTITY CONSTRUCTION TENDS TO draw heavily on negotiated stories from the past. Religious images and figures play a significant role in identity work, and new times, new questions, and new challenges encourage us to look for new Biblical figures to engage with. In this chapter I focus on the Egyptian slave girl Hagar, a character that is marginal in the Genesis story of Abraham, and on how the memory of her can represent a new point of departure for overcoming marginality.[1]

Jews, Christians, and Muslims identify themselves as children of Abraham. In Genesis, Abraham and his wife Sarah were originally childless, but Hagar gave Abraham his firstborn son; later Sarah gave birth to her own son, by God's intervention, and Hagar was forced into the desert. Though the Biblical figure of Hagar has merely a marginal position in the collective memory of the West,[2] she is an important figure in some specific contexts: Hagar has become an icon for African American womanhood,[3] she is a symbol within Israeli peace movements and scholarship,[4] and in

---

1. Many of the ideas and reflections discussed in this chapter are central to a research project Anne Hege Grung and I have developed at the University of Oslo. See also Grung and Kartzow, "Samtaler om Hagar."

2. See Haag and Sölle, *Grosse Frauen der Bibel in Bild und Text*, 32–47. See also Faltin and Wright, *The Religious Roots of Contemporary European Identity*. Castelli talks about "the nagging persistence in the collective imagination of the West of the figure of Hagar," in Castelli, "Allegories of Hagar," 228.

3. Williams, "Hagar in African American Biblical Appropriation," 176.

4. See the introduction to the first volume of the Israeli journal, "Hagar."

Islam she is a pioneering woman who enabled the establishment of a new civilization.[5] Hagar (Hajar in Arabic) is not mentioned by name in the Qur'an, but in the Hadith (oral traditions of the Prophet Muhammad), and she plays a prominent role as the "mother of monotheism."[6] All three religions share that Hagar is the mother of Abraham/Ibrahim's oldest son Ishmael, and that she at one point together with her son was left alone in the wilderness struggling for their common survival.

By starting the reflection from positions that are marginal to Western cultural and religious landscapes, the character of Hagar may help us highlight issues of hegemony and dominance and give "marginalized subjects" an epistemic advantage.[7] Hagar's desert location and social mobility may function as a matrix to discuss intersections of gender, class, race, and religion. She has become a traveling concept that has moved out of the Biblical and religious discourses and been given new meanings.[8] Stories of Hagar's survival in past and present contexts have the potential to create new spaces for conversation and dialogue. The memory of Hagar highlights the multiple possibilities embedded in most social settings, while at the same time reflecting the overriding impact of power and hierarchy. In this chapter I am interested in "thinking about Hagar," "thinking with Hagar," and "thinking beyond Hagar," to use Penner and Stickele's distinctions.[9]

THE CHILDREN OF ABRAHAM

Abraham, who represents important elements of shared ancestry, has always been a central character in Biblical scholarship and in recent discussions on religious dialogue.[10] The figure of Hagar in the Genesis narrative, the enslaved surrogate mother,[11] may help us create a differ-

---

5. Hassan, "Islamic Hagar and Her Family," 154.

6. Ibid., 149. See also Trible and Russell, "Unto the Thousandth Generation," 10.

7. See Nash, "Re-Thinking Intersectionality," 3.

8. Bal, *Travelling Concepts in the Humanities*.

9. See the introduction to Vander Stichele and Penner, *Contextualizing Gender in Early Christian Discourse*.

10. Among a number of examples, from a variety of genre and channels, see Hendel, *Remembering Abraham*, Benyik, "The Formation and Interpretation of the Bible and of the Qur'an," Moberly, *The Bible, Theology, and Faith*, Haddad and Eposito, *Daughters of Abraham*.

11. Nuzi law in Mesopotamia, which may have been followed, allowed a free woman who was barren to choose a slave to give her a child, Williams, "Hagar in African

ent vision of the past and provide a more dynamic model than that of Abraham's children. This approach may be located in the verbal echo between what Edward Said calls *filiation* and *affiliation*. His point is that the first concept represents continuity in reproduction and biological terms, while the latter deals with institutions, associations, and community.[12] To move from filiation to affiliation may be a journey from biology to world vision, from nature to culture, as Said sees it.[13] Although both Abraham and Hagar have elements of filiation and affiliation, Hagar may help us see the problematic aspects of the idea of Abraham as a shared forefather. According to Genesis, one of the mothers in the story was a foreign slave who was forced to give her owners a child. Hagar represents a different myth and symbol than Abraham: Abraham is "the father of all," while Hagar does not provide an illusion of a harmonious and static line of shared family origin. She may therefore correspond better to challenges in our global context of cultural complexity.[14] Shift in focus from Abraham to Hagar represents a major shift in meaning.[15] This shift may also challenge the shared—although differently articulated and practiced—male dominance in all three traditions.[16]

By employing an intersectional approach to recovered memory, this chapter will pay particular attention to the dynamics of the archive; Hagar is part of active memory for Muslims, while stored away in the archive for most Christians and Jews. Memory theory deals with power, status, and struggle over canon,[17] and Hagar's role as representing common memory for the three monotheistic traditions seems to have great potential.

American Biblical Appropriation," 181. See also Adamo and Eghwubare, "The African Wife of Abraham," 287.

12. Said, *The World, the Text, and the Critic*, 17.

13. Ibid., 19–20.

14. Bal argues that the Genesis figure of Abraham as a model for religious life has a lot to account for: "he had cast out his firstborn son, Ishmael, and the lad's mother, Hagar. Then (. . .) God asks Abraham to prove his faith by sacrificing his 'only' son—'the one you love.'" As a father he has in fact already sacrificed his son when he casts out Ishmael. How can Abraham then work as a unifying figure for the three monotheistic religions? Bal, *Loving Yusuf*, 19.

15. Trible and Russell, "Unto the Thousandth Generation," 24. Castelli suggests that shifting focus to Hagar is "nonhegemonic." See "Allegories of Hagar," 245.

16. Abugideiri, "Hagar." See also von Braun and Auga, "Beyond Boundaries," 5–6.

17. See the introduction to Danbolt et al, *Lost and Found*. See also Olick, "Products, Processes, and Practices."

RENEWED INTEREST IN SARAH AND HAGAR

In a recent anthology, the roles of Sarah and Hagar in the three traditions have been discussed, providing useful overviews of the source material and discussing the role of these two women today.[18] Although I am most interested in Hagar, many sources and current discussions deal with Hagar and Sarah as contrast figures, circling around how the two women competed for Abraham's and God's favor.[19] By highlighting Hagar as a figure in her own terms and not necessarily in opposition to or rivalry with Sarah, I want to avoid stereotypical notions about the female which primarily divide women into good or bad.[20]

Also within Islamic feminist studies Hagar has been given a role with great potential: Abugideiri talks about Hagar as a historical model for gender jihad.[21]

HAGAR IN EARLY CHRISTIAN AND JEWISH MEMORY

How do the various ancient thinkers understand Hagar's gender, class, race, and religion? I only aim at opening up the discussion; the text material dealing with Hagar is strikingly ambiguous and will need to be studied in detail. By presenting the various texts briefly, I want to emphasize the variety and invite others to see the potential and join the conversation.

In the Jewish historian Philo, for example, Hagar is a figure on the borderline.[22] In a dialogue with Abraham, Sarah characterizes her as "bodily a slave, but of free and noble race ... an Egyptian by birth, but a Hebrew by her choice/rule of life" (*De Abrahamo* 251).[23] Philo also has a

---

18. Trible and Russel, *Hagar, Sarah, and Their Children*.

19. Russel, "Children of Struggle," 186. Note that it has been argued that Islamic interpretations are not so concerned with contrasts and competition between Sarah and Hagar, praising instead both women for their motherhood; see Abugideiri, "Hagar."

20. "Splitting the female always serves male dominating interests," as suggested in Pabst, "The Interpretation of the Sarah-Hagar-Stories in Rabbinic and Patristic Literature," 8. See also Scholz, "Gender, Class, and Androcentric Compliance in Rapes of Enslaved Women in the Hebrew Bible," 6.

21. See Abugideiri, "Hagar."

22. Borgen, "Some Hebrew and Pagan Features in Philo's and Paul's Interpretation of Hagar and Ishmael," 161.

23. Greek text: τὸ μὲν σῶμα δούλην, ἐλευθέραν δὲ καὶ εὐγενῆ τὴν διάνοιαν and γένος μὲν Αἰγυπτίαν, τὴν δὲ προαίρεσιν Ἑβραίαν. For English translation, see ibid., 155–56.

positive attitude to children born within "mixed marriages," considering Ishmael a legitimate son of Abraham and adopted by Sarah (*Abr.* 250).

In the rich body of Rabbinic literature, the general impression is that Sarah is superior to Hagar, but the rabbis in question are not blind to the moral dilemmas of the story, nor uniform in their judgment of the situation.[24] Many rabbis focus on the problem of Sarah's infertility, and some blame her for her mistreatment of Hagar.[25] Sometimes Hagar's national origin plays an important role, reflecting the ambiguous attitude to Egypt in Jewish thought.[26] She also appears as the daughter of Pharaoh; he preferred to give her to Abraham as a slave than to another man as a wife, a way to recognize Abraham's relation to God.[27]

Hagar functions as a prototype for later Egyptian woman who were incorporated into Jewish history, such as Aseneth. In the discussion of *Joseph and Aseneth* in chapter 3 we saw that Aseneth's idolatry made her an outsider. In some rabbinic sources, it is recognized that Hagar may have worshipped God as long as she was in Abraham's household, but the moment she left she started to worship the pagan gods again.[28] This was in marked contrast to the free and elite Egyptian woman Aseneth, who was like a Hebrew woman after her conversion.

In *Genesis Rabbah* (45:7), Hagar's slave status is confirmed: sharing a husband with Sarah does not mean she has access to Sarah's social status. The text compares Hagar with a donkey, not due to her ethnicity or sexuality, but because Hagar as a slave is a work animal.[29] In general, *Genesis Rabbah* 45 is a fascinating text to study when the aim is to destabilize Hagar's role as a figure in the archive: it also discusses why pregnancy was so difficult for Sarah, and negotiates the value of a woman who cannot bear children.[30]

Other Jewish sources also mention Hagar: A hymn by Baruch in praise of wisdom describes how no one ever succeeded in finding

---

24. Reinhartz and Walfish, "Conflict and Coexistance in Jewish Interpretation," 105.
25. See Russel, "Children of Struggle," 189.
26. The ambiguous role of Egypt is discussed in Ilana Pardes, *Countertraditions in the Bible*.
27. Reinhartz and Walfish, "Conflict and Coexistance in Jewish Interpretation," 106.
28. Ibid.
29. Ibid., 107.
30. Discussed in ibid., 107–8.

Wisdom, and Hagar and her sons seem to be involved.[31] Hagar also appears in the Qumran writings: the so-called "war scroll" takes a negative attitude to Hagar's lineage, seeing Ishmael as the progenitor of the "Sons of Darkness," the main enemies of the Qumran community (1 QM 2.13).[32] These last two texts dealing with the role of Hagar remain little examined in scholarship on Hagar.

Among the Christian church fathers, Hagar and Sarah became codes for the synagogue and the church, building on the allegorical interpretation of Paul in Galatians 4.[33] As Origen sees it, those who are born according to the flesh, as Hagar's son was, fail and lack in many things.[34] In Tertullian, Sarah represents "our mother, the holy Church," and the Christians "are not children of the bondwoman but of the free."[35] In addition to being a useful figure in Christian anti-Jewish polemic, Hagar is also used as a metaphor for Gnosticism, in debates over marriage and asceticism.[36] But Hagar did not only become the image of Jews who did not accept Christ as a savior or of gnostic Christians or other "heretics" who misunderstood the truth; she also became a figure guilty of "unchristian" sexual behavior.[37] Hagar came to be a very flexible symbol among the church fathers, and was never considered a sympathetic character.[38]

Taking into account all the interest in Hagar in early Jewish texts and the church fathers, Hagar and Sarah's absence from the canonical Gospels and Acts in the New Testament is striking. Hagar is only mentioned in the allegory in Gal 4:21–31. Paul not only labels the agitators as slaves, but compares them with a slave woman and her offspring.[39] En route from Genesis to Galatians, some important elements of the story have been negotiated. Paul's interpretation of the Genesis story creates a different

---

31. See *The Wisdom Poem* 3, 22–23. For text, translation, and discussion, see Burke, *The Poetry of Baruch*, 2, 68–69 and 92–96.

32. Tsang, *From Slaves to Sons*, 94.

33. E. A. Clark, "Interpretive Fate Amid the Church Fathers," 129.

34. See the discussion in Pabst, "The Interpretation of the Sarah-Hagar-Stories in Rabbinic and Patristic Literature," 5–6.

35. *Adversus Marcionem* 5.4.8. See also ibid., 3.

36. E. A. Clark, "Interpretive Fate Amid the Church Fathers," 129–31.

37. Ibid., 143.

38. Ibid.

39. Tsang, From Slaves to Sons, 102.

meaning, he "read[s] the Bible with lively creativity," as Brad R. Braxton argues.[40]

In Rom 9:6–13 Hager can be identified as the mother who produces the children of the flesh, those who are not the children of the promise or counted as descendents. Paul is concerned with the true "Israelites" who have the privilege of "divine filiation" (vv. 4–5, cf. Said's distinction above).[41] The son Abraham had by Hagar is not a heir, similar to the social practices at Paul's time in which a slave mother's children became part of their owner's property and did not have any legal father. In the subsequent verses the Ishmael/Isaac analogy represents a parallel to that of Rebecca's twins by Isaac.[42]

HAGAR IN ISLAM

The memory of Hagar in Islam highlights a specific set of features of the story, and her slave status, gender, and Egyptian origin seem to be far less problematic. Although she is entrusted by God to give birth to a prophet, "her divine instruction entailed much more than childbirth," as phrased by Abugideiri.[43] Seen as a matriarch, her name and message came to be part of Islam's sacred history and ritual.[44] In Islamic tradition, Hagar was not left alone in the wilderness, but Abraham kept on visiting her and her son.[45]

According to Riffat Hassan

> The dramatic story of Hagar's life shows that class or color is not a deterrent to any person who has faith in God and is resolutely righteous in action. So Hagar does not see herself as a victim of Abraham and Sarah, or of a patriarchal, class- and race-conscious culture.[46]

---

40. Braxton, "Galatians," 342.
41. Byrne, *Romans*, 291.
42. This passage is compact and complex and I think there is more to discuss here than what Yuval finds: "Hence, it is the divine promise, not ethnic-biological pedigree, that determines the status of the chosen one." The intersection of ethnicity, class, and motherhood may offer a better explanation. Yuval, *Two Nations in Your Womb*, 13.
43. Abugideiri, "Hagar," 85.
44. Ibid., 87.
45. Hassan, "Islamic Hagar and Her Family," 149–67.
46. Ibid., 155.

Seen from an intersectional perspective, this way of describing the memory of Hagar in Islam is of great interest, as Jennifer Glancy also notices when discussing slavery and early Christianity.[47] This almost looks like an optimistic interpretation of Gal 3:28, as discussed in chapter 9. Perhaps the Islamic Hagar may be a good place to start when looking for discourses that destabilize marginality?

HAGAR IN INTERRELIGIOUS DIALOGUE

While the model of "Abraham's children" is taken from a family metaphor, Hagar may represent a more conflicting or controversial starting point. For a long time the metaphor of Abraham's children has been vital for interreligious dialogue, but what role may the figure of Hagar play in such conversations?

Anne Hege Grung has recently shown that circling around Hagar may bring new themes to the interreligious dialogue, such as human trafficking and ritualization.[48] She has facilitated and analyzed discussions between Muslim and Christian women in Norway based on readings of texts on Hagar in the two traditions.[49] Hagar was a central character for these Muslim women, but Hagar also engaged the various Christian women, who had hardly heard of her before.

I think this pioneer work shows that the figure of Hagar has great potential for future dialogues. Also the recent attempts by Israeli intellectuals to employ Hagar—"the other women" for Jews, who consider Sarah their foremother—as a critical tool in political discourse seem very promising.[50]

CONCLUSION

Hagar is a figure at the margins in early Christian memory, suffering under intersecting power systems that regulate gender, sexually, race, and class. It is telling that those who have the most vivid memory of Hagar among Christians today, African American womanists, build on the story from Genesis and not from early Christian sources.

---

47. Glancy, "Early Christianity, Slavery, and Women's Bodies," 156–57.
48. Grung and Kartzow, "Samtaler om Hagar," 213.
49. See Grung, "Gender Justice in Muslim-Christian Readings."
50. See the Israeli journal "Hagar."

In the story of Genesis, as Reinhartz and Walfish observe, "fertility destabilizes the fixed hierarchy between Hagar and Sarah."[51] Hagar's reproductive capital gives her the access to motherhood that her owner lacks, but this motherhood is indeed marked by Hagar's gender, class, and race. When asking the other question and looking for female slaves in motherhood discourses in the Pastoral Epistles or in the household codes, Hagar may be a model for such profiles. Although she is marginal due to issues of class, gender, and race, she possesses some resources and capital that have the potential to help her overcome marginality. Hagar is

> the faithful maiden exploited, the black woman used by the male and abused by the female of the ruling class, the surrogate mother, the resident alien without legal resources, the pregnant young woman alone, the expelled wife, the homeless woman, the welfare mother.[52]

Perhaps because she is such a complex character in the first story, she is transformed into a wide variety of different roles and functions as the memory of her has been negotiated. I find the mobile memory of Hagar very challenging but also hopeful, and I think Hagar is a very promising point of departure for addressing current global challenges:

1. She seems to be a productive character to generate discussions of intersectional oppression.
2. She is a shared character for the three monotheistic religions.
3. She functions as a model for demonstrating that the margins can be destabilized.

The slave girl of Abraham and Sarah is named in Genesis. This naming has a huge impact on how she is remembered and cannot be overestimated. By her name we recognize her in the Hadith, although her marginal status is not highlighted in the Islamic tradition.

Somehow the memory of Hagar is a possible model for overcoming marginality: she did not end her life as a foreign slave who was forced to be a surrogate mother for her owners, but was transformed to be a founder of a ritual, important for the establishment of a new religion. This is most fascinating and promising. I believe the memory of Hagar indeed has a future role as continuing the process of destabilizing the margins.

51. Reinhartz and Walfish, "Conflict and Coexistance in Jewish Interpretation," 107.
52. Trible, *Texts of Terror*, 28.

Conclusion

INTRODUCTION

In this book I have followed the generally accepted idea that we use memory of the religious and cultural past to construct our present reality. In regard to early Christian texts I have argued that we need to be critical of how this past is re-constructed in order to uncover the intersecting power relations embedded in the memory process. If these texts are broadly acknowledged as part of what is worth remembering, we have a major task in highlighting the multilayered nature of these texts, the complex processes in antiquity that produced marginality, and the ambiguity of several Biblical characters.

In what ways can the Biblical texts offer help to reflect upon a fast-changing world? If we are looking for a dialogue partner in early Christian memory, one who can play a role in a complex and divided world that faces extreme weather, natural catastrophes, terror, crises, wars, conflicts, and violence, we cannot invoke the stable, unchanging, conservative force that canonical texts often represent. The old wisdom must be made anew, and this task requires critical and creative tools.

I think the Bible needs a body, a voice, social relationships, and a name before she can help us. I envision the Bible as an old, wise woman—let us call her Claudia. She is a former slave, who has lived long and survived several childbirths and experienced much suffering. She remains clear in her head and encounters the news with curiosity and engagement every day. This old lady's memory is excellent and she is full of details, although it should be admitted that she has forgotten things from the past. She is perhaps marginal and only infrequently visited by her closest family, but she walks around in her neighborhood and is enthusiastic about meeting old and new friends.

Some would argue that this old woman is not the solution, but part of the problem: Perhaps the Bible is not what the world needs to be a more human place? Old power structures, gender hierarchies, and global injustice are openly or more subtly legitimized by Biblical ideas, for example in the case of modern-day arrangements that resemble slavery. On the other hand, I am not rejecting the Bible as an important text to both religious believers and to the wider culture. It has been, is, and will remain an important constitutive text for various groups. Some passages of the Bible have had the power to change and liberate people in history, and resistance to the slave trade and slave conditions has used the Bible as a liberating force.

Part of my aim with this book has been to negotiate these perspectives. I am skeptical of the overly enthusiastic attitude that people have to read the Bible in order to understand our culture or get important impulses to find their own identity. The Bible is a complex text and it presents ideas about God and humans that at times are problematic, violent, oppressive, and discriminative, as this book has demonstrated. I just think that early Christian texts should be read with more critical distance, by all categories of readers. I have tried to show that a possible way to balance enthusiasm and suspicion towards the Bible is to open up for marginal and strange characters and texts passages that may represent more variety and broaden the horizon. By asking the other question, intersecting fragments often turn out to be essential in order to understand a given text.

BODIES, VOICES, RELATIONSHIPS, AND NAMED SLAVES: INTERSECTIONAL CHALLENGES

By use of memory theory and intersectionality I have studied the margins of early Christian texts. The four parts of this book have highlighted discourses of embodiment, speech and talk, relationship pairs, and named female slaves.

It can indeed be argued that early Christian bodies are contested and negotiated in the various texts read in Part One. In order to understand the function of these bodies at the margins I have argued that not only gender needs to be taken into consideration, but also other categories such as class, race/religion, and sexuality. Violence, castration, virginity, circumcision, and motherhood connected to marginal characters in early Christian discourse show that the body cannot be conceptualized without dealing with intersections of a variety of social categories.

In the Lukan parable violence among slaves is gendered and sexualized, but punished, but when the slave owner cuts his slave into pieces, it seems to be according to standardized procedure. Violence is regulated along class and gender lines. The story in Acts about the Ethiopian eunuch not only deals with complex intersections of race/religion and sex/gender, but also class. If a eunuch was a slave before he was castrated, his gender status was already disturbed, since male slaves lacked masculinity. It was rare for virginity to be promoted as an ideal for both men and women, but in *Joseph and Aseneth* complex intersections of gender and race/religion construct virginity as different concepts for a man and a woman. In the Pastoral Epistles motherhood is obviously an ideal for freeborn women, but could female slaves who produced children also be counted among those who were saved through childbirth? Further, circumcision was a religious sign on the male body, but when these epistles talk about "those of the circumcised," we have to ask whether male slaves and women of all categories could be included in this category.

Part Two discussed who was heard, remembered, silenced, or overheard in ancient texts. The conventional idea that men were heard while women were silenced has been destabilized by asking the other question. Some talking characters of the margins not only suffer due to their gender, but of intersecting hierarchies of oppression.

In gospel studies a growing awareness of the fact that early Christianity was an aural-oral community has reinvigorated the attention to speech and talk. The stories of the women at the empty tomb pertain not only to gender, since orality also relates to issues of class and the role of language as an expression of cultural diversity. Issues of speech and talk seem central to the ideal masculine discourse constructed in the Pastoral Epistles, but not only gender seems to regulate whose voices could be heard: slaves, strangers, various categories of female characters, and ethnic groups such as Cretans or Jews are also blamed. The gendered discourse of gossip in the Pastoral Epistles blames in particular one specific but ambiguous group of women: widows. They could have certain power positions but were vulnerable due to their sexual reputation, reproduction/motherhood, and age. This category of women is repeatedly associated with gossip in early Christian discourse, and most likely a similar connection can be found in the Lukan parable of the widow and the judge. Paul in Acts is portrayed as healing a fortune-telling slave girl who is possessed by a strange spirit that represents an unclean religious power. Being owned by others, she is at the bottom of most applicable hierarchies. In contrast to Paul, she is for the most part a forgotten figure of the archive. By highlighting that she actually speaks the truth, she can be categorized as a female prophet: Paul's "healing" of her functions to silence a talking woman in the community of early Christians.

Bodies, speech, and talk function to organize and regulate communities. In the various relationship pairs represented in early Christian texts, identity and hierarchy are negotiated, as addressed in Part Three. Since a person did not only have one identity marker—a slave could be female, could be a mother, could have a partner, and so forth—the relationship pairs of Gal 3:28 and the Colossian household codes generate certain dilemmas and conflicts for those who were supposed to apply them and live by them.

Female slaves were thrice vulnerable in regard to class, gender, and sexuality: they are among the most marginal characters in early Christian memory. When some of them are mentioned by name, it somehow destabilizes this negative picture. Two of these female slaves were the focus in Part Four. A name functions to give an individual a certain position and it has a major impact on the memory process. Among several anonymous characters we find some named female slaves: the slave girl Blandina is transformed into an ideal, masculine Christian, while Hagar is remembered in ambiguous ways by early Jewish and Christian thinkers and becomes a pioneer woman in Islam.

FUTURE QUESTIONS TO BE ASKED

As I argued in the introduction to this book, I see this study more like an experiment or a suggestion than the final conclusion. So, to honor that statement, I think the best conclusion will be to outline possible new areas or directions of research that this work has opened up. "The other question" seems to generate an endless road of new questions:

1. Destabilizing the female: In the various texts treated, I have found a rather diverse and complex picture of a female ideal. As an unmarried and foreign woman, Aseneth needs to be a pure virgin to convert, while as a married women her role as wife and mother is downplayed. In the Pastoral Epistles the ideal is completely the opposite: a proper woman must be mother, and preferably wife or decent widow. When it comes to the Egyptian slave girl Hagar,

it is obvious that she was neither virgin nor proper wife, but her role as mother was emphasized, however negatively in Galatians 4. Blandina, in contrast, is a female slave who is not connected to either virginity, marriage, or motherhood, but still manages to perform ideal masculine and feminine values. I think this variety in ideals for female characters of all categories somehow destabilizes the fixed and one-dimensional perceptions about the female in early Christian circles. Several aspects of this complexity invites further research.

2. Realizing the connection between ethnicity/race/religion and class/gender: In several texts, strangeness is described in terms that testify to the blurred line between systems that organize what we would call race, culture, or religion. Do terms such as Ethiopian, Jewish, circumcised, or possessed give information related to race, nationality, ethnicity, culture, or religion? Excellent work has already been done on these complex issues, but I think we need to emphasize how these ambiguous categories also relate to gender and class. Did slaves have ethnicity, and did they belong to any religion? Could women be counted among those of the circumcision? Was a free women's ethnicity/religion stable, and if not, what was needed for conversion? To reflect on these various intersections seem crucial in current discussions on religious dialogue and extremism.

3. Highlighting men at the margins: more needs to be done on male virginity, circumcision, male slaves' reproductive possibilities, eunuchs, castration, and violence against men in early Christian texts from perspectives that integrate issues of class, ethnicity, and masculinity. The intersectional questions asked here in regard to beaten male slaves, the Ethiopian eunuch, the patriarch (and former slave) Joseph, Jewish men, and fatherhood reveal that we have little knowledge from antiquity of men at the margins. If we realize that also other categories than gender regulated ancient society, nuances and differentiation are needed not only among women but also among men. We also see that it was not enough to be a man to be on top, and that several men suffered in a system that valued certain types of masculinity.

Several other points could be added to these three in relation to using intersectionality to read ancient texts. I think all kinds of interpreters and readers have work to do in finding characters and texts in the archive to destabilize the margins. Biblical practices such as religious usage, cultural usage, scholarship, and translation all have challenging tasks related to these issues.

IMPACT OF MEMORY: THE COMPLEXITY OF REMEMBERING EARLY CHRISTIAN TEXTS

New Testament users contribute to construct the present by relating to the past. To theorize the gaps or search for early Christian dreams, visions, and possibilities that correspond to present-day hopes may be an important contribution of knowledge production. If we want to take the interdisciplinary character of Biblical studies seriously, we cannot embrace merely historical or literary theories, but also open up for a variety of other impulses and perspectives. By employing theories of complexity, diversity, and multiple identities based on studies of individuals and social interaction in present-day cultures, my aim has been to bring ancient texts and "our time" into a shared space, and to investigate the complex dynamics of the memory process.

But this production of knowledge also affects current issues of marginality. Present-day usage of the Bible deals in particular with how the ancient texts are translated and made accessible in modern languages. Translation practices and the publication industry are indeed important parts of the memory process that make the Biblical texts relevant for present identity work and culture making. I agree with scholars who want the strangeness, complexity and brutality of the ancient texts to be made visible. The examples I have cited include: use "slaves" and not "servants" whenever the texts talk about enslaved persons; male or female slaves should not be hidden behind categories that construct them as free men and women (Luke 12:45); use the term "eunuch" for the Ethiopian and not let him look like any other court official (Acts 8:26–40), and make it explicit that the Pastoral Paul compares false teaching with old wives' tales, not any gender-neutral or ageless chatter (1 Tim 4:7). In these few examples several intersections of gender, sexuality, class, ethnicity, and age should be recognized in the translations, inviting various Bible readers and users to explore the texts' potential to correspond to our fast-changing world and contexts of cultural complexity.

In addition, if we want to learn anything from the ancient texts we have to direct the critique of inhumane treatment of marginalized people to our own world order. The idea that early Christianity represented a break with inequality and mistreatment of women, slaves, children, or strangers can be upheld as a vision, although we acknowledge that the social realities for those who encountered this new marginal sect probably did not change much.

What would Claudia do (WWCD)? I think she would have believed in this vision and looked for similar structures of injustice today. She would have started by searching the archive and encountering the margins.

If the Bible is seen as part of various canons, it cannot be only the stories with existential value or high literary quality that are highlighted. Gendered slave systems and God as a mass murderer are challenges that all Bible users need to take seriously. The power dynamics of the memory processes need to be questioned, if not we risk using the Bible to uphold power structures and renew systems of injustice. In the archive we also find struggling survivors and hybrid personalities, who may function to annoy us, inspire us, or blame us.

To remember the past is essential for identity construction, but such memory may also function to challenge or critique the present and give hope for a better future. I believe that early Christian memory may have the potential to destabilize the margins in our contexts of cultural complexity.

Bibliography

Abrahamsen, Valerie. "Women at Philippi: The Pagan and Christian Evidence." *JFSR* 3, (1987) 17–30.

Abugideiri, Hibba. "Hagar: A Historical Model for 'Gender Jihad.'" In *Daughters of Abraham: Feminist Thought in Judaism, Christianity, and Islam*, edited by Yvonne Yazbeck Haddad and John L. Esposito, 81–107. Gainesville: University Press of Florida, 2001.

Adamo, David Tuesday, and Erivwierho Francis Eghwubare. "The African Wife of Abraham: An African Reading of Genesis 16:1–16 and 21:8–21." In *Genesis*, edited by Athalya Brenner et al., 275–92. Minneapolis, MN: Fortress, 2010.

Assmann, Aleida. "The Religious Roots of Cultural Memory." *NTT* 4:109 (2008) 271–92.

Assmann, Jan. *Religion and Cultural Memory: Ten Studies*. Translated by Rodney Livingstone. Cultural Memory in the Present. Stanford: Stanford University Press, 2006 (2000).

Bailey, Randall C. et al., eds. *They Were All Together in One Place? Towards Minority Biblical Criticism*. Atlanta: SBL, 2009.

Baker, Cynthia M. "'From Every Nation under Heaven': Jewish Ethnicities in the Greco-Roman World." In *Prejudice and Christian Beginnings: Investigating Race, Gender, and Ethnicity in Early Christian Studies*, edited by Laura Nasrallah and Elisabeth Schüssler Fiorenza, 79–99. Minneapolis, MN: Fortress, 2009.

Bal, Mieke. *Loving Yusuf: Conceptual Travels from Present to Past*. Chicago: The University of Chicago Press, 2008.

———. *Travelling Concepts in the Humanities: A Rough Guide*. Toronto: University of Toronto Press, 2002.

Barclay, John M. G. "Paul, Philemon and the Dilemma of Christian Slave-Ownership." *NTS* 37 (1991) 151–86.

Bartchy, Scott S. "Slavery/New Testament." In *The Anchor Bible Dictionary*, edited by David Noel Freedman, 65–73. New York: Doubleday, 1992.

Bassler, Jouette M. *1 Timothy, 2 Timothy, Titus*, Abingdon New Testament Commentaries. Nashville, TN: Abingdon, 1996.

Bauckham, Richard. *Gospel Women: Studies of the Named Women in the Gospels*. Grand Rapids: Eerdmans, 2002.

Beattie, Gillian. *Women and Marriage in Paul and His Early Interpreters*, JSNTsup. 296. London: T. & T. Clark, 2005.

Beavis, Mary Ann. "Christian Origins, Egalitarianism, and Utopia." *JFSR* 23:2 (2007) 27–49.

Benyik, György. "The Formation and Interpretation of the Bible and of the Qur'an." *Studia Universitatis Babes-Bolyai* 53:2 (2008) 36–58.

Bernhard, Andrew E. *Other Early Christian Gospels: A Critical Edition of the Surviving Greek Manuscripts*. London: T. & T. Clark, 2006.

Betz, Hans Dieter. *Galatians: A Commentary on Paul's Letter to the Churches in Galatia*, Hermeneia: A Critical and Historical Commentary on the Bible. Philadelphia: Fortress, 1979.

Blount, Brian K., gen. ed, Cain Hope Felder et al., eds. *True to Our Native Land: An African American New Testament Commentary*. Minneapolis, MN: Fortress, 2007.

Boomershine, Thomas E. *Story Journey: An Invitation to the Gopspel as Storytelling*. Nashville: Abingdon, 1988.

Borgen, Peder. "Some Hebrew and Pagan Features in Philo's and Paul's Interpretation of Hagar and Ishmael." In *The New Testament and Hellenistic Judaism*, edited by Peder Borgen et al., 151–64. Aarhus: Aarhus University Press, 1995.

Boyarin, Daniel. "Thinking with Virgins: Engendering Judaeo-Christian Difference." In *A Feminist Companion to the New Testament Apocrypha*, edited by Amy-Jill Levine and Maria Mayo Robbins, 216–44. London: T. & T. Clark, 2006.

Braxton, Brad R. "Galatians." In *True to Our Native Land: An African American New Testament Commentary*, edited by Brian K. Blount, 333–45. Minneapolis, MN: Fortress, 2007.

Bremmer, Jan N. "Performing Myths: Women's Homes and Men's *Leschai*." In *Myth and Symbol II*, edited by Synnøve des Bouvrie, 123–40. Athens: The Norwegian Institute at Athens, 2005.

Briggs, Sheila. "Slavery and Gender." In *On the Cutting Edge: The Study of Women in Biblical Worlds: Essays in Honor of Elisabeth Schüssler Fiorenza*, edited by Jane Schaberg et al., 171–92. New York: Continuum, 2004.

Broadbent, Ralph. "The First and Second Letters to Timothy and the Letter to Titus." In *A Postcolonial Commentary on the New Testament Writings*, edited by Fernando F. Segovia and R. S. Sugirtharajah, 323–28. London: T. & T. Clark, 2007.

Brooten, Bernadette J. "Feminist Sexual Ethics Project." Online: http://www.brandeis.edu/projects/fse/.

Brooten, Bernadette J. (with assistance of Jacqueline L. Hazelton), ed. *Beyond Slavery: Overcoming Its Religious and Sexual Legacies*. New York: Palgrave Macmillan, 2010.

Brundage, W. Fitzhugh. "Introduction: No Deed but Memory." In *Where These Memories Grow: History, Memory, and Southern Identity*, edited by W. Fitzhugh Brundage, 1–28. Chapel Hill: The University of North Carolina Press, 2000.

Buell, Denise Kimber. "God's Own People: Specters of Race, Ethnicity, and Gender in Early Christian Studies." In *Prejudice and Christian Beginnings: Investigating Race, Gender, and Ethnicity in Early Christian Studies*, edited by Laura Nasrallah and Elisabeth Schüssler Fiorenza, 159–90. Minneapolis, MN: Fortress, 2009.

———. *Why This New Race: Ethnic Reasoning in Early Christianity*, Gender, Theory, and Religion. New York: Columbia University Press, 2005.

Bunge, Marcia J., gen. ed., Beverly R. Gaventa, and Terence E. Fretheim, eds. *The Child in the Bible*. Grand Rapids: Eerdmans, 2008.

Burchard, Christoph. "The Importance of Joseph and Aseneth for the Study of the New Testament: A General Survey and Fresh Look at the Lord's Supper." *NTS* 33 (1987) 102–34.

———. "Joseph and Aseneth: A New Translation and Introduction." In *The Old Testament Pseudepigrapha: Expansions of the "Old Testament" and Legends, Wisdom and Philosophical Literature, Prayers, Psalms, and Odes, Fragments of Lost Judeo-Hellenistic Works*, edited by James H. Charlesworth, 177–247. London: Darton, Longman & Todd, 1985.

Burke, David G. *The Poetry of Baruch: Reconstruction and Analysis of the Original Hebrew Text of Baruch 3:9—5:9*, Septuagint and Cognate Studies. Missoula, MT: Scholars, 1982.

Burman, Erica. "From Difference to Intersectionality: Challenges and Resources." *European Journal of Psychoterapy and Counselling* 6:4 (2003) 293–308.

Burrus, Virginia. "The Gospel of Luke and the Acts of the Apostles." In *A Postcolonial Commentary on the New Testament Writings*, edited by Fernando F. Segovia and R. S. Sugirtharajah, 133–55. London: T. & T. Clark, 2007.

———. *Saving Shame: Martyrs, Saints, and Other Abject Subjects*. Philadelphia: University of Pennsylvania Press, 2008.

Butler, Shane. "Notes on a *Membrum Disiectum*." In *Women and Slaves in Greco-Roman Culture: Differential Equations*, edited by Sandra R. Joshel and Sheila Murnaghan, 236–55. London: Routledge, 1998.

Byrne, Brendan. *Romans*, Sacra Pagina Series. Collegeville, MN: Liturgical, 1996.

Byron, Gay L. "Ancient Ethiopia and the New Testament: Ethnic (Con)Texts and Racialized (Sub)Texts." In *They Were All Together in One Place? Towards Minority Biblical Criticism*, edited by Randall C. Bailey et al., 161–90. Atlanta: SBL, 2009.

———. *Symbolic Blackness and Ethnic Difference in Early Christian Literature*. London: Routledge, 2002.

Byron, John. *Recent Research on Paul and Slavery*. Sheffield: Phoenix, 2008.

Byrskog, Samuel. *Story as History—History as Story: The Gospel Tradition in the Context of Ancient Oral History*, Wissenschaftliche Untersuchungen Zum Neuen Testament; 123. Tübingen: Mohr Siebeck, 2000.

Camp, Clauda V. "Oralities, Literacies, and Colonialisms in Antiquity and Contemporary Scholarship." In *Orality, Literacy, and Colonialism in Antiquity*, edited by Jonathan A. Draper, 193–217. Boston: Brill, 2004.

Casey, Edward S. *Remembering: A Phenomenological Study*. 2nd ed. Bloomington: Indiana University Press, 2000.

Castelli, Elizabeth A. "Allegories of Hagar: Reading Galatians 4:21–31 with Postmodern Feminist Eyes." In *The New Literary Criticism and the New Testament*, edited by Elizabeth Struthers Malbon and Edgar V. McKnight, 228–50. Sheffield: Sheffield Academic, 1994.

———. *Martyrdom and Memory: Early Christian Culture Making*, Gender, Theory, and Religion. New York: Columbia University Press, 2004.

———. "Romans." In *Searching the Scriptures. A Feminist Commentary*, edited by Elisabeth Schüssler Fiorenza, 272–300. New York: Crossroad, 1994.

Chesnutt, Randall D. "Joseph and Aseneth." In *The Anchor Bible Dictionary*, edited by David Noel Freedman, 969–71. New York: Doubleday.

Christiansen, Ann. "Får all makt i himmel og på jord." *Aftenposten*, January 9, 2011, http://www.aftenposten.no/kul_und/article3979873.ece.

Clark, Elizabeth A. *History, Theory, Text: Historians and the Linguistic Turn*. Cambridge: Harvard University Press, 2004.

———. "Ideology, History, and the Construction of 'Woman' in Late Ancient Christianity." *JECS* 2:2 (1994) 155–84.

———. "Interpretive Fate Amid the Church Fathers." In *Hagar, Sarah, and Their Children: Jewish, Christian, and Muslim Perspectives*, edited by Phyllis Trible and Letty M. Russell, 127–47. Louisville, KY: Westminster John Knox, 2006.

Clark, Gillian. "Bodies and Blood: Late Antique Debate on Martyrdom, Virginity and Resurrection." In *Changing Bodies, Changing Meanings: Studies on the Human Body in Antiquity*, edited by Dominic Montserrat, 99–115. London: Routledge, 1998.

Collins, John J. *Between Athens and Jerusalem: Jewish Identity in the Hellenistic Diaspora*. 2nd ed, The Biblical Resource Series. Grand Rapids: Eerdmans, 2000.

———. "*Joseph and Aseneth*: Jewish or Christian?" *JSP* 14:2 (2005) 97–112.

Collins, Patricia Hill. "It's All in the Family: Intersections of Gender, Race, and Nation." *Hypatia* 13:3 (1998) 62–82.

Connerton, Paul. *How Societies Remember*, Themes in the Social Sciences. Cambridge: Cambridge University Press, 1989.

Conway, Colleen M. *Behold the Man: Jesus and Greco-Roman Masculinity*. Oxford: Oxford University Press, 2008.

Corley, Kathleen E. *Women and the Historical Jesus: Feminist Myths of Christian Origins*. Santa Rosa, CA: Polebridge, 2002.

Cotter, Wendy C. S. J. "The Parable of the Feisty Widow and the Threatened Judge (Luke 18:1–8)." *NTS* 51 (2005) 328–43.

Craffert, Pieter F. *The Life of a Galilean Shaman: Jesus of Nazareth in Anthropological-Historical Perspective*. Matrix: The Bible in Mediterranean Context, Vol. 3. Eugene, OR: Cascade Books, 2008.

Crenshaw, Kimberlé. "Demarginalizing the Intersection of Race and Sex: A Black Feminist Critique of Antidiscrimination Doctrine, Feminist Theory, and Antiracist Politics." *University of Chicago Legal Forum*, Volume 1989, 139–67.

D'Angelo, Mary R. "Women in Luke-Acts: A Redactional View." *JBL* 109:3 (1990) 441–61.

Danbolt, Mathias et al., eds. *Lost and Found: Queering the Archive*. Copenhagen: Kunsthallen Nikolaj, 2009.

Davis, Kathy. "Intersectionality as Buzzword: A Sociology of Science Perspective on What Makes a Feminist Theory Successful." *Feminist Theory* 9 (2008) 67–83.

De los Reyes, Paulina, and Diana Mulinari. *Intersektionalitet: Kritiska reflektioner över (o)jämlikhetens landskap*. Stockholm: Liber, 2005.

Derrett, J. Duncan M. "Law in the New Testament: The Parable of the Unjust Judge." *NTS* 18 (1971–1972) 178–91.

Dewey, Joanna. "1 Timothy." In *Women's Bible Commentary*, edited by Carol A. Newsom and Sharon H. Ringe, 444–49. Louisville, KY: Westminster John Knox, 1998.

———. "From Oral Stories to Written Text." In *Women's Sacred Scriptures*, edited by Pui-lan Kwok and Elisabeth Schüssler Fiorenza, 20–28. London: SCM, 1998.

———. "From Storytelling to Written Text: The Loss of Early Christian Women's Voices." *Biblical Theology Bulletin* 26 (1996) 71–78.

———. "Women on the Way: A Reconstruction of Late First-Century Women's Storytelling." In *The Bible in Ancient and Modern Media: Story and Performance*, edited by Holly E. Hearon and Philip Ruge-Jones, 36–48. Eugene, OR: Cascade Books, 2009.

Dixon, Suzanne. *The Roman Family*, Ancient Society and History. Baltimore: John Hopkins University Press, 1992.

Draper, Jonathan A. "Orality, Litracy, and Colonialism in Antiquity." In *Orality, Litracy, and Colonialism in Antiquity*, edited by Jonathan A. Draper, 1–6, 2004.

Dube, Musa W. *Postcolonial Feminist Interpretation of the Bible*. St. Louis, MO: Chalice, 2000.

DuBois, Page. *Slaves and Other Objects*. Chicago: University of Chicago Press, 2003.

Edwards, Catharine. *The Politics of Immorality in Ancient Rome.* Cambridge: Cambridge University Press, 1993.
Eriksen, Thomas Hylland. "What Is Cultural Complexity?" In *Jesus Beyond Nationalism: Constructing the Historical Jesus in a Period of Cultural Complexity*, edited by Halvor Moxnes et al., 9–24. London: Equinox, 2009.
Faltin, Lucia, and Melanie J. Wright. *The Religious Roots of Contemporary European Identity.* London: Continuum, 2007.
Fatum, Lone. "1 Thessalonians." In *Searching the Scriptures*, edited by Elisabeth Schüssler Fiorenza, 250–62. New York: Crossroad, 1993.
———. "Christ Domesticated: The Household Theology of the Pastorals as Political Strategy." In *The Formation of the Early Church*, edited by Jostein Ådna, 175–207. Tübingen: Mohr Siebeck, 2005.
———. "Images of God and Glory of Man: Women in the Pauline Congregations." In *Image of God and Gender Models in Judaeo-Christian Tradition*, edited by Kari Elisabeth Børresen, 56–137. Oslo: Solum, 1991.
Fitzmyer, Joseph A. *The Gospel According to Luke: Introduction, Translations and Notes*, The Anchor Bible. Garden City, NJ: Doubleday, 1981.
Foster, Erik K. "Research on Gossip: Taxonomy, Methods, and Future Directions." *Review of General Psychology* 8:2 (2004) 78–99.
Fowler, Robert M. "Why Everything We Know About the Bible Is Wrong: Lessons from the Media History of the Bible." In *The Bible in Ancient and Modern Media: Story and Performance*, edited by Holly E. Hearon and Philip Ruge-Jones, 3–18. Eugene, OR: Cascade Books, 2009.
Foxhall, Lin. "Introduction." In *When Men Were Men: Masculinity, Power and Identity in Classical Antiquity*, edited by Lin Foxhall and John Salmon, 1–9. London: Routledge, 1998.
Gamble, Sarah, ed. *The Routledge Companion to Feminism and Postfeminism*, Routledge Companions. London: Routledge, 2001.
Gerhardsson, Birger. "The Secret of the Transmission of the Unwritten Jesus Tradition." *NTS* 51 (2005) 1–18.
Gilhus, Ingvild Sælid et al. *Farsmakt og moderskap i antikken.* Oslo: Spartacus, 2009.
Glancy, Jennifer A. *Corporal Knowledge: Early Christian Bodies.* New York: Oxford University Press, 2010.
———. "Early Christianity, Slavery, and Women's Bodies." In *Beyond Slavery: Overcomming Its Religious and Sexual Legacies*, edited by Bernadette J. Brooten, 143–58. New York: Palgrave Macmillan, 2010.
———. "Jesus, the Syrophoenician Woman, and Other First-Century Bodies." *Biblical Interpretation* 18:4–5 (2010) 342–63.
———. "Protocols of Masculinity in the Pastoral Epistles." In *New Testament Masculinities*, edited by Stephen D. Moore and Janice Capel Anderson, 235–64. Atlanta: SBL, 2003.
———. "Review Essay: Slavery, Historiography, and Theology / Response to Harrill." *Biblical Interpretation* 15:2 (2007) 200–11 / 22–24.
———. *Slavery in Early Christianity.* Oxford: Oxford University Press, 2002.
Gleason, Maud W. *Making Men: Sophists and Self-Presentation in Ancient Rome.* Princeton: Princeton University Press, 1995.
Gressgård, Randi. "Mind the Gap: Intersectionality, Complexity and 'the Event.'" *Theory and Science* (2008).

Grung, Anne Hege. "Gender Justice in Muslim-Christian Readings: Christian and Muslim Women in Norway Making Meaning of Texts from the Bible, the Koran, and the Hadith." University of Oslo (Doctoral Thesis), 2010.

———. "Makt og kontekst i Susanna-fortellingen." *Kirke og Kultur* 4 (2011) 288–301.

Grung, Anne Hege, and Marianne Bjelland Kartzow. "Samtaler om Hagar: Tekster, fortellinger og religionsmøter." *Kirke og Kultur: Religion og samfunn* 3 (2011), 204–17.

Haddad, Yvonne Yazbeck, and John Eposito, eds. *Daughters of Abraham: Feminst Thought in Judaism, Christianity and Islam*. Gainesville: University Press of Florida, 2001.

Hagar: Studies in Culture, Polity and Identities. Online: http://hsf.bgu.ac.il/hagar/.

Harding, Sandra G. *Is Science Multicultural? Postcolonialisms, Feminisms, and Epistemologies*. Race, Gender, and Science. Bloomington: Indiana University Press, 1998.

Harrill, J. Albert. "The Dramatic Function of the Running Slave Rhoda (Acts 12:13–16): A Piece of Greco-Roman Comedy." *NTS* 46 (2000) 150–57.

———. "The Vice of Slave Dealers in Greco-Roman Society: The Use of a *Topos* in 1 Timothy 1:10." *JBL* 118:1 (1999) 97-122.

———. *The Manumission of Slaves in Early Christianity*. Hermeneutische Untersuchungen zur Theologie, Vol. 32. Tübingen: Mohr, 1995.

Hassan, Riffat. "Islamic Hagar and Her Family." In *Hagar, Sarah, and Their Children: Jewish, Christian, and Muslim Perspectives*, edited by Phyllis Trible and Letty M. Russell, 149–67. Louisville, KY: Westminster John Knox, 2006.

Hearon, Holly E. "The Implications of 'Orality' for Studies of the Biblical Text." *Oral Tradition* 19:1 (2004) 96–107.

———. "The Interplay between Written and Spoken Word in the Second Testament as Background to the Emergence of Written Gospels." *Oral Tradition* 25:1 (2010) 57–74.

———. *The Mary Magdalene Tradition: Witness and Counter-Witness in Early Christian Communities*. Collegeville, MN: Liturgical, 2004.

———. "The Storytelling World of the First Century and the Gospels." In *The Bible in Ancient and Modern Media: Story and Performance*, edited by Holly E. Hearon and Philip Ruge-Jones, 21–35. Eugene, OR: Cascade Books, 2009.

Hendel, Ronald. *Remembering Abraham: Culture, Memory, and History in the Hebrew Bible*. New York: Oxford University Press, 2005.

Herzog, William R. *Parables as Subversive Speech: Jesus as Pedagogue of the Oppressed*. Louisville, KY: Westminster/John Knox, 1994.

Hezser, Catherine. *Jewish Slavery in Antiquity*. New York: Oxford University Press, 2005.

Hirsch, Marianne, and Valerie Smith. "Feminism and Cultural Memory: An Introduction." *Signs: Journal of Women in Culture and Society* 28:1 (Gender and Cultural Memory) (2002) 1–19.

Hornsby, Teresa J. "The Annoying Woman: Biblical Scholarship after Judith Butler." In *Bodily Citations: Religion and Judith Butler*, edited by Ellen T. Armour and Susan M. St. Ville, 71–89. New York: Columbia University Press, 2006.

Hornschuh, Manfred. *Studien zur Epistula Apostolorum*, Patristische Texte und Studien; 5. Berlin 1965.

Horsley, Richard A. "Oral Traditions in New Testament Studies." *Oral Traditions* 18:1 (2003) 34–36.

Humphrey, Edith McEwan. *Joseph and Aseneth*, Guides to Apocrypha and Pseudepigrapha. Sheffield: Sheffield Academic, 2000.

Hunter, Virginia. "Gossip and the Politics of Reputation in Classical Athens." *Phoenix Classical Association of Canada* 44:4 (1990) 299–325.
Haag, Herbert et al., eds. *Grosse Frauen der Bibel in Bild und Text*. Freiburg, Basel, Vienna: Herder, 1993.
Ilan, Tal. *Integrating Women into Second Temple History*. Peabody, MA: Hendrickson, 1999.
———. *Jewish Women in Greco-Roman Palestine: An Inquiry into Image and Status*. Tübingen: Mohr, 1995.
———. *Lexicon of Jewish Names in Late Antiquity*. Tübingen: Mohr, 2002.
Inowlocki, Sabrina. *Le roman d'Aséneth. Des idoles mortes et muettes au Dieu vivant*, Monothéismes et philosophie. Turnhout, Belgium: Brepols, 2002.
Ipsen, Avaren. *Sex Working and the Bible*. London: Equinox, 2009.
"Jesus in Cultural Complexity." Project at the Univeristy of Oslo, Online: www.tf.uio.no/jc.
Johnson-Debaufre, Melanie. *Jesus among Her Children: Q, Eschatology, and the Construction of Christian Origins*. Cambridge: Harvard University Press, 2005.
Johnson, Luke Timothy. *The First and Second Letters to Timothy: A New Translation with Introduction and Commentary*. The Anchor Bible, Vol. 35A. New York: Doubleday, 2001.
———. *The Gospel of Luke*. Edited by S. J. Daniel J. Harrington. Sacra Pagina Series, Vol. 3. Collegeville, MN: Liturgical, 1991.
———. *Letters to Paul's Delegates: 1 Timothy, 2 Timothy, Titus*, The New Testament in Context. Valley Forge, PA: Trinity Press International, 1996.
Johnstone, Steven. "Cracking the Code of Silence: Athenian Legal Oratory and the Histories of Slaves and Women." In *Women and Slaves in Greco-Roman Culture: Differential Equations*, edited by Sandra R. Joshel and Sheila Murnaghan, 221–34. London: Routledge, 1998.
Joshel, Sandra R., and Sheila Murnaghan, eds. *Women and Slaves in Greco-Roman Culture: Differential Equations*. London: Routledge, 1998.
Kartzow, Marianne Bjelland. "'Asking the Other Question': An Intersectional Approach to Galatians 3:28 and the Colossian Household Codes." *Biblical Interpretation* 18: 4–5 (2010) 364–89.
———. "The Complexity of Pairing: Reading Acts 16 with Plutarch's *Parallel Lives*." In *Reading Acts in the Second Century*, edited by Rubén Dupertuis and Todd Penner. London: Equinox Publishing (forth).
———. "Female Gossipers and Their Reputation in the Pastoral Epistles." *Neotestamentica* 39:2 (2005) 255–72.
———. *Gossip and Gender: Othering of Speech in the Pastoral Epistles*. BZNW Vol. 164. Berlin: Gruyter, 2009.
———. "Resurrection as Gossip: Representations of Women in Resurrection Stories of the Gospels." *Lectio Difficilior* (2010) 1–28.
Kee, Howard C. "The Socio-Religious Setting and Aims of 'Joseph and Aseneth.'" In *Society of Biblical Literature Seminar Papers Series*, edited by George MacRae, 183–92. Missoula, MN: Scholars, 1976.
Kelber, Werner H. "The Case of the Gospels: Memory's Desire and the Limits of Historical Criticism." *Oral Tradition* 17:1 (2002) 55–86.
———. "The Generative Force of Memory: Early Christian Traditions as Processes of Remembering." *Biblical Theology Bulletin* 36:1 (2006) 15–22.

King, Karen L. *The Gospel of Mary of Magdala and the First Woman Apostle*. Santa Rosa, CA: Polebridge, 2003.

Knapp, Gudrun-Axeli. "Race, Class, Gender: Reclaiming Baggage in Fast Travelling Theories." *European Journal of Women's Studies* 12:3 (2005) 249–65.

Knust, Jennifer Wright. *Abandoned to Lust: Sexual Slander and Ancient Christianity*, Gender, Theory, and Religion. New York: Columbia University Press, 2006.

Kraemer, Ross Shepard. "The Book of Aseneth." In *Searching the Scriptures: Volume Two: A Feminist Commentary*, edited by Elisabeth Schüssler Fiorenza, 859–88. New York: Crossroad, 1995.

———. "Recycling Aseneth." In *Recycling Biblical Figures. Papers Read at a Noster Colloquium in Amsterdam, 12–13 May 1997*, edited by Athalya Brenner and Jan Willem van Henten, 234–65. Leiden: Deo, 1999.

———. *When Aseneth Met Joseph: A Late Antique Tale of the Biblical Patriarch and His Egyptian Wife, Reconsidered*. New York: Oxford University Press, 1998.

Kuefler, Mathew. *The Manly Eunuch: Masculinity, Gender Ambiguity, and Christian Ideology in Late Antiquity*, The Chicago Series on Sexuality, History, and Society. Chicago: University of Chicago Press, 2001.

Kwok, Pui-lan. *Discovering the Bible in the Non-Biblical World*. Maryknoll, NY: Orbis, 1995.

Lawrence, William Frank Jr. "The History of the Interpretation of Acts 8:26–40 by the Church Fathers Prior to the Fall of Rome." New York: Union Theological Seminary, 1984.

Leach, Mary. "Feminist Figurations: Gossip as a Counterdiscourse." In *Working the Ruins: Feminist Poststructural Theory and Methods in Education*, edited by Wanda S. Pillow and Elizabeth St. Pierre, 223–36. New York: Routledge, 2000.

Lewis, Naphtali, and Ann Ellis Hanson. *On Government and Law in Roman Egypt: Collected Papers of Naphatali Lewis*. Atlanta: Scholars, 1995.

Liddell, Henry George, and Robert Scott. *Greek-English Lexicon: Revised Supplement*. Edited by P. G. W. Glare and A. A. Thompson. Oxford: Clarendon, 1996.

Lieu, Judith M. *Neither Jew nor Greek? Constructing Early Christianity*, Studies of the New Testament and Its World. London: T. & T. Clark, 2002.

———. "The 'Attraction of Women' in/to Early Judaism and Christianity: Gender and the Politics of Conversion." *JSNT* 72 (1998) 5–22.

Lind-Solstad, Katrine Intelhus. "La de små barna komme til meg? En analyse av Markusevangeliets fortellinger om barn." Masters thesis, University of Oslo, 2010.

Lohse, Eduard. *The New Testament Environment*. London: SCM, 1976.

MacDonald, Dennis Ronald. *The Legend and the Apostle: The Battle for Paul in Story and Canon*. Philadelphia: Westminster, 1983.

———. "Lydia and Her Sisters as Lukan Fictions." In *A Feminist Companion to the Acts of the Apostles*, edited by Amy-Jill Levine with Marianne Blickenstaff, 105–10. London: T. & T. Clark, 2004.

MacDonald, Margaret Y. "Beyond Identification of the Topos of Household Management: Reading the Household Codes in Light of Recent Methodologies and Theoretical Perspectives in the Study of the New Testament." *NTS* 57 (2010) 65–90.

———. *Colossians and Ephesians*. Edited by Daniel J. Harrington. Sacra Pagina Series, Vol. 17. Collegeville, MN: Liturgical, 2000.

———. *Early Christian Women and Pagan Opinion. The Power of the Hysterical Woman*. Cambridge: Cambridge University Press, 1996.

———. "A Place of Belonging: Perspectives on Children from Colossians and Ephesians." In *The Child in the Bible*, edited by Marcia J. Bunge (gen. ed), Terence E. Fretheim, and Beverly Roberts Gaventa, 278–304. Grand Rapids: Eerdmans, 2008.

———. "Slavery, Sexuality and House Churches: A Reassessment of Colossians 3.18–4.1 in Light of New Research on the Roman Family." *NTS* 53 (2008) 94–113.

Malina, Bruce J., and John J. Pilch. *Social-Science Commentary on the Book of Acts*, Social-Science Commentary. Minneapolis, MN: Fortress, 2008.

Marshall, John W. "'I Left You in Crete': Narrative Deception and Social Hierarchy in the Letter to Titus." *JBL* 4 (2008) 781–803.

Martin, Clarice J. "The Acts of the Apostles." In *Searching the Scriptures*, edited by Elisabeth Schüssler Fiorenza, 762–99. New York: Crossroad, 1993.

———. "A Chamberlain's Journey and the Challenge of Interpretation for Liberation." In *Interpretation for Liberation*, edited by Katie Geneva Cannon and Elisabeth Schüssler Fiorenza: SBL, 1989.

———. "Womanist Interpretations of the New Testament: The Quest for Holistic and Inclusive Translation and Interpretation." *JFSR* 6 (1990) 41–61.

Martin, Dale B. *Sex and the Single Savior: Gender and Sexuality in Biblical Interpretation*. Louisville, KY: Westminster John Knox, 2006.

———. "Slave Families and Slaves in Families." In *Early Christian Families in Context: An Interdisciplinary Dialogue*, edited by Carolyn Osiek and David L. Balch, 207–30. Grand Rapids: Eerdmans, 2003.

———. *Slavery as Salvation: The Metaphor of Slavery in Pauline Christianity*. New Haven: Yale University Press, 1990.

Martyn, J. Louis. *Galatians: A New Translation with Introduction and Commentary*. The Anchor Bible, Vol. 33A. New York: Doubleday, 1998.

Maseno, Loreen Iminza, and Marianne Bjelland Kartzow. "Widows, Intersectionality and the Parable in Luke 18." *International Journal for Sociology and Anthropology* 2:7 (2010) 140–48.

Mason, Steve. "Jews, Judeans, Judaizing, Judaism: Problems of Categorization in Ancient History." *Journal for the Study of Judaism* 38:4–5 (2007) 457–512.

Matsuda, Mari J. "Beside My Sister, Facing the Enemy: Legal Theory out of Coalition." *Stanford Law Review* 43 (1990) 1183–92.

Matthews, Shelly. "Elite Women, Public Religion, and Christian Propaganda in Acts 16." In *A Feminist Companion to the Acts of the Apostles*, edited by Amy-Jill Levine, 111–33. London: T. & T. Clark, 2004.

Mattsson, Katarina. "Genua och vithet i den intersektionella vändingen." *Tidsskrift för genusvetenskap* 1–2 (2010) 7–22.

McCall, Leslie. "The Complexity of Intersectionality." *Signs: Journal of Women in Culture and Society* 30:3 (2005) 1771–800.

Meeks, Wayne A. *The First Urban Christians: The Social World of the Apostle Paul*. New Haven: Yale University Press, 2003 (1983).

———. "The 'Haustafeln' and American Slavery: A Hermeneutical Challenge." In *Theology and Ethics in Paul and His Interpreters: Essays in Honor of Victor Paul Furnish*, edited by Jerry L. Sumney et al., 232–54. Nashville, TN: Abingdon, 1996.

Mendels, Doron. *Memory in Jewish, Pagan and Christian Societies of the Graeco-Roman World*, Library of Second Temple Studies 45. London: T. & T. Clark, 2004.

Methuen, Charlotte. "Widows, Bishops and the Struggle for Authority in the *Didascalia Apostolorum*." *Journal of Ecclesiastical History* 46:2 (1995) 197–213.

Metz, Annette. "How a Woman Who Fought Back and Demanded Her Rights Became an Importunate Widow: The Transformation of a Parable of Jesus." In *Jesus from Judaism to Christianity: Continuum Approaches to the Historical Jesus*, edited by Tom Holmén, 49–86. London: T. & T. Clark, 2007.

Meyers, Carol. "Mowinkel Lecture." Oslo, 2008.

Meyers, Carol L., ed. *Women in Scripture: A Dictionary of Named and Unnamed Women in the Hebrew Bible, the Apocryphal/Deuterocanonical Books, and the New Testament*. Grand Rapids: Eerdmans, 2001.

Millard, Alan. *Reading and Writing in the Time of Jesus*. Sheffield: Sheffield Academic, 2000.

Miller, Robert J., ed. *The Complete Gospels*. San Francisco: Harper, 1994.

Misztal, Barbara A. *Theories of Social Remembering*, Theorizing Society. Maidenhead, England; Philadelphia: Open University Press, 2003.

Moberly, R. W. L. *The Bible, Theology, and Faith: A Study of Abraham and Jesus*. Cambridge: Cambridge University Press, 2000.

Moderne slaveri [Modern slavery]. Directed by Thomas Robsahm and Tina Davis. Oslo: Speranza Film, 2009. Online: http://www.nfi.no/english/norwegianfilms/show.html?id=706.

Moi, Toril. *What Is a Woman? And Other Essays*. Oxford: Oxford University Press, 1999.

Mounce, William D. *Pastoral Epistles*. Word Biblical Commentary, Vol. 46. Nashville, TN: Nelson, 2000.

Moxnes, Halvor. "From Unique Personality to Charismatic Movement: 100 Years of Shifting Paradigms in Historical Jesus Research." In *Religion in Late Modernity: Essays in Honor of Pål Repstad*, edited by Inger Furseth and Paul Leer-Salvesen, 187–200. Trondheim: Tapir, 2007.

———. *Putting Jesus in His Place: A Radical Vision of Household and Kingdom*. Louisville, KY: Westminster John Knox, 2003.

Moxnes, Halvor, and Marianne Bjelland Kartzow. "Complex Identities: Ethnicity, Gender and Religion in the Story of the Ethiopian Eunuch, Acts 8:26–40." (forthcoming).

Musurillo, Herbert, ed. *The Acts of the Christian Martyrs*, Oxford Early Christian Texts. Oxford: Clarendon, 1972.

———, ed. *The Acts of the Pagan Martyrs. Acta Alexandrinorum*. Oxford: Clarendon, 1954.

Nadar, Sarojini. "The Bible in and for Mission: A Case Study of the Council of World Mission." *Missionalia* 37:2 (2009) 210–28.

Nash, Jennifer C. "Re-Thinking Intersectionality." *Feminist Review* 89 (2008) 1–15.

Nazer, Mende, with Bernadette J. Brooten. "Epilogue." In *Beyond Slavery: Overcoming Its Religious and Sexual Legacies*, edited by Bernadette J. Brooten and Jacqueline L. Hazelton, 309–18. Basingstoke: Palgrave Macmillan, 2010.

Nickelsburg, G. W. E. "Joseph and Aseneth." In *Jewish Writings of the Second Temple Period: Apocrypha, Pseudepigrapha, Qumran Sectarian Writings, Philo, Josephus*, edited by Michael E. Stone, 65–71. Philadelphia: Fortress, 1984.

Nussbaum, Martha C. *Not for Profit: Why Democracy Needs the Humanities*. Princeton: Princeton University Press, 2010.

Nåsström, Britt-Mari. *The Abhorrence of Love: Studies in Rituals and Mystic Aspects in Catullus' Poem of Attis*. Uppsala: Almqvist & Wiksell, 1989.

O'Toole, Robert F. "Slave Girl at Philippi." In *The Anchor Bible Dictionary*, edited by David Noel Freedman, 57–58. New York: Doubleday, 1992.

Oden, Thomas C. *Ancient Christian Commentary on Scripture: Acts.* Vol. 5. Downers Grove, IL: InterVarsity, 2006.
Olick, Jeffrey K. "Products, Processes, and Practices: A Non-Reificatory Approach to Collective Memory." *Biblical Theology Bulletin* 36 (2006) 5–14.
Osiek, Carolyn. "Female Slaves, *Porneia*, and the Limits of Obedience." In *Early Christian Families in Context: An Interdisciplinary Dialogue. Religion, Marriage, and Family*, edited by Carolyn Osiek and David L. Balch, 255–74. Grand Rapids: Eerdmans, 2003.
———. "The Widow as Altar: The Rise and Fall of a Symbol." *Second Century* 3 (1983) 159–69.
———. "The Women at the Tomb: What Are They Doing There?" *Ex Auditu* 9 (1993) 97–107.
Osiek, Carolyn, and David L. Balch. *Families in the New Testament World: Households and House Churches*, The Family, Religion, and Culture. Louisville, KY: Westminster John Knox, 1997.
Osiek, Carolyn, and Margaret Y. MacDonald, with Janet H. Tulloch. *A Woman's Place: House Churches in Earliest Christianity.* Minneapolis, MN: Fortress, 2006.
Pabst, Irene. "The Interpretation of the Sarah-Hagar-Stories in Rabbinic and Patristic Literature: Sarah and Hagar as Female Representations of Identity and Difference." *Lectio Difficilior* 1 (2003) 1–19.
Pardes, Ilana. *Countertraditions in the Bible: A Feminist Approach.* Cambridge: Harvard University Press, 1992.
The Perseus Digital Library. http://www.perseus.tufts.edu/.
Pervo, Richard I. *Acts: A Commentary.* Edited by Harold W. Attridge, Hermeneia: A Critical and Historical Commentary on the Bible. Minneapolis, MN: Fortress, 2009.
———. "Aseneth and Her Sisters: Women in Jewish Narratives and in the Greek Novels." In *"Women Like This": New Perspectives on Jewish Women in the Greco-Roman World*, edited by Amy-Jill Levine, 145–60. Atlanta: Scholars, 1991.
Phoenix, Ann, and Pamela Pattynama, eds. *European Journal of Women's Studies (Issue on Intersectionality).* Vol. 13, 2006.
———. "Intersectionality." *European Journal of Women's Studies* 13:3 (2006) 187–92.
Portefaix, Lilian. *Sisters Rejoice: Paul's Letter to the Philippians and Luke-Acts as Seen by First-Century Philippian Women*, Coniectanea Biblica. New Testament Series 20. Stockholm: Almqvist & Wiksell, 1988.
Price, Robert M. *The Widow Traditions in Luke-Acts: A Feminist-Critical Scrutiny*, Dissertation Series / Society of Biblical Literature no. 155. Atlanta: Scholars, 1997.
Quinn, Jerome D., and William C. Wacker. *The First and Second Letters to Timothy: A New Translation with Notes and Commentary.* Edited by David Noel Freedman and Astrid B. Beck, Eerdmans Critical Commentary. Grand Rapids: Eerdmans, 2000.
Reid, Barbara E. O. P. "A Godly Widow Persistently Pursuing Justice: Luke 18:1–8." *Biblical Research* 45 (2000) 25–33.
Reinhartz, Adele, and Miriam-Simma Walfish. "Conflict and Coexistance in Jewish Interpretation." In *Hagar, Sarah, and Their Children: Jewish, Christian, and Muslim Perspectives*, edited by Phyllis Trible and Letty M. Russell, 101–25. Louisville, KY: Westminster John Knox, 2006.
Rienecker, Fritz. *A Linguistic Key to the Greek New Testament.* Translated by Cleon L. Rogers. Grand Rapids: Regency Reference Library, 1980.

Rodríguez, Rafael. *Structuring Early Christian Memory: Jesus in Tradition, Performance, and Text*. London: T. & T. Clark, 2010.

Rohrbaugh, Richard L. "Gossip in the New Testament." In *Social Scientific Models for Interpreting the Bible*, 239–59. Leiden: Brill, 2001.

Roller, Lynn E. "The Ideology of the Eunuch Priest." In *Gender and the Body in the Ancient Mediterranean*, edited by Maria Wyke, 118–35. Oxford: Blackwell, 1998.

Roloff, Jürgen. *Der erste Brief an Timotheus*. EKK, Vol. XV. Zurich: Benziger, 1988.

"Roundtable Discussion on the Future of Feminist Biblical Studies." *Journal of Feminist Studies in Religion* 25:2 (2009) 125–43.

Rowley, Jane, and Louise Wolthers. "Lost and Found: Queering the Archive." In *Lost and Found: Queering the Archive*, edited by Mathias Danboltet al., 9–23. Copenhagen: Kunsthallen Nikolaj, 2009.

Russel, Letty. "Children of Struggle." In *Hagar, Sarah, and Their Children: Jewish, Christian, and Muslim Perspectives*, edited by Phyllis Trible and Letty Russel, 185–97. Louisville, KY: Westminster John Knox, 2006.

Saga, Stine Kiil. "Teologi for hundene? Norske presteblikk på Jesu møte med en fremmed kvinne." *Kirke og kultur: Religion og samfunn* 3 (2011), 229–38.

Said, Edward W. *The World, the Text, and the Critic*. Cambridge: Harvard University Press, 1983.

Scholz, Susanne. "Gender, Class, and Androcentric Compliance in the Rapes of Enslaved Women in the Hebrew Bible." *Lectio Difficilior* 1 (2004) 1–33.

Schottroff, Luise. *The Parables of Jesus*. Minneapolis, MN: Fortress, 2006.

Schüssler Fiorenza, Elisabeth. *Discipleship of Equals: Critical Feminist Ekklesia-Logy of Liberation*. London: SCM, 1993.

———. "Discipleship of Equals: Memory and Vision." *Journal of the European Society of Women in Theological Research* 16 (2008) 67–90.

———. *In Memory of Her: A Feminist Theological Reconstruction of Christian Origins*. London: SCM, 1983.

———. *In Memory of Her: The Tenth Anniversary Edition*. New York: Crossroad, 1994.

———. "Introduction: Exploring the Intersections of Race, Gender, Status, and Ethnicity in Early Christian Studies." In *Prejudice and Christian Beginnings: Investigating Race, Gender, and Ethnicity in Early Christian Studies*, edited by Laura Nasrallah and Elisabeth Schüssler Fiorenza, 1–23. Minneapolis, MN: Fortress, 2009.

———. *Jesus and the Politics of Interpretation*. New York: Continuum, 2000.

———. *The Power of the Word: Scripture and the Rhetoric of Empire*. Minneapolis, MN: Fortress, 2007.

———. *Rhetoric and Ethic: The Politics of Biblical Studies*. Minneapolis, MN: Fortress, 1999.

———. "Slave Wo/Men and Freedom: Some Methodological Reflections." In *Postcolonial Interventions. Essays in Honor of R. S. Sugirtharajah*, edited by Tat-siong Benny Liew, 123–46. Sheffield: Sheffield Phoenix, 2009.

———. "Transforming the Margin—Claiming Common Ground: Charting a Different Paradigm of Biblical Studies." In *Still at the Margins: Biblical Scholarship Fifteen Years after Voices from the Margin*, edited by R. S. Sugirtharajah, 22–39. London: T. & T. Clark, 2008.

———. "'What She Has Done Will Be Told . . .': Reflections on Writing Feminist History." In *Distant Voices Drawing Near: Essays in Honor of Antoinette Clark Wire*, edited by Holly E. Hearon, 3–18. Collegeville, MN: Liturgical, 2004.

Schäfer, Peter. *Judeophobia: Attitudes toward the Jews in the Ancient World.* Cambridge: Harvard University Press, 1997.
Scott, Bernard Brandon. *Hear Then the Parable: A Commentary on the Parables of Jesus.* Minneapolis, MN: Fortress, 1989.
Seim, Turid Karlsen. *The Double Message: Patterns of Gender in Luke-Acts,* Studies of the New Testament and Its World. Edinburgh: T. & T. Clark, 1994.
Sengupta, Shuddhabrata. "I/Me/Mine—Intersectional Identities as Negotiated Minefields." *Signs: Journal of Women in Culture and Society* 31:3 (2006) 629–39.
Shauf, Scott. "Locating the Eunuch: Characterization and Narrative Context in Acts 8:26–40." *The Catholic Biblical Quarterly* 71 (2009) 762–75.
Skinner, Marilyn B. "*Ego Mulier*: The Construction of Male Sexuality in Catullus." In *Catullus,* edited by Julia Haig Gaisser, 445–75. Oxford: Oxford University Press, 2007.
Smith, Abraham. "A Second Step in African Biblical Interpretation: A Generic Reading Analysis of Acts 8:26–40." In *Reading from This Place,* edited by Fernando F. Segovia and Mary Ann Tolbert, 213–28. Minneapolis, MN: Fortress, 1995.
Smith, Daniel A. *Revisiting the Empty Tomb: The Early History of Easter.* Minneapolis, MN: Fortress, 2010.
Snyder, R. Claire. "What Is Third-Wave Feminism? A New Directions Essay." *Signs: Journal of Women in Culture and Society* 34:1 (2008) 175–96.
Solevåg, Rebecca. "Birthing Salvation: Salvation and Childbirthing in Early Christian Discourse." PhD diss., University of Oslo, 2011.
Solevåg, Rebecca, and Marianne Bjelland Kartzow. "Hvem bryr seg om Pastoralbrevene? Nyere trender i pastoralbrevsforskningen." *NTT* 111:4 (2010) 255–69.
———. "Who Loves the Pastorals and Why?" *SBL Annual Meeting, The Disputed Paulines session* (2007).
Spacks, Patricia Meyer. *Gossip.* New York: Knopf, 1985.
Spelman, Elizabeth V. *Inessential Woman: Problems of Exclusion in Feminist Thought.* Boston: Beacon, 1988.
Spencer, F. Scott. *The Portrait of Philip in Acts: A Study of Roles and Relations.* JSNTsup. 67. Sheffield: Sheffield Academic, 1992. Staley, Jefferey L. "Changing Woman: Postcolonial Reflections on Acts 16:6–40." *JSNT* 73 (1999) 113–35.
Standhartinger, Angela. *Das Frauenbild im Judentum der hellenistischen Zeit: Ein Beitrag anhand von 'Joseph und Aseneth.'* Arbeiten zur Geschichte des antiken Judentums und des Urchristentums 26. Leiden: Brill, 1995.
———. "The Epistle to the Congregation in Colossae and the Invention of the 'Household Code.'" In *A Feminist Companion to the Deutero-Pauline Epistles,* edited by Amy-Jill Levine and Marianne Blickenstaff, 88–97. Cleveland, OH: Pilgrim, 2003.
———. "'Wie die verehrteste Judith und die besonnenste Hanna.' Traditionsgeschichtliche Beobachtungen zur Herkunft der Witwengruppen im entstehenden Christentum." In *Dem Tod nicht glauben. Sozialgeschichte der Bibel. Festschrift für Louise Schottroff zum 70. Geburtstag,* edited by Frank Grüsemann et al., 103–26. Gütersloh: Gütersloher Verlagshaus, 2004.
Stegemann, Wolfgang. "Anti-Semitic and Racial Prejudices in Titus 1:10–16." In *Ethnicity and the Bible,* edited by Mark G. Brett, 271–94. Leiden: Brill, 1996.
Stein, Dina. "A Maidservant and Her Master's Voice: Discourse, Identity, and Eros in Rabbinic Texts." *Journal of the History of Sexuality* 10:3/4 (2001) 375–97.

Stenström, Hanna. "Masculine or Feminine? Male Virgins in *Joseph and Aseneth* and the Book of Revelation." In *Identity Formation in the New Testament*, edited by Bengt Holmberg and Mikael Winninge, 199–222. Tübingen: Mohr Siebeck, 2008.

Sta[set umlaut over a]hlin, Gustav. "χήρα." In *Theological Dictionary of the New Testament*, edited by Gerhard Friedrich, 440–65. Grand Rapids: Eerdmans, 1985.

Sugirtharajah, R. S., ed. *Still at the Margins: Biblical Scholarship Fifteen Years after Voices from the Margin*. London: T. & T. Clark, 2008.

———. *Voices from the Margin: Interpreting the Bible in the Third World*. Maryknoll, NY: Orbis, 1991.

Thesaurus Linguae Graecae: A Digital Library of Greek Literature. Online: http://www.tlg.uci.edu/.

Thurston, Bonnie Bowman. "The Widow as the 'Altar of God.'" In *SBL 1985 Seminar Papers*, edited by Kent Harold Richards, 279–89. Atlanta: Scholars, 1985.

———. *The Widows: A Women's Ministry in the Early Church*. Minneapolis, MN: Fortress, 1989.

Torjesen, Karen Jo. *When Women Were Priests: Women's Leadership in the Early Church and the Scandal of Their Subordination in the Rise of Christianity*. San Francisco: HarperSanFrancisco, 1993.

Trible, Phyllis. *Texts of Terror: Literary-Feminist Readings of Biblical Narratives*, Overtures to Biblical Theology 13. Philadelphia: Fortress, 1984.

Trible, Phyllis, and Letty Russel, eds. *Hagar, Sarah, and Their Children: Jewish, Christian, and Muslim Perspectives*. Louisville, KY: Westminster John Knox, 2006.

Trible, Phyllis, and Letty M. Russell. "Unto the Thousandth Generation." In *Hagar, Sarah, and Their Children: Jewish, Christian, and Muslim Perspectives*, edited by Phyllis Trible and Letty Russel, 1–29. Louisville, KY: Westminster John Knox, 2006.

Tsang, Sam. "Are We 'Misreading' Paul? Oral Phenomena and Their Implications for the Exegesis of Paul's Letters." *Oral Tradition* 24:1 (2009) 205–25.

———. *From Slaves to Sons: A New Rhetoric Analysis on Paul's Slave Metaphors in His Letter to the Galatians*. New York: Lang, 2005.

van der Toorn, Karel. "Torn between Vice and Virtue: Stereotypes of the Widow in Israel and Mesopotamia." In *Female Stereotypes in Religious Traditions*, edited by Ria Kloppenborg and Wouter J. Hanegraaff. Leiden: Brill, 1995.

Vander Stichele, Caroline, and Todd Penner. *Contextualizing Gender in Early Christian Discourse: Thinking Beyond Thecla*. London: T. & T. Clark, 2009.

Verloo, Mieke. "Multiple Inequalities, Intersectionality and the European Union." *European Journal of Women's Studies* 13:3 (2006) 211–28.

von Braun, Christina, and Ulrike Auga. "Beyond Boundaries: Introduction." In *Gender in Conflict: Palestine, Israel, Germany*, edited by Christina von Braun and Ulrike Auga, 1–11. Berlin: Lit, 2006.

Walcot, Peter. "On Widows and Their Reputation in Antiquity." *Symbolae Osloenses* LXVI (1991): 5–26.

Walker, Barbara G. *The Woman's Encyclopedia of Myths and Secrets*. San Francisco: Harper and Row, 1983.

Walton, Stephen J. *Skaff deg eit liv! Om biografi*. Oslo: Samlaget, 2008.

Williams, Delores S. "Hagar in African American Biblical Appropriation." In *Hagar, Sarah, and Their Children: Jewish, Christian, and Muslim Perspectives*, edited by Phyllis Trible and Letty Russel, 171–84. Louisville, KY: Westminster John Knox, 2006.

Wire, Antoinette Clark. *The Corinthian Women Prophets: A Reconstruction through Paul's Rhetoric*. Minneapolis, MN: Fortress, 1990.

———. *Holy Lives, Holy Deaths: A Close Hearing of Early Jewish Storytellers*. Edited by Sharon H. Ringe. Studies in Biblical Literature, Vol. 1. Atlanta: SBL, 2002.

Wright, David P. "'She Shall Not Go Free as Male Slaves Do': Developing Views About Slavery and Gender in the Law of the Hebrew Bible." In *Beyond Slavery: Overcoming Its Religious and Sexual Legacies*, edited by Bernadette J. Brooten, 125–42. New York: Palgrave Macmillan, 2010.

Yuval-Davis, Nira. "Intersectionality and Feminist Politics." *European Journal of Women's Studies* 13:3 (2006) 193–209.

Yuval, Israel Jacob. *Two Nations in Your Womb: Perceptions of Jews and Christians in Late Antiquity and the Middle Ages*. Translated by Barabara Harshav and Jonathan Chipman. Berkeley: University of California Press, 2006.

Økland, Jorunn. "Sex, Gender and Ancient Greek: A Case-Study in Theoretical Misfit." *Studia Theologica* 57:2 (2003) 124–42.

Økland, Jorunn, and Roland Boer, eds. *Marxist Feminist Criticism of the Bible*. Sheffield: Sheffield Phoenix, 2008.

Subject Index

Actress, 138
Africa, 7, 54, 57, 67, 165, 172
African American womanists, 9, 15, 172
Age, 35, 100, 105, 108, 113, 135
   Ageless, 179
Anti-racist, 15
Anonymous, 87
Ancestry, 166
Apostles, 106
Archive, 1, 23, 33, 127, 179
Asceticism, 71
Ask the other question, 18
Asylum seekers, 78
Aural-oral communities, 79, 176
Authority, 137

Babblers, 115
Baby/babies, 75
Baptism, 46, 53, 122, 125, 141
Baptism formula, 26, 141, 159
Bishops, 106
Black eye, 111, 119
Bloodline, 67
Body/bodies, 14, 23–24, 27, 29, 31, 40, 46, 51, 59, 65, 75, 131, 147, 177
   Female slave's body vs. a wife's body, 161
Brother/s, 87
Brotherhood, 54
Busybodies, 104, 115

Canon, 19, 45, 180
Canon, religious and cultural, 1
   Cultural 2, 7

Canon and archive, 12, 26, 44, 122, 130
Cast-off son, 138–40
Castration/castrated, 24, 29, 46, 49–52, 175–76
Chastity, 66, 68, 113
Child/children, 34–36, 45, 49, 55, 63–64, 72, 77, 96, 143, 180
   Adopted children, 150
   Boys and girls, 35–36
   Childless, 169
   Children of Abraham, 165–67, 172
   Child soldiers, 152
   Child prostitutes, 152
   Exposed children, 150
   Freeborn children, 35, 149
   Slave children, 36, 38
   Step-children, 150
Childbirth, 24, 41, 72, 148, 152, 174, 176
Church order, 157
Circumcision/circumcised, 24, 29, 66, 70, 74–77, 106, 175
Concubine, 66, 163
Conflict, 174
Countermemory, 14
Counterdiscourse, 22
Colonialization, 4, 22
Confrontation (between widow and judge), 118
Conversion, 61, 68, 126
Complexity, 5–8
Couples/double figures/pair, 122–25
Cultural complexity, 14, 180

Subject Index

Daughter, 63
Deacons, 106, 114
Deaconesses, 104
Destabilize, 7–8, 27
Destabilizing potential, 21, 77, 94, 105, 130
Dialogue, 109
    Dialogue partner, 174
    Interreligious dialogue, 172
    Religious dialogue, 178
Disability, 112, 125
Discipleship of equals, 89
Discrimination/discriminating, 17, 19, 74, 157, 175
Divorced woman, 113
DNA tests, 149
Domination, 2
Dream/s, 94, 132

Eunuch, 2, 7, 10, 14, 23, 24, 46–58, 67, 176
Empty tomb, 87–89
Erotic, 56
"Etc.," 17
Ethnic strangers, 97
Ethnicity, 4, 14, 16, 19, 24–25, 47, 60, 66, 76, 98, 108, 127, 129, 133, 135–47, 151, 158–59, 169, 178
Ethics of interpretation, 57
Exotic, 6, 8, 56
Exclusion and silencing, 93
Extremism, 178

Face-to-face communication, 121
Father/s, 144
Fatherhood, 37, 41, 63, 149
Family, 31–34, 44, 75, 112, 144, 148–50
    Family patterns, 157
Fasting, 61, 76
Female beauty, 67
Female elders, 104
Female householders, 104

Female leader 126
Feminist, 18, 43–44, 70–71, 82, 94, 168
Feminist theory, 13–16, 89–92, 125
Flexibility, 27
Folktale, 90
Forgetting/forgotten, 5, 19, 26, 44, 88, 99, 174, 177
Foreignness, 68
Foremother/s, 126
Forefather/s, 167
Fornicators, 77, 105
Freedom in family, church and society, 133
Friends, 36, 50, 120, 174
"Frozen" memory, 19

Gender/race/class, 2, 4, 133, 135–53
Gender-bending, 161
Gender jihad, 168
Gender neutral, 179
Gospel, 84
Gossip/gossipy, 25, 35, 79, 81–82, 91, 95, 103, 110–11, 114, 176
Gossip network, 120
Gossip/slander, 104
Grandchildren, 101

Half-brothers, 36
Half-sisters, 36
Health, 14, 17, 122
Hegemony, 6, 98
Hetero(gender), 40, 62, 125
Hierarchy, 18, 23, 43–44, 77, 137
    Female hierarchy, 139
Household, 31, 39, 41, 122, 145–50
    Household codes, 12, 26, 34, 133, 143–46
Husband, 34, 68, 72, 112
Husband and wife, 37, 143
Hybrid personalities, 180
Hysterical woman, 87–88

Illegal immigrants, 78

Illegitimate son, 140
Imaginary, 27
Inclusion and exclusion, 59, 67, 76
Infant, 73
Infertility, 169
Informal female networks, 95
Information flows, 114
Injustice, 93, 180
    Global injustice, 175
Interreligious dialogue, 172
Intersectionality, 1, 9–23, 175–77
Intersectional turn, 9, 94
Islam, 23, 166, 171

Judaism, Christianity and Islam, 78, 165
Jew/s, 10, 24, 55–56, 65, 74–75, 89, 106, 138, 142, 167, 170, 176
Jew and Greek, 151

Kerygma summaries, 86
Kyriarchy, 22

Language, 39, 97, 100
Liars, 77, 105–7
Liberating agendas, 93
Liberating credo, 133, 136
Liberating project, 93
Liberation and freedom, 131
Literates, 97, 100–101
LGBT, 7, 58

Male and female, 151
Male beauty, 67
Male dominance, 92, 126, 167
Male urban elite, 97
Manumission/manumitted, 39, 152
Margin/marginal, 5, 7–8
Marginalization and exclusion, 102
Marketplace, 130
Martyr acts, 164
Martyrdom, 12, 161
Marriage, 38, 61, 64, 143, mixed 169

Masculine/masculinity, 22, 25, 48–50, 53, 55, 62, 68, 75, 106, 108, 113, 121, 161, 176
Media, 114
Men at the margins, 178
Metaphor/metaphorical, 31, 34, 54, 67, 75, 129
    Metaphorical language, 127
Methodology, 21
Memory theory, 9–23
Midwives, 96
Mother/s, 63, 66, 72, 78, 104, 139, 144, 162
Motherhood, 17, 23, 29, 63, 70, 72–74, 77, 175
Musician, 138
Myths, 107

Naming, 26–27, 85, 155, 177
Naming and blaming, 106
Neighbors/neighborhood, 120, 174
News channels, 114
Nonsense, 86
Nurses, 96

Offspring, 152, 170
Old wives' tales, 104
Opposition, 2, 22
Oppression, 14, 17, 23, 26, 43, 73, 157, 176
Oral/orality, 25, 81
    Female orality, 89
    Female orality network, 90
    Oral genres, 81, 101
    Oral performance, 83
    Oral texts, 86
    Oral transmission, 18
    Oral traditions, 83, 86, 94
Orphans, 112
Othering, 82, 93
Otherness, 158
Outcast, 51
Outsider, 67

Paganism, 68
Parable, 31–33
Parents/parenthood, 35, 38, 67, 143
Parable, 23, 31, 37, 40, 42, 110–21, 127
Parallel stories/pairs/contrast figures, 123–32
Past and present, 11
Phallus, 48, 147, 149
Pilgrimage, 46
Place, 27, 44
Power, 1, 5, 19, 21, 26, 35, 37, 68, 79, 83, 95, 98–99, 106, 121
    Power dynamics, 180
    Power structure, 145
    Power systems, 109
Pray/prayer, 76, 110, 122
Pregnant/pregnancy, 36, 72, 169
Prejudice/s, 160
Private and public, 114
Procreation, 152
Production of knowledge, 57
Prophets, 106
    Female prophet/s, 123, 131, 177
Proselyte, 46
Prostitute, 72, 128, 139
Pseudoepigraphy, 71

Queer, 2, 46, 57, 161
Qumran writings, 170
Qur'an, 3, 166

Rabbinic texts, 169
Racism, 1, 17, 22, 78
Readers at the margins, 3
Recovering memory, 94
Relationship pairs, 141
Remarriage, 112
Reproduction, 38, 40, 72, 148
Reproductive capital, 73
Reputation, 120, 176
Resurrection, 81, 86
Ritual/ritualization, 50, 53, 66, 76, 172

Romance, 67
Roman law, 37
Roma women, 78
Rumors, 63, 114, 120

Sameness and difference, 59
Same sex relationships, 40, 145
Servant/s, 58, 128
Sexism, 18, 43, 78
Sex and gender, 147
Sex workers, 77
Sharing, 99
Silence/silenced, 24, 26, 33, 79, 103
Skin color, 39, 56
Slander, 105
Slave/s, 2, 23, 34, 68, 70–78, 120, 180
    Enslavement, 75, 142
    Fellow slaves, 35
    Female slave/s, 21, 23, 27, 38, 40, 51, 60, 97, 101, 106, 113, 132, 147, 148, 160; childless 152
    Foreign slaves, 97
    Fortune-telling slave girl, 122–32
    Freed slave/s, 48
    House slaves, 153
    Male slaves, 48–53, 74–76, 96, 101, 106, 132, 147
    Master and slave, 31
    Re-naming of slaves, 158
    Runaway slaves, 39, 50–51
    Slave and free, 10, 151; babies, 36; women, 104, 161
    Slave babies, 36, 38
    Slave body, 14, 31, 45, 129
    Slave children, 36, 145
    Slave father/s, 41, 72
    Slave girl, 25, 79, 122–32, 177
    Slave mother/s, 38–39, 41, 71–74
    Slave of God, 20, 26, 128–29
    Slave owners, 43, 145
    Slave pair, 123–32
    Slave-holding system; 37, gendered, 132

Slave/s (cont.)
    Slave-holding families, 43
    Slave trade/traders, 77, 105, 175
    Slavery language, 51, 127–28
    Slaves as secretaries/scribes, 91, 101
    Structures of slavery, 33
Social biography, 52
Social imagination, 20, 101
Social space, 36
Sodomites, 77, 105
Son/s, 72, 138–40
Sorcery, 87
Space, 44, 78
    Female space, 95
    Male space, 50
Speech and talk, 79, 81–132
Status, 19
Stereotype/s, 26, 78, 82, 92–93, 101–3, 108–9, 121, 160
Stigma/stigmatize/stigmatization, 14, 46, 51, 56, 58
Storytelling, 13, 53, 81, 83, 88–89, 91, 94, 101
Strangeness, 158
Surrogate mother, 27; enslaved, 166, 173
Surrogate body, 38
Synoptic, 31, 36
    The synoptic problem, 82

Tales, 105
Tattoo, 51
Terror, 174

Text of terror, 1
Teachers, 106
Trafficking, 45, 153, 172
Transformation, 2, 22, 61, 66
Translation, 97
Translation practices, 6, 33, 45, 104, 179
Transmitted, 86
Traveling concepts, 166
Tolerance, 109
Twins, 171

Unmarried daughters, 123

Violence, 2, 23, 29, 31, 34, 38, 42, 175
    Physical violence, 45
    Psychological violence, 45
    Sexual violence, 41, 45, 73
Virgin/virginity, 24, 29, 58, 60–61, 63, 175
    Male virginity, 64
Virgin/wife/widow, 112
Vision/s, 94, 132, 179–80
Voice/s, 24, 26, 79, 96, 102

Wet nursing, 148
Widow/s, 2, 72, 79, 111–12, 162, 176
    Widowhood, 112
    Widows old and young, 104
Wife/Wives, 34, 66, 104, 162
    Free or freeborn wives, 96, 101

Xenophobia, 78

Scripture Index

Genesis
41:45	59
41:50	59
46:20	59

Isaiah
53:7–9	52

Jeremiah
13:23	

Matthew
24:42–51	35
24:49	35
28:1	85

Mark
16:1	85
16:8	86
16:11	86

Luke
2:36–38	
2:37	110
12:35–48	32, 34, 43, 127
12:45	14, 23, 35, 43, 179
12:45–46	31
17:3–10	34
18:1	111
18:1–8	110
18:2–5	25, 110–11, 117, 121
18:6–8	111
19:11–27	34
24:10	85
24:11	86

John
20:1	85

Acts
2:18	132
2:31–33	87
8	52
8:26–40	23, 46, 179
8:27–28	48
8:32–33	52
13:29–37	87
14	125
16	126–27
16:16–18	20, 25, 119, 122–23
21:9	123

Romans
9:4–5	171
9:6–13	171

1 Corinthians
12:13	141
15	84, 86, 88–89
15:4–7	87

Galatians
3:28	12–13, 26, 78, 133, 135–37, 140–43, 146–53, 158–59, 164, 172, 177
4:21–31	170

Colossians
3–4	158
3:11	141

Colossians (cont.)

3:18—4:1	137, 140, 143–53
3:20–21	144–45

1 Timothy

1:4	74
1:10	77–78, 105
2:9–15	72, 163
2:15	148
3:11	104, 115
4:7	103, 115, 179
5	112
5:2	72
5:3	115
5:3–16	110
5:5	110
5:13–14	110
5:13	104
5:14	72
5:3–16	25
6:1–2	77, 105, 163

2 Timothy

4:21	162, 164

Tit

1:10	74
1:12–14	106
1:14	74
2:3	104
2:3–5	72
2:9–10	105, 163
2:10	77

www.ingramcontent.com/pod-product-compliance
Lightning Source LLC
Chambersburg PA
CBHW070324230426
43663CB00011B/2211